T0100755

iPhone for Work

Increasing Productivity for Busy Professionals

Ryan J. Faas

Apress®

iPhone for Work: Increasing Productivity for Busy Professionals

Copyright © 2009 by Ryan J. Faas

All rights reserved. No part of this work may be reproduced or transmitted in any form or by any means, electronic or mechanical, including photocopying, recording, or by any information storage or retrieval system, without the prior written permission of the copyright owner and the publisher.

ISBN-13 (pbk): 978-1-4302-2445-7

ISBN-13 (electronic): 978-1-4302-2446-4

Printed and bound in the United States of America 9 8 7 6 5 4 3 2 1

Trademarked names may appear in this book. Rather than use a trademark symbol with every occurrence of a trademarked name, we use the names only in an editorial fashion and to the benefit of the trademark owner, with no intention of infringement of the trademark.

Lead Editors: Clay Andres, Matthew Moodie
Technical Reviewer: Kunal Mittal
Editorial Board: Clay Andres, Steve Anglin, Mark Beckner, Ewan Buckingham, Tony Campbell, Gary Cornell, Jonathan Gennick, Michelle Lowman, Matthew Moodie, Jeffrey Pepper, Frank Pohlmann, Ben Renow-Clarke, Dominic Shakeshaft, Matt Wade, Tom Welsh
Project Manager: Denise Santoro Lincoln
Copy Editor: Damon Larson
Compositor: Angie MacAllister
Indexer: Rebecca Hornyak

Distributed to the book trade worldwide by Springer-Verlag New York, Inc., 233 Spring Street, 6th Floor, New York, NY 10013. Phone 1-800-SPRINGER, fax 201-348-4505, e-mail `orders-ny@springer-sbm.com`, or visit `http://www.springeronline.com`.

For information on translations, please contact Apress directly at 233 Spring Street, New York, NY 10013. E-mail `info@apress.com`, or visit `http://www.apress.com`.

Apress and friends of ED books may be purchased in bulk for academic, corporate, or promotional use. eBook versions and licenses are also available for most titles. For more information, reference our Special Bulk Sales–eBook Licensing web page at `http://www.apress.com/info/bulksales`.

The information in this book is distributed on an "as is" basis, without warranty. Although every precaution has been taken in the preparation of this work, neither the author(s) nor Apress shall have any liability to any person or entity with respect to any loss or damage caused or alleged to be caused directly or indirectly by the information contained in this work.

Dedicated to Kris, along with all the love and thanks I'm capable of giving

Contents

PART 3 ■ ■ ■ Getting Even More Done with Additonal Apps

About the Author

 **Ryan Faas** is a freelance technology journalist and network consultant who has been writing about Apple products and the mobile industry for over a decade. His first book, written while serving as Mac hardware guide/editor for About.com, was *Troubleshooting, Maintaining, and Repairing Macs* (Osborne/McGraw-Hill, 2000), followed by *Essential Mac OS X Panther Server Administration* (O'Reilly, 2005) and *Creating a Widget in Dashcode* (Peachpit, 2007).

Ryan is also a prolific writer of shorter works. His articles and how-to guides have been featured by Computerworld, InformIT, Peachpit Press, About.com, and Jupiter Media's Datamation news service. In 2008, he was awarded a Neal National Business Journalism award for his work featured in Computerworld's Week of Leopard series.

In addition to writing, Ryan has spent a large portion of the past 15 years in the systems and network management fields as a systems administrator, trainer, and all around cross-platform technology consultant. His client list has ranged from human service nonprofits and private schools to Fortune 500 companies and major media agencies. Living in upstate New York, he continues to offer training, documentation and editing, and network consulting services to organizations around the world.

Despite his focus on covering all things technology, Ryan still lays the thanks for his entire career to his high school journalism teacher, who was the first person to ever sit him down in front of a Mac (or any computer beyond a 1980s-era Commodore 64) and introduce him as teenager lacking in direction to the worlds of writing, modern technology, and Apple products (at the time a Mac IIci).

About the Technical Reviewer

Kunal Mittal serves as an Executive Director of Technology at Sony Pictures Entertainment, where he is responsible for the SOA and Identity Management programs. He provides a centralized engineering service to different lines of business and consults on open source technologies, content management, collaboration, and mobile strategies.

Kunal is an entrepreneur who helps startups define their technology strategy, product roadmap, and development plans. With strong relations with several development partners worldwide, he is able to help startups and even large companies build appropriate development partnerships. He generally works in an advisor or consulting CTO capacity, and serves actively in the project management and technical architect areas.

He has authored and edited several books and articles on J2EE, cloud computing, and mobile technologies. He holds a master's degree in software engineering and is an instrument-rated private pilot.

Acknowledgments

I owe a great deal of thanks to many people for the advice, help, and support that made this book possible. First, thanks to Clay Andres, Matt Moodie, Denise Santoro Lincoln, Damon Larson, and everyone at Apress for your hard work and patience over the past several months. And a big thanks to Kunal Mittal for every piece of feedback as my tech reviewer.

I have to give a great deal of thanks to Joanna Palladino and her decision to buy an iPhone as a business tool to replace her Blackberry. Without that seed of inspiration and all the questions she asked me last winter, the concept of this book probably wouldn't have even occurred to me. She also provided lots of suggestions for the original outline of this book, as well as ongoing suggestions, anecdotes, the occasional quote, and lots of moral support along the way.

A great many other iPhone users also offered their stories about using the iPhone professionally and suggestions for business apps that they depend on to be included in Part 3 of this book. Some of them are old friends, some are colleagues, and some were complete strangers that I occasionally walked up to on the street because I saw them using an iPhone. In particular, the following people made great contributions to this book, and I thank you all very much: Amanda Brinke, Sean Wendell, Dan Valente, Cynthia Dobe, Phil Clarke, Nancy Lott, John Cirrin, Janet Womachka, and Ken Mingis.

Bill Baker and Alykhan Jetha deserve special thanks for giving me a good perspective on iPhone business tools and uses from a developer's point of view, which helped immensely.

Several people offered support without directly contributing content to the book, including Gary Hobbs for reminding more than once that balance is important in life, Henric Post for general patience during the last few months, and Veronica Cole for advice, laughter, and friendship.

Of course, I have to give much thanks to my parents Frank and Pat Faas. Without them, nothing I've accomplished would be possible.

And last but certainly not least, I have to thank Kris Anderson for years of love and support without which this book (and probably almost anything else I've written in the past six years) could never have happened. Thank you.

Ryan Faas

Introduction

Since Apple announced it in January of 2007, the iPhone has repeatedly revolutionized the world of mobile phones. The iPhone was the first phone to utilize a touchscreen as the sole input technology. It was the first phone that proved that average consumers were willing to pay for a well-designed smart phone that was also a media player, and it was the first smart phone to truly display web content as well as a computer. Those accomplishments were achieved the day the first iPhone shipped.

With Apple's first major refresh to the iPhone's hardware and software, the company dramatically expanded the device's capabilities with faster network connectivity, GPS capabilities, and integration with Microsoft Exchange (the most commonly used collaborative suite in the business world). But, more significantly, Apple gave third-party software developers the ability to create new applications for the iPhone and leveraged the power of the iTunes Store to make it easy and convenient for users to browse these new applications, and to buy, download, and install them in one easy step. Within months, iPhone users had access to tens of thousands of applications that ran the gamut from virtual whoopee cushions to business and project management solutions, and everything in between.

Between the ever-expanding options of additional applications and Apple's introduction of some core business features to the iPhone, it came as no surprise to me last year when I began to get asked if the iPhone could be a real solution for business in the way that the Blackberry or Windows Mobile devices were. The answer, of course, was yes. And over the past year, I've seen companies of all sizes, as well as individual workers and consultants, purchase and integrate the iPhone into their workflows.

This book is based on partly my personal experience as a technology consultant/trainer and as an iPhone owner. It is also based on many conversations with iPhone-toting professionals from many fields. My goal is to provide you with a reference that is part how-to book, but also takes each feature of the iPhone (including some of the more consumer-oriented features, like YouTube and text messaging) and provides practical ways that you can use it in your professional life.

To that end, you'll see a lot of basic iPhone knowledge to get you started. You'll also see the occasional quote from iPhone users highlighting helpful business uses for specific features, as well as tips and sidebars that offer suggestions on more detailed ways that you can use the iPhone for professional networking, task management, daily work-related tasks, and professional development. Even if you know a lot of the basics about the iPhone, each chapter probably has some helpful tidbit, regardless of your field or industry.

In Part 1 of this book, I'll cover all the basic things you need to know about purchasing, activating, and getting started with your iPhone. In Part 2, you'll learn all the details about the built-in applications that come with the iPhone (both how to use them and how use them in business settings). Part 3 covers the App Store, where you can find and purchase an amazing array of business and productivity tools (and a lot of apps that are just plain fun—after all, the iPhone is a fun device to use).

In addition to introducing you to the App Store, the final part of this book provides an introductory guide to many business applications for the iPhone. This includes general tools that can be helpful for almost any iPhone-owning professional and any type of business. It also includes guides to applications that are helpful for people in specific professions such as doctors, lawyers, real estate agents, and teachers.

At the end of this book, you'll have a clear idea of how to use your iPhone and how to apply it to your specific career and job needs. But, as I note more than once in Part 3, the range of applications is always growing, and Apple is continuing to push the iPhone forward with new features and capabilities. So, while this book will be a great starting point for your iPhone-enabled career, it is just that—a place to get started—because I have no doubt that Apple and third-party iPhone developers will expand the potential of the iPhone for business users and consumers alike.

PART 1

■ ■ ■

iPhone Basics

Chapter 1

Buying and Activating Your iPhone

Getting Ready to Get Down to Work with the iPhone

The iPhone may be generally considered a consumer device, but Apple has built an incredible amount of professional and business-grade features into it, including access to Microsoft Exchange and other industry collaborative tools (messaging, calendar, and contacts), as well as secure and on-demand access to remote network resources—each of which we'll explore throughout this book. In this first chapter, however, let's focus on the immediate questions that you'll need to know when you go to the store to pick out your iPhone, and when you come home, activate it for use and sync data between it and your computer for the first time.

iPhone Models and the iPod touch

Compared to some smart phone platforms, the iPhone is probably the simplest platform to understand when making a purchase. Apple has kept the iPhone lineup very streamlined, and it currently includes only two shipping models: the iPhone 3G (originally introduced in July 2008) and the newer iPhone 3GS (introduced in June 2009). A third model, the original iPhone introduced in July 2007, is no longer being produced by Apple (though used models continue to be available). Although all three models run the same software and are functionally very similar, there are notable differences between them.

The iPhone 3GS

Introduced in June 2009, the iPhone 3GS (Apple has described the *S* in the name as being for "speed") is the most recent iPhone model. Although it has the same design and interface elements as the other two models, it offers notably better performance for many tasks due to a faster processer and more built-in memory than either of the earlier models (which were functionally very similar). As a result, operations such as launching applications, rendering web sites, and loading graphics-intense application data are on average two to three times faster on an iPhone 3GS (though Internet access performance may still be limited by the type of Internet connection).

In addition to the increased speed, the iPhone 3GS boasts a few other hardware upgrades over previous models. It includes a higher-resolution camera (3 megapixels to the 2-megapixel camera on both previous models) that includes autofocus capabilities, performs better in low-light situations, and has the ability to shoot video as well as still images. The iPhone 3GS also includes a built-in electronic compass that allows it to determine which way the device is pointed, and offers navigation features beyond the iPhone 3G's GPS-only navigation (the original iPhone didn't ship with any built-in GPS capabilities). It also boasts improved battery life over previous models.

As of this writing, the iPhone 3GS is available in 16GB and 32GB storage capacities with either a black or white case. The storage in the iPhone is not upgradable—which means that if you choose the smaller model and outgrow its capacity, you'll need to either pare down the amount of data stored on it or completely upgrade to a new, larger phone.

The iPhone 3G

The iPhone 3G, which Apple continues to produce in an 8GB capacity (originally it was available in both 8GB and 16GB versions), offers a half-price alternative to the iPhone 3GS. Although it offers slower overall performance, the iPhone 3G is still adequate for most tasks. Like the iPhone 3GS, it can connect to modern 3G mobile networks for Internet access, though the iPhone 3GS supports a somewhat faster version of 3G networking that is not currently available via AT&T (the sole US carrier of the iPhone). In fact, the majority of built-in and third-party applications function the same on both models.

As a result of the hardware differences between the iPhone 3G and iPhone 3GS, however, some additional features are not available. As noted, this includes the compass and certain camera features. It also means that some software features, such as the ability to use Apple's built-in voice control and voiceover (which allows the iPhone 3GS to speak feedback to the user) are not available.

One feature only available on the iPhone 3GS that should be noted for business users is the ability to fully encrypt all data on the device. This adds a significant layer of security to the iPhone 3GS because even if the device is lost or stolen, retrieving data from a fully encrypted and passcode-protected device is virtually impossible without knowing the passcode. Unencrypted devices can often be accessed by someone with the proper tools and forensic skills even if they are protected by a passcode.

The Original iPhone

This iPhone 3G and 3GS are currently the only iPhone models available, the original iPhone (also sometimes called the 2G or 2.5G iPhone, or the first-generation iPhone) may be found used or refurbished from private resellers. The original iPhone cannot make use of 3G mobile networks and must rely on the older (and significantly slower) EDGE technology for data services like web browsing or sending and receiving e-mail. The iPhone 3G (as you might guess from the name) was designed to function with the newer 3G technology to offer much faster data performance. Since 3G networks are not deployed everywhere (particularly in rural areas), the iPhone 3G and 3Gs will still function with EDGE networks if needed.

Another big difference between the original iPhone and the iPhone 3G and iPhone 3GS is the inclusion of a GPS antenna in the iPhone 3G. GPS (global positioning system) is a network of 16 satellites that GPS devices (including the iPhone 3G) can rely upon to acquire an accurate location anywhere on the earth. Typically GPS is accurate to within a few feet.

GPS is a major feature of the iPhone 3G and iPhone 3GS, and is used in a wide range of applications by Apple, Google, and other developers. While the original iPhone lacks GPS capabilities, it can access some location services by triangulating its distance from the cellular towers to which it is connected at any given time, and by using a global database of known Wi-Fi hotspots (known as Skyhook). The results are often far less accurate than GPS, and the degree of accuracy can vary from a few yards to a mile or more. As with 3G networking, the iPhone 3G and iPhone 3GS can also use these technologies to plot their locations if they cannot acquire signals from GPS satellites (such as when inside many older brick buildings—such structures can also impede network performance, though of the various technologies in any iPhone model, GPS is the most easily blocked).

The iPod touch

While not an iPhone, the iPod touch runs the same operating system software and many of the same applications as the iPhone. This means that, even though the iPod touch cannot be used as a phone, it can still function as an Internet-enabled business device. An iPod touch can be used for e-mail, web browsing, maintaining calendar and contact data, and viewing media files (music, photos, videos, and podcasts), and can work with the vast majority of iPhone applications. The primary limitations of the iPod touch are that it cannot make or receive phone calls and it must rely on Wi-Fi hotspots or networks to access the Internet (unlike the iPhone, which can rely on a mobile carrier's data network). The iPod touch also lacks the camera built into the iPhone.

> **TIP:** Although the iPod touch cannot make calls using a wireless carrier, Voice over IP (VoIP) applications including Skype, Truphone, and fring are available from Apple's App Store that can be used with the iPod touch to make phone calls over the Internet when connected to a Wi-Fi network. However, you will need to purchase a separate headset with a built-in mic in order to use these apps, as the iPod touch doesn't include a built-in mic.

These may be somewhat significant limitations for some professionals, but the iPod touch has a couple of things to chalk up in its favor. The device is available in 8GB, 32GB, and 64GBstorage capacities and it does not require you to sign an extended service agreement or even purchase service with AT&T (or another carrier outside the United States). Depending on your needs or the options available at your company, an iPod touch coupled with a more traditional phone may be a viable option.

Since the iPhone an iPod touch are very similar, you will be able to apply the majority of information in this book to either device. I will make note, however, of features that are specific to the iPhone that will not apply to the iPod touch.

Understanding iPhone Activation and Rate Plans for Individuals and Businesses

If you are purchasing an iPhone as an individual, you can do so directly from the carrier (AT&T in the United States), an Apple retail store, or another retailer (such as Best Buy or Wal-Mart). This is because the actual full cost of the iPhone is subsidized by the carrier, who sells the iPhone to you at a reduced rate that has been negotiated with Apple as part of its agreement to support and sell the iPhone.

The fully subsidized cost is $199 for the 16GB iPhone 3GS or $299 for the 32GB model (some retailers, such as Wal-Mart or Best Buy, may further reduce the cost, though major markdowns are rare because of the terms between Apple and retailers). The fully subsidized price for the 8GB iPhone 3G is $99, representing a notable cost savings. The cost outside the United States may vary, as may the contract terms depending on local laws and the agreements that Apple has made with other carriers. This subsidized pricing actually drops the initial purchase cost of the iPhone below the retail pricing for the iPod touch (the entry-level model of which sells for $199).

Regardless of where you purchase and activate your iPhone, the process will be similar. If you are an existing customer of AT&T, you may be eligible to receive the iPhone at these prices, or you may be asked to pay more depending on your upgrade eligibility— this is determined by how long it has been since you last signed a new contract with the carrier.

AT&T, like most wireless carriers, will offer you subsidized pricing only a periodic basis, as this helps ensure that you will either remain a customer long enough to repay the investment in subsidizing the cost of your phone or be forced to pay an early termination fee. You can check your upgrade eligibility by calling the carrier or checking your account status online.

You can also choose to buy an unsubsidized iPhone 3GS, though the costs are much steeper, with models selling for $599 (16GB) and $699 (32GB)—and may not be worth avoiding the two-year commitment in countries such as the United States, where there is only a single exclusive carrier from whom you can purchase service.

If you are a new customer, you'll need to sign a contract, you'll be subject to a credit check, and photo ID will be required. At this time, AT&T doesn't offer the ability to purchase and activate an iPhone using a pay-as-you-go account (though this may vary in other countries). You will have the option of porting your current phone number to your new iPhone or activating the iPhone with a brand-new number.

With the paperwork done, your iPhone may be activated by the retailer using iTunes in the store, or you may be asked to activate the iPhone at home or the office by connecting it to iTunes (as illustrated in Figure 1-1). In addition to being a media player and online media store, iTunes is the primary tool for managing the iPhone. If you purchase an iPhone in an Apple store, it will likely be activated using iTunes on one of the demo Macs throughout the store. Other retailers will typically use a stripped-down/activation-only version of iTunes on their store point-of-sale computers. In either case, this initial connection serves only to activate the phone, and no information is actually synced to it.

> **TIP:** The same activation process occurs in iTunes on your computer as in the store. In fact, if your iPhone needs to be restored (completely erased) as part of troubleshooting, you will also be asked to activate it through iTunes after the restore, answering basic questions about your wireless account.

Figure 1-1. *Activating an iPhone using iTunes*

Consumer vs. Business Rate Plans

The rate plans associated with the iPhone will vary by country and carrier. In the United States, AT&T draws distinctions between business and consumer plans. If you are purchasing an iPhone for a small business or a larger enterprise environment, you will need to purchase directly from AT&T. There are a number of plan options for businesses, but the majority are similar to the plans available to consumers. Business consultants within AT&T can help you assess your business needs.

If you are purchasing an iPhone as an individual, you will be asked to choose both a data plan (required with iPhone activation) and a voice plan. AT&T has provided several iPhone-specific plans that include both the required 3G data plan (which includes unlimited data transfer for $30/month) and voice plans. If you are activating an iPhone as part of a family plan, you may want to investigate what options are available in terms of family plans that share minutes, as it is possible to choose from AT&T's more general voice and feature plans and simply add the iPhone data plan to it. The same is true for businesses that include both iPhones and other phone models.

If you are activating a used or existing original iPhone as an additional line on the same account as an iPhone 3G or iPhone 3GS, be sure to fully investigate the options and compare the costs of shared-minute plans and traditional independent line plans. The original iPhone requires a different $20/month EDGE data plan that includes unlimited text messaging (the iPhone 3G data plan does not). As a result, comparing the combination of plans is important because the costs can vary based on the type of plan you choose. Likewise, if you are activating an iPhone on a family or business plan with other types of phones, you should investigate all the plan options before making a decision. In this respect, purchasing from an AT&T store or business consultant can be useful because they are typically more familiar with certain options, and may be able to offer options that other retailers cannot.

Getting Used to iTunes As the Hub of Your Personal and Business Data

Over the years, Apple has turned the iTunes media application from a simple music jukebox into a repository for all types of digital media and a hub for managing devices like the iPhone and iPod. Managing your business life (as well as your music, movies, and podcasts) through iTunes may be one of the strangest concepts for professional users to accept about the iPhone. Conceptually, it isn't that much different from other multifunction applications, including Microsoft's Outlook, which combines e-mail, calendars, and personal folders, but the very name iTunes doesn't immediately conjure up the word *professional* in most people's minds.

Nonetheless, that's where management of iPhone data primarily takes place. Whether or not you use iTunes for listening to music or watching movies and TV shows, you'll need it as a place to manage your iPhone. This is the place where you update your iPhone's software, download and install third-party applications, choose which contacts and calendars to sync, purchase or install ringtones, and (of course) choose what music, photos, and videos you want to put on the iPhone. iTunes is also charged with backing up the contents of your iPhone every time it syncs (including things like settings and text messages, which are included in the backup process even though you never see them in iTunes itself).

What If the IT Department Made Your Life Easier by Preconfiguring Your iPhone?

Being a device that is designed for both end users and business customers, the iPhone supports some preconfiguration by IT departments. This configuration is done through the use of special files called *configuration profiles*, which are created using Apple's iPhone Configuration Utility. Configuration profiles can be installed on the iPhone by IT staff directly or sent to the iPhone via e-mail or a weblink. Appendix A discusses some of the details about how to perform preconfiguration of one or multiple iPhones using configuration profiles created using Apple's iPhone Configuration Utility. (Additional information can be found in Apple's iPhone Enterprise Deployment Guide, which is available online at http://manuals.info.apple.com/en_US/Enterprise_Deployment_Guide.pdf.)

If you have received your iPhone from your company's IT department, you may find that many of the options for the device have been preset for you. This level of preset can vary. For example, you might receive an iPhone that is completely preconfigured with Wi-Fi networking, as well as all your user information, shared contacts, and calendar servers already on it. Or your iPhone might simply be activated with a basic e-mail server (but no username or password information) being prepopulated. You may also find that your IT department has set some access restrictions on your iPhone. These might include things such as the requirement of a passcode to unlock the iPhone, the ability to purchase content from the iTunes Store, or disabling of your ability to use some applications (such as YouTube, Safari, or the built-in camera). If your iPhone has arrived in such a preconfigured state, you should ask the IT staff member providing it about what features have been configured, which ones you may need to configure yourself, and any security restrictions that have been imposed.

IT can also update the configuration and security settings on the device by updating the configuration profiles after you receive your iPhone. When this happens, you will typically receive an e-mail from an IT staff member with an attachment that contains the new profile. Opening the attachment will cause the iPhone to ask if you want to install it (doing so may overwrite some or all of the settings in place from an existing profile). Similarly (and somewhat more securely), IT may direct you to load a profile from a company web server by going to an appropriate web page using the Safari web browser on you iPhone.

Typically, you will want to install these updates, as they probably relate to your ability to access your company's network. However, you may wish to confirm with a staff member that the updates are genuine, and what settings the updates will change, before installing them. Although there is little chance of malicious damage to the iPhone from configuration profiles, they can affect your ability to access a variety of features, including corporate Wi-Fi networks and e-mail servers. Also, they may implement new security restrictions, though they will typically not affect your ability to sync data or content through iTunes (the exception being the ability of configuration profiles to block access to content in iTunes that is flagged as explicit or adult).

Initial Setup and First Sync

After initial activation, you'll be able to use your iPhone to make calls. You'll also be able to launch any of the built-in applications, including the Safari web browser and the Mail e-mail application. The real power of the iPhone, however, comes after you've activated the phone and connected it to your computer for the first time.

When you first connect the iPhone to your Mac or PC (after downloading the latest version of iTunes from www.apple.com/itunes, or using the software update feature in Mac OS X's System Preferences or the Windows Control Panel if iTunes is already installed), you'll be asked to identify or name your new iPhone and confirm the carrier and account information (such as phone number) associated with it, as shown in Figure 1-2. If you've already synced an iPhone to a computer, it may ask if you want to restore the new iPhone from backup (unless you're troubleshooting a problem after restoring or replacing an iPhone, say no).

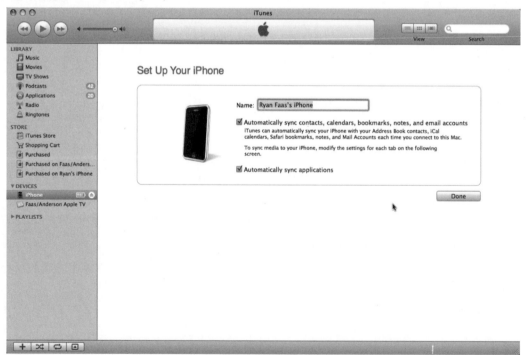

Figure 1-2. *Initial iPhone setup in iTunes*

Once this is complete, you'll see the iPhone appear in the iTunes sidebar (see Figure 1-3). Select the iPhone in the Devices section of the sidebar, and then you'll be able to view information about the iPhone and choose what information you want to sync to it. As you can see, there are eight tabs available in iTunes for managing the iPhone:

- Summary
- Info
- Ringtones
- Music
- Photos
- Podcasts
- Video
- Applications

Figure 1-3. *The iPhone Summary pane in iTunes*

Regardless of which of these tabs you're looking at, you'll see a Sync button in the lower-right corner of the window, which allows you to update your iPhone with any changes you've made to settings or content immediately. You'll also always see a bar along the bottom of the display that illustrates the amount of storage space available on your iPhone and how much of it is currently being taken up by different types of data (such as music, photos, video, and application files).

The Summary Pane

I'll look through each of these panes at various points throughout this book as I discuss specific features of the iPhone. For now, the important two to look at are the Summary pane and the Info pane. The Summary pane (shown previously in Figure 1-3) provides you with general status information about your iPhone, including the name, serial number, operating system software version, overall storage capacity (this may be listed as smaller than the actual capacity because it represents the available capacity after the device has been formatted to accept data), and phone number.

There are also a handful of options, including a button to update the installed iPhone software. Apple periodically issues updates to the iPhone (and iPod touch) operating system software that add new features and/or fix known problems. iTunes will check for new iPhone software automatically once a month (and will display the date of the next check on this pane). You can manually check for and update software using this button at any time.

Another button allows you to restore the iPhone. Restoring an iPhone is most commonly done as a troubleshooting step. The entire contents of the iPhone (operating system software, applications, data, and settings) are erased, and the most recent version of the iPhone software is loaded onto the device—effectively restoring it as if it were a brand-new phone. This process can also be performed if you want to give or sell your iPhone to someone else and remove any content first.

The final options on the Summary pane allow you to control the sync process. You can choose to have your iPhone sync automatically whenever it is connected to your computer or only when you click the Sync button in iTunes. Automatic syncing ensures that your iPhone's contents remain current, but it can get bothersome if you are only plugging your iPhone in to charge it through your computer's USB port.

You also have an option to sync only checked songs and videos. If you have songs or videos in iTunes that you don't want synced to your iPhone (either because of the content or simply to save space), you can select this option. You can then deselect the check box next to those items that you don't want to sync in your library (select the Music, Movies, or TV Shows items in the sidebar to view your library).

Finally, you can choose to manually manage music and videos on your iPhone. When this option is selected, iTunes will not sync any music, movies, or TV shows to your iPhone (even if you click the Sync button). Instead, you will need to drag and drop individual songs, albums, movies, audio books, TV shows, podcasts, or playlists onto the iPhone's icon in the sidebar to copy them to it.

With this option, iTunes will treat your iPhone almost as if it's a playlist—allowing you to add and remove content whenever you like (though new purchases or downloads will not automatically be copied to the iPhone). This option is particularly helpful if you regularly attach your iPhone to more than one computer, as you can copy media from multiple iTunes libraries to a single iPhone (though all those computers will need to be associated with a single iTunes Store account to play protected content from the iTunes Store).

The Info Pane and Where iTunes Finds Your Information

Your iPhone can store and sync a variety of personal and professional data. Some of that data resides in iTunes itself—namely music, movies, TV shows, and podcasts. Other data resides elsewhere on your computer and is typically stored or managed by other programs. Although iTunes will be the tool that you use to manage the iPhone, it will act as a gatekeeper rather than a source for most professional information, including e-mail accounts, contacts, and calendars.

The Info pane in iTunes (shown in Figure 1-4) determines what non-iTunes data is synced with your iPhone. You can choose to sync contacts, calendars, e-mail accounts, and web browser bookmarks. In many ways, syncing this data from your computer makes setup of services on the iPhone extremely simple (particularly for e-mail accounts) because iTunes will prepopulate everything based on how your computer is set up.

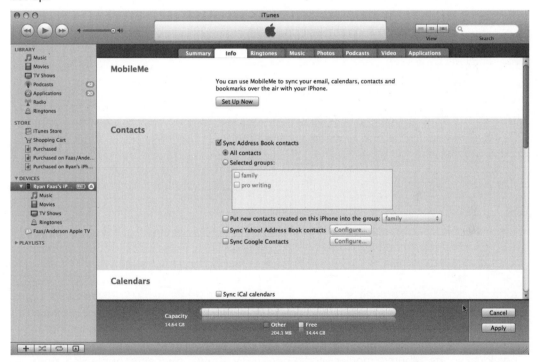

Figure 1-4. *Choosing what to sync using the Info pane for an iPhone in iTunes under Mac OS X*

Mac OS X

Since Mac OS X and Windows differ slightly in terms of what applications store information, we'll look at each separately. If you are using a Mac, iTunes will sync contacts to your iPhone (which include people's names, phone numbers, e-mail addresses, physical mail addresses, and similar information) from Mac OS X's Address

Book. Address Book is also accessible to many Mac OS X applications, most notably the Mail e-mail application and the iChat instant messenger.

> **TIP:** You can also choose to sync contacts from popular web services including those offered by Yahoo! and Google.

Calendars and event information will be synced from Apple's iCal. If you have multiple calendars created in iCal, you can choose which ones to sync. You also have the option of not syncing data for events that have already passed using the "Do not sync events older than X days" check box and number field.

If you choose to sync e-mail accounts, you have the option of copying the settings (server, username, and password) for each e-mail account that you've configured in Apple's Mail program. Again, you can choose to sync any or all accounts that have been configured on your Mac. This does not, however, sync your messages. It will only sync the information about the e-mail account. iTunes will also offer to sync bookmarks with the Safari web browser. This can be a very helpful tool, as any bookmarks you have on your Mac will be copied to your iPhone.

> **NOTE**: Although you can sync e-mail accounts, e-mail signatures are not synced to the iPhone—though as you'll learn in Chapter 6, you can configure a signature on the iPhone itself (the default signature being "Sent from my iPhone"). However, the iPhone only supports one signature that is used across every e-mail account it is configured to access (as opposed to having separate signature for each account).

Finally, at the bottom of the Summary pane is an Advanced section. This allows you to designate that specific items on your computer (contacts, calendar events, e-mail account information, and bookmarks) will override and replace whatever data is currently stored on the iPhone during the next sync. This can be helpful if you have duplicate data or as a troubleshooting solution if there are conflicts between data on the computer and on the iPhone. Typically, you should avoid this section, however, as unilaterally replacing information can lead to data loss if you've updated information on the iPhone but not on your computer.

> **NOTE:** If you're a Mac user that relies on Microsoft's Entourage rather than the built-in Apple tools just listed, you will see the option to sync contacts, calendars, and e-mail accounts from Entourage as well.

Windows

If you are using a Windows PC (see Figure 1-5), iTunes will also offer to sync the same information as it can sync in Mac OS X on the Info pane, as discussed in the last section. The difference is that iTunes will pull that same information from different sources. You can choose to sync contacts from Windows Address Book/Outlook Express, Microsoft Outlook, or the supported web services described earlier. You can sync e-mail account information from either Outlook Express or Outlook. You can sync calendars from Outlook. If you have Safari for Windows installed, you can choose to sync either Safari bookmarks or Internet Explorer bookmarks.

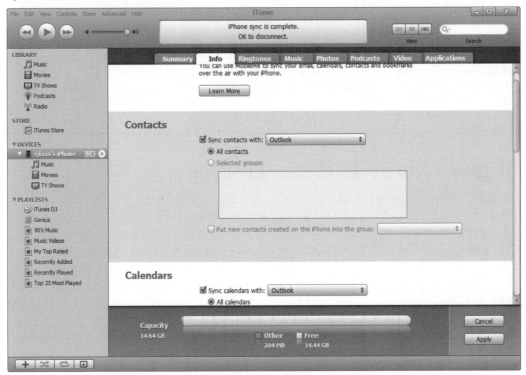

Figure 1-5. *Choosing what to sync using the Info pane for an iPhone in iTunes under Windows*

Aside from using different tools to manage the data that you sync to your iPhone, when using an iPhone with Windows, you will only be able to sync information from one source (such as e-mail accounts from either Outlook or Outlook Express, but not both). Although this generally doesn't create any problems (particularly for most professional users, who rely on Outlook as a central source for contacts, e-mails, and calendars), it is a contrast to Mac OS X, which can sync data from multiple sources to the iPhone.

CHOOSING WHAT AND WHERE TO SYNC

Although iTunes can sync a variety of information to your iPhone, you don't need to sync absolutely everything to it. If you're using the iPhone in a professional situation, it may actually make a good deal of sense to not sync personal music or photos, particularly if the device is owned by your employer. When choosing what to sync, consider what data is critical to your job and begin from there. Also consider any acceptable use policies for your company's mobile phones, computer, and Internet access.

Another issue to consider for professional users is where to sync your iPhone. Once synced to a computer, the iPhone relies primarily on that computer for any information you choose to sync to it. At a time when most of us use multiple computers in a day, you may want to give some thought to whether to use a home or office computer as the primary source for syncing your iPhone.

iTunes Sync vs. Over-the-Air Sync

So far, I've talked about syncing an iPhone with iTunes. This is the primary sync solution and it is the one that is required for iPhone activation. The iPhone does, however, support over-the-air (wireless) syncing as well. You can configure the iPhone to sync contacts, calendars, and bookmarks over the air using either Apple's MobileMe service (which costs $99/year) or Microsoft's ActiveSync protocol with Exchange server.

MobileMe

MobileMe is a consumer-oriented service, but for individual professionals and small businesses, it can be a useful tool. It includes over-the-air syncing with the iPhone, as well as a web storage space called an *iDisk* that can be used for sharing files between computers, hosting a web site, online photo/video galleries, and an @me.com e-mail address that supports push notification (which allows MobileMe to inform your iPhone immediately when new e-mail arrives). MobileMe can also be used to sync a variety of settings between multiple computers, and allows you to access all your synced information through the MobileMe web site (Figure 1-6).

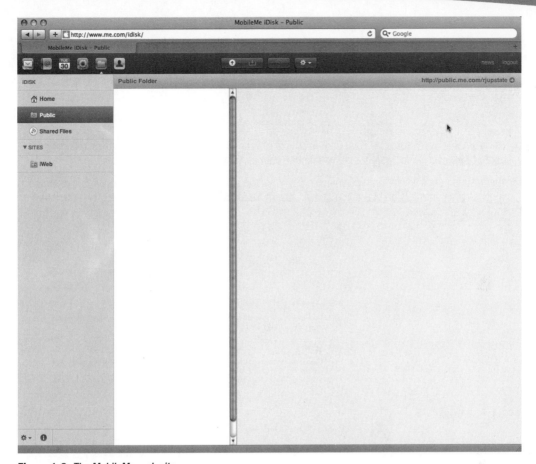

Figure 1-6. *The MobileMe web site*

One particularly advantageous feature of MobileMe for iPhone users beyond over-the-air sync is Find My iPhone. As you can see in Figure 1-7, Find My iPhone allows you to locate a missing iPhone (using its built-in location and GPS features to plot its location on a map), and it can also be used to send a message that is displayed on the phone and play an alert sound (even if the phone is locked or in silent mode). This can be helpful if your iPhone is lost or stolen, or even if you've just misplaced it somewhere in your home or office.

You can also issue a command to remotely wipe all data from your iPhone (an excellent feature if it is stolen or contains confidential information). When you issue this command, the iPhone will lock and begin resetting itself to its factory defaults—erasing all your settings, information, and any media that you've synced to it. If you recover the iPhone, you can restore your data by connecting it to your computer and using the option to set up using the backup made during its last sync.

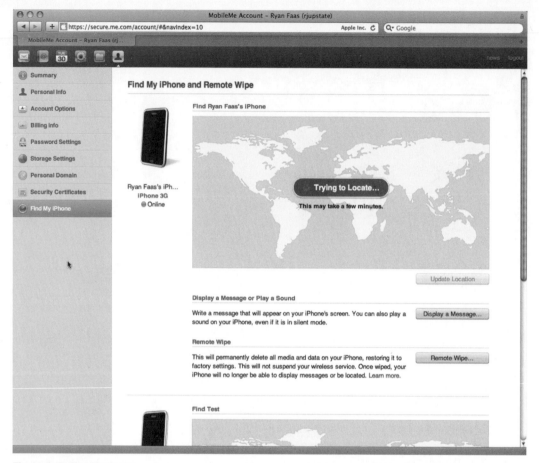

Figure 1-7. *Find My iPhone*

NOTE: MobileMe provides a Find My iPod touch service as well, though its results may be poorer, as the iPod touch can only approximate its location based on Skyhook's Wi-Fi hotspots database, and because the iPod touch must be connected to a Wi-Fi network in order for MobileMe to communicate with it at all.

Exchange

Syncing to an Exchange server also allows you to wirelessly sync contacts and calendars. Exchange is a powerful messaging and collaboration suite from Microsoft that interfaces with all the features available in Microsoft Outlook. I'll cover Exchange and ActiveSync in detail in Chapter 9, and I'll further touch on MobileMe in various chapters, beginning with Chapter 6. But first, in the next chapter, I'll walk you through the process of actually using the iPhone's basic features for the first time.

Summary

This chapter covered the initial steps of purchasing, activating, and syncing an iPhone to your computer. In the next chapter, you'll learn the basics of the iPhone's interface and how to use it, followed by how to get connected to the Internet on your company's network in Chapter 3. Then, in Part 2 of this book, you'll look at each of the built-in applications and features on the iPhone, how to use them, and how to apply them in business and professional settings.

Chapter 2

Using Your iPhone for the First Time

Setting Up and Getting to Know the iPhone

Once your iPhone (or iPod touch) is activated and has been synced to iTunes for the first time, you're ready to actually get started using it. In this chapter, I'll introduce you to the basic features and interface of the iPhone and iPod touch. Then we'll take a look at how to configure some of the basic settings and how to make sure your device and the data on it remain secure.

Getting to Know the Physical Hardware

Let's start the introduction to your iPhone or iPod touch with a short overview of the physical buttons and ports on these devices. If you've already played with your device and gotten familiar with the physical components, feel free to skip to the next section, where I'll discuss the iPhone/iPod touch user interface and how to work with it.

Dock and Headphone Ports

The iPhone and iPod touch both share the same physical ports: a headphone jack and an iPod-style dock connector. The headphone jack can accept the standard Apple headphones as well as any standard 1/8th-inch miniplug headphones. These include the majority of headphones on the market for any device (helpful if you find Apple's earbud-style headphones uncomfortable or want higher-quality headphone options). The headphone jack is located on the top edge of the iPhone near the left side (if you are holding the iPhone facing yourself). The iPod touch has the headphone jack located on the bottom edge near the right side.

> **NOTE:** The original iPhone's headphone jack was slightly recessed, which made it incompatible with many standard headphones. Adapters from both Griffin Technology and Belkin, however, allow you to use standard headphones with the original iPhone.

While the iPod touch ships with the standard Apple-issued iPod headphones, all iPhone models ship with headphones that include a small button/mic combination about halfway down the right headphone. This allows the headphones to also serve as a hands-free headset for talking during phone calls. The button allows you to answer an incoming call simply by clicking it. You can also click the button to pause/play while listening to music, or double-click to skip past the currently playing song.

The dock connector runs along the center of the bottom edge of both the iPhone and iPod touch. The dock connector is used via a standard iPhone/iPod dock cable to connect to your computer's USB port. This USB end of the cable also plugs into the AC adapter included with the iPhone to work as a power charger. Finally, the dock connector can be used with various docking devices and other accessories (including basic audio devices and car chargers, as well as a range of new devices introduced since the summer of 2009 that can expand the capabilities of the iPhone, such as portable projectors and turn-by-turn navigation devices). On the iPhone, speakers for internal sound and pickups for your voice when speaking on a call are located on either side of the dock connector.

SIM Card Tray

The iPhone's SIM card tray is located in the center of the top edge of the iPhone (as you may have noticed when you purchased and activated your iPhone). The tray can be ejected by inserting a straightened-out paper clip in the hole on the tray. Once ejected, the SIM card can be lifted off the tray. Typically, you will only need to eject the SIM card if you are selling or replacing an iPhone, or as part of troubleshooting.

Physical Buttons

For the most part, the iPhone and iPod touch rely on virtual onscreen icons and buttons to perform actions. However, there are four physical buttons that you will end up using pretty frequently.

The Home Button

The Home button is located just below the iPhone/iPod touch screen. The primary purpose of this button is to quit an application and return to the home screen. If you have created multiple home screens, clicking it from any home screen will return you automatically to the first home screen (I'll cover multiple home screens in just a bit). If you are on the first home screen, clicking the Home button will bring you to the Spotlight search screen, which you can use to search for items (applications, notes, e-mail, appointments, etc.) stored on your iPhone across many apps. It can also be used to wake an iPhone/iPod touch from sleep.

On the iPhone, double-clicking the Home button can also be set to launch the iPhone's Phone application and immediately display your list of favorite contacts, to bring you immediately to the search screen, to bring up the iPod application, or to launch the

Camera app to snap photos (the default setting is to launch the Phone app). It can also be set to bring up a minidisplay that allows you to pause or skip backward and forward through the currently playing music without needing to launch the iPod application. (I'll cover how to set this behavior later in this chapter when we talk about configuring general settings.)

Sleep/Wake Button

The Sleep/Wake button is located along the top edge of the iPhone (to the right) and iPod touch (on the left-hand side). This button allows you to put the device into sleep mode, turning off the screen and locking the device. When in sleep/locked mode, clicking this button will wake it and allow you to unlock it. Sleeping a device is not the same as turning it off—music will continue to play, e-mail will continue to be periodically checked, and calls will be received while a device is locked or sleeping.

Volume Controls

Located along the left side of the iPhone and iPod touch are a pair of connected buttons that control volume. As you might guess, the upper one turns the volume up and the lower one turns it down. This will adjust the volume of a currently playing song, the sound from a running application, the volume of a current call, or (if no application is running and there is no call) the ring volume of the iPhone.

Vibrate/Silent Switch

Located directly above the volume controls on the iPhone is a small switch that can be used to turn on silent/vibrate mode. One thing worth noting about this switch is that while it will silence ringtones for incoming calls, as well as sounds for incoming text messages, voicemails, and e-mails, it will not silence any alarms set in the iPhone's Clock application.

The side button which silences the phone is extremely useful. Unlike other "smartphones" I've had where you had to do multiple things to ensure the phone would be quiet, the iPhone keeps it very simple.

Phil Clarke, IT Manager

Multitouch

With the exception of the buttons I just mentioned, all interaction with the iPhone and iPod touch is done using the touchscreen and a technology Apple calls *multitouch*. Multitouch goes beyond being a simple touchscreen, because it also allows you to scroll through displays by dragging your finger up and down along the surface of the screen. It also allows you to place two fingers on the screen and pinch them together to zoom out or spread them apart to zoom in while viewing photos, documents, and web pages. Multitouch is completely intuitive, and it will take you only a couple of minutes of use to grasp.

The very first instance of multitouch that you will see is when you first turn on or wake an iPhone or iPod touch, when you will see the screen shown in Figure 2-1 asking you to use your finger to move a virtual slider to unlock the device.

Figure 2-1. *The unlock screen of the iPhone*

> **TIP:** In any application that supports scrolling content, you can always tap the information bar containing the time, battery life, and carrier information at the top of the screen to immediately jump to the top of the application's content.

The Home Screen

The home screen (shown in Figure 2-2) is the launchpad for every function of the iPhone and iPod touch. It contains icons for every available application (both the built-in ones and those that you install). Launching an application is as simple as tapping its icon once with your finger. Quitting an application and returning to the home screen is as simple as pressing the Home button.

If the home screen becomes full, the iPhone or iPod touch will automatically create additional home screens to accommodate additional icons (up to 11 home screens are supported). When additional screens are created, you will see a series of white dots at the bottom of the each screen, with each dot representing one home screen (the dot indicating your current screen will be brighter than the others). You can switch to adjacent screens by swiping your finger right or left across the surface of the current screen, or by clicking a dot representing a specific screen (and as I mentioned earlier, you can double-click the Home button to return to the first screen).

There is also a four-icon dock at the bottom of home screen display. This dock will display the same four icons no matter which home screen you are using. By default, the dock will contain the Phone, Mail, Safari, and iPod applications on the iPhone, and Music, Videos, Photos, and iTunes Store on the iPod touch. The next section shows how to alter the dock.

Figure 2-2. *The home screen*

> **TIP:** One of the big things to keep in mind about the iPhone and iPod touch is that every available feature is really an application. If you want to make a phone call, you will launch the Phone app. If you want to play music, videos, or podcasts, you will launch the iPod app. If you want to adjust general device and some application-specific settings, you will launch the Settings app (which I'll talk about later in this chapter). This means that every feature is accessible from an icon on the home screen.

Organizing the Home Screen

Although the built-in applications follow the layout shown in Figure 2-2 (and additional applications are added after the built-in applications in the order in which they are downloaded and installed), you can organize applications however you want. You can even change which applications are displayed in the dock shown at the bottom of every home screen.

To do this, press and hold on any icon on the home screen for a few seconds until you see the icons being to jiggle (see Figure 2-3). At this point, you can place your finger on any icon and drag it to a different location. The existing icons will shift to make room for any icon you reposition. If you want to replace an icon in the dock, simply drag one of the other icons to its position in the dock. When you're satisfied with the changes, click the Home button again to return to normal use.

Figure 2-3. *The home screen ready to reposition applications*

You can also move icons from one home screen to another. All you need to do is drag an icon to the right or left edge of the current home screen. As you hold the icon at the edge of one home screen, the next will slide into view and the icon will move to it. You can even create additional home screens before the home screen (or screens) is full by dragging the icon to the right edge of the rightmost home screen (or the right edge if you currently have only one home screen).

If you've installed additional applications, you'll notice that when their icons jiggle, they will include an X icon in the upper-left corner. Clicking this X will delete the application (you will see a confirmation asking if you want to actually delete the icon, so don't worry about accidentally deleting them—in fact, Apple will ask you to rate an application when you delete it and will factor your rating into the ratings listed in the App Store).

TIP: The ability to organize apps across one or more home screens and choose which apps appear in the dock is a powerful tool. It allows you to group your most commonly used apps together for easy access. You can even create home screens that are devoted to specific types of applications, particularly once you begin adding applications beyond those that come with the iPhone or iPod touch. You might, for example, create one home screen for all your e-mail, messaging, and social networking apps, another for travel- and weather-related apps, and another related to specific types of business apps.

The Search Screen

With the iPhone OS 3.0 update that Apple released in the summer of 2009, a special home screen addition known as the Spotlight search screen was added. This screen, shown in Figure 2-4, can be accessed by clicking the Home button from the first home screen, by flicking right past the first home screen, or by tapping the small magnifying glass icon next to the row of dots representing your home screens.

Figure 2-4. *The Spotlight search screen*

As I mentioned earlier, the search screen allows you to search across all of your iPhone applications. This gives you a great one-stop place to go if you need to locate anything on your iPhone. Simply begin typing your query using the onscreen keyboard. As you type, you'll see any matching results. The search is a live search, which means that results are displayed as you type—so, you typically only need to type a few letters to find what you want, rather than having to type multiple words or phrases.

> **TIP:** The search screen can serve as a quick application launcher because it includes applications in searches. This can be really helpful if you've installed a large number of applications across many home screens and need to find them quickly. Also, because of this, you can install more apps (there is actually no limit to the number of apps you can install except storage space) on the iPhone than would fit on the 11 possible home screens), because it can serve as a way of finding and launching apps even if they aren't displayed on a home screen.

> **Tip:** Most of the built-in applications also offer application-specific search boxes, though they aren't always displayed. To see them, simply flick up past the top of the screen, and they will pop into view.

The Built-In Apps

The iPhone and iPod touch both ship with a number of built-in applications. These include applications that offer traditional phone and PDA features (such as calling and managing contacts), as well as several dedicated applications for other, often Internet-related, functions. The following list is an overview of the built-in applications (items with an asterisk are included only on the iPhone). With the exception of the Settings app, which I'll cover later in this chapter, each of the applications is detailed in Part 2 of this book.

- **Phone:** The Phone app, as you might guess, is used to place and manage phone calls. It also manages the iPhone's Visual Voicemail feature and can be used to view contact information and call histories.*

- **Mail:** Mail is the built-in e-mail application for the iPhone and iPod touch. It can be used to send and receive e-mails, as well as manage e-mail accounts.

- **Safari:** Safari is the mobile version of Apple's web browser, and is the primary web browser for the iPhone and iPod touch.

- **iPod:** The iPod app provides all the iPod functionality of the iPhone and iPod touch, including playing music, movies, and TV shows, and podcasts that have synced from iTunes (on the iPod touch, this app is broken into separate apps: Music and Video).

- **Contacts:** This is the contact management tool. It includes contacts synced from a computer, through MobileMe, or from an Exchange server (it also provides access to the Global Address List feature of Exchange). You can view, add, and edit contacts directly in the Contacts app.

- **Messages:** Messages is the SMS/text and multimedia messaging application for the iPhone.*

- **Calendar:** This is the calendar application for the iPhone and iPod touch. It supports viewing and editing multiple calendars, and can sync to a computer through MobileMe, or to an Exchange server.

- **Camera:** The Camera app provides the ability to take photos using the iPhone's built-in camera. Note that some apps can also access the camera, though this is the primary interface for it.*

- **Photos:** The Photos app is the photo library manager for the iPhone and iPod touch. It allows you to browse and view slide shows of photos synced from your computer, downloaded from Safari, sent in e-mail attachments, or taken from the Camera app. It also allows you to e-mail photos, upload them to MobileMe's web galleries, and set them as the iPhone's wallpaper (displayed on the lock screen).

- **YouTube:** This is the dedicated YouTube browser that allows you to search/browse and view YouTube videos.

- **Maps:** Maps is the Google Maps application that allows you to view your current location using the iPhone's location services, look up addresses and business, view maps (with or without satellite imagery), and get directions (by car, by public transportation, or on foot).

- **Calculator:** As its name implies, this is a fully functional calculator.

- **Weather:** The Weather app allows you to see current weather conditions and a basic five-day forecast for one or more cities.

- **Clock:** Clock is an application that provides a number of time-related features, including a world clock for views of the current time in varying global locations, an alarm clock (multiple alarms are supported), a stopwatch, and a countdown timer.

- **Settings:** The Settings app allows you to manage a number of different configuration options for the iPhone and iPod touch.

- **App Store:** The App Store provides direct access to Apple's App Store for purchasing, downloading, and installing additional third-party applications. Purchases are backed up the next time you sync with your computer.

- **iTunes:** Similar to the App Store, iTunes provides direct access to purchase and download music and podcasts (but not movies or TV shows) from the iTunes Store. Purchases are added to your computer's iTunes library the next time you sync.

- **Notes:** The Notes app allows you to type multiple notes to yourself (each note appears as a page of yellow legal paper).

- **Stocks:** Similar to Weather, Stocks allows you to track multiple stock prices in real time.

- **Voice Memos:** Voice Memos allows you to make audio recordings, such as voice notes, lectures, and even your own podcasts. Recordings are automatically copied as audio files into your iTunes library when you sync your iPhone.

NOTE: The iPhone 3GS also includes a Compass application that can be used to display your current direction.

Using the Onscreen Keyboard

The iPhone and iPod touch use an onscreen keyboard (shown in Figure 2-5) for text input in any application. In many ways, this is an effective solution, and it allows the iPhone platform to make use of the entire face of the device as a touchscreen. But I won't lie—it does take some getting used to, particularly if you're used to the physical keyboards common on other smart phones such as most Blackberry models.

The keyboard will automatically be displayed whenever you tap your finger on a text field either in an application or on a web page. It will display as a standard QWERTY keyboard (unless you've chosen a non-English language, in which case it will display as the standard keyboard layout for that language). An up arrow key functions like a Shift key, allowing you to type capital letters, and a number/symbol key allows you to view numbers and special characters in place of the standard QWERTY display. In some instances (mostly when working with Internet-related data), you may also see keys at the bottom of the standard keyboard with the @ symbol and ".com," allowing you to type these items more quickly.

NOTE: When you tap the uppercase key, the next letter you tap will be typed in uppercase. If you hold the key, any letters you tap while holding it will be typed in uppercase.

TIP: Holding the .com key will display a pop-up menu over the key allows you to select similar Internet suffixes like .org and .edu.

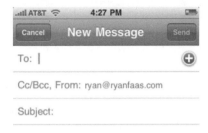

Figure 2-5. *The standard portrait keyboard*

Landscape vs. Portrait Typing

Because the iPhone and iPod touch can determine the angle at which you're holding them (horizontally or vertically), many applications can rotate to display in either orientation. In some but not all applications (including most built-in applications) that accept text input, you can rotate the device to landscape orientation. This provides a much wider, and for many people, easier-to-type-on, keyboard (as shown in Figure 2-6).

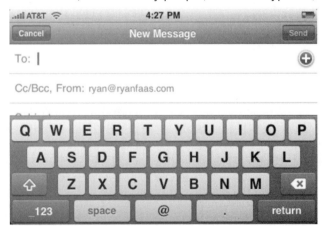

Figure 2-6. *Typing in landscape mode*

Make Auto-Correct Your Friend (Or Turn It Off)

Another feature to be aware of when typing on the iPhone or iPod touch is the auto-correct feature. This feature, shown in Figure 2-7, attempts to correct potentially misspelled words as you type. If auto-correct thinks you're mistyping a word, it will display potentially correct spellings. Hitting the spacebar will accept a correction. Tapping the X in the correction pop-up will reject it.

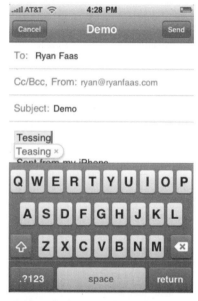

Figure 2-7. *The auto-correct feature*

Auto-correct can be a useful feature, particularly since it tends to learn from your typing habits as you reject its suggestions for things that you consider words that it doesn't. In fact, after enough use, it will start suggesting words that were not part of its original dictionary. After enough use, it can even function as an auto-complete feature by suggesting words when you have only partially finished typing them, which is very helpful.

Unfortunately, auto-correct can also be annoying—never more so than when you first start using an iPhone or iPod touch, before it has learned your typing habits (including your common errors as well as personal vocabulary). When you first start typing, the natural inclination is to type an entire word and hit the spacebar. Unfortunately, until you and auto-correct get used to each other, doing this can easily end up with a word other than the one you intended being substituted.

My advice is to use auto-correct, but don't expect it to be perfect. It may take you a few weeks to become used to the feature, and it may take auto-correct weeks or months to get used to your typing habits. Eventually, you'll probably make friends with each other. However, if you find it too distracting and frustrating to make it through this trial-and-error period, you can disable this feature in the Settings application.

Cut, Copy, and Paste

With the iPhone OS 3 release, Apple introduced the ability to cut/copy and paste text and images throughout the iPhone applications, similar to how you can use these features on a computer. This feature works in any application for copying and pasting text, and in several applications for working with images.

To select text to copy or cut, simply tap and hold on a piece of text for a few seconds. You'll see cartoon bubble–like pop-up that will give you the option to select text to copy, and will include Select and Select All. To select all the text, simply tap Select All (see Figure 2-8). To select specific text, click Select. The iPhone will select the current word automatically and place blue anchor dots on either side. To select more text, simply drag the anchor dots to encompass the additional text (Figure 2-8).

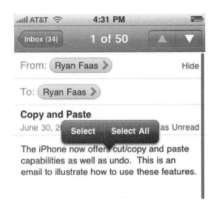

Figure 2-8. *Selecting text*

With your text selected, click the Copy pop-up that appears during selection. If you're copying from an editable text field (such as in a web form or an e-mail), you'll also see a Cut option. To paste text, simply tap and hold in an editable text field and tap the Paste pop-up (Figure 2-9).

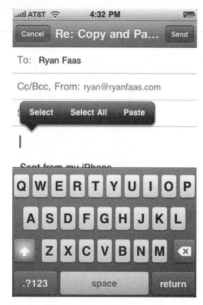

Figure 2-9. *Pasting text*

> **TIP:** In some instances, when you first tap and hold, you'll see a magnifying glass icon allowing you to position a cursor at a specific point between letters in a word when making a text selection or pasting. In these instances, select a position and lift your finger to see the various select and paste pop-ups.

> **NOTE:** Some applications have specific options when it comes to copying and pasting (including the ability to copy and paste images). I'll cover those situations throughout this book where appropriate to the app.

Undo

The iPhone also supports the undo feature common in many computer applications that allows you to undo mistakes such as text deletions, but implements it in a novel yet effective way. If you make a major mistake while typing or editing something, simply shake the iPhone up and down. An undo alert will appear, giving you the option to undo your last action or cancel (in case you have shaken the iPhone by accident).

Meet the Settings App

The Settings app, shown in Figure 2-10, is the tool that you'll use to customize your iPhone or iPod touch. By default, the Settings app includes 13 settings options, though third-party applications can also use Settings as a central location for configuration options. So, once you've installed additional applications, you may notice that the list of options in the Settings app gets longer.

Figure 2-10. *The Settings app*

> **NOTE:** The exact appearance and options in Settings will vary a little between the iPhone and iPod touch.

You may also notice that certain options in the Settings app are grouped together. The first two options all relate to network connectivity (Airplane Mode and Wi-Fi), which I'll cover in the next chapter. Similarly, the three options that allow you adjust the overall look and feel of you iPhone (Sounds, Brightness, and Wallpaper) are also grouped together as a trio. The remaining six default options (General; Mail, Contacts, Calendars; Phone; Safari; iPod; and Photos) are also grouped together, as will be the case for any options for third-party apps that you install.

I'll cover most of these options in chapters throughout this book, but let's begin with the General option of any mobile device—which provides information about your device and can be used to secure the device and your data in case it is ever lost or stolen.

The setup was quick and easy. It actually shocked me how simple it was. I kept thinking to myself "I must be missing something." Turns out—it was just that easy.

Joanna Palladino, State Government Workforce Development Specialist

General Options

Each of these options can be set using the General option in the Settings application (see Figure 2-11), which also displays information about your device, including general details like name, network, and current contents, and device-specific information like serial number, device hardware details (Figure 2-12), and current usage statistics (Figure 2-13).

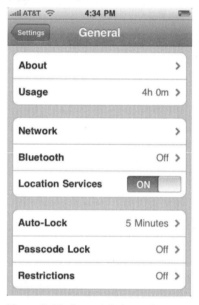

Figure 2-11. *General device options*

Figure 2-12. *About a device*

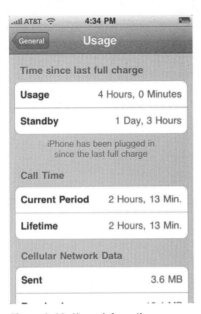

Figure 2-13. *Usage information*

Network and Service Options

The Network option allows you to determine which network technologies are enabled on your device. Obviously, this will vary slightly between the original and 3G iPhone models as well as between an iPhone and iPod touch, but the options will be similar to what you see in Figure 2-14.

Figure 2-14. *Network options*

All iPhone OS devices will include the ability to enable and configure Wi-Fi and VPN (secure virtual tunnels through the Internet to a company network), which I'll cover in the next chapter. iPhones will also include the option to disable international data roaming when traveling abroad (an important feature, as data roaming charges can vary and be quite costly when you go from one country to another, and thus one carrier to another).

The iPhone 3G and 3GS models also include the option to disable higher-speed 3G cellular networks. 3G networks are significantly faster than older data networks (known as EDGE networks), but connecting using 3G networks is often more taxing on an iPhone's battery life. Thus, disabling 3G networking can save power, but data access will be much slower.

Bluetooth

Bluetooth is a wireless technology that allows multiple devices and accessories to automatically discover each other and pair together. The primary example of this with the iPhone is the ability to pair with wireless headsets. Another example is a computer pairing with a wireless keyboard. Bluetooth can also allow you to tether a computer to your iPhone and connect to the Internet using your iPhone's Internet connection (typically through your mobile carrier's network).

> **NOTE:** Bluetooth can theoretically pose a security risk (which is part of the reason devices are paired with each other using a passcode, as shown in Figure 2-15). Using a random passcode can help secure devices, as can simply leaving Bluetooth disabled. Bluetooth can also have a negative impact on battery life, as it essentially is an additional transmitter that the iPhone must power.

Location Services

Location Services enables an iPhone or iPod touch to automatically determine your location based on GPS (in the iPhone 3G and iPhone 3GS) by triangulating against known cell phone towers (for the original iPhone or iPhone 3G/iPhone 3GS if a GPS signal can't be achieved—an issue for indoor uses), or by using a database of known Wi-Fi hotspots called Skyhook (for the iPhone and iPod touch). The accuracy of the location information may vary depending on which technologies are in use, though typically a GPS signal can result in location being accurately determined to within a few feet.

Location Services can be used by a device in many ways. It can plot your location using the built-in Maps application, it can encode location data in your photos, and it can be provided to a variety of third-party applications such as social networking sites. Whether you want to enable Location Services at all is up to you and how private or public your want your location to be. However, even if you have Location Services turned on, most applications will ask you before actually transmitting your location (the notable exception being the camera, which will simply encode it as part of a photo).

Securing Your Device

There are a number of ways to secure an iPhone or iPod touch, and you should consider a mix of the various options. Ultimately, you will want to choose a combination of options that provide you an optimal blend of security and usability of features. The exact blend you choose will come down to how comfortable you are with potential compromises of data vs. the tasks that you need to perform. Even if you don't make use of all of the options, you should be aware of what they are.

> **NOTE:** In some cases, your employer or IT department may actually decide how secure your device needs to be. In these situations, you may find that certain security features are automatically enabled on your iPhone or iPod touch when you receive it, or that they may be automatically updated using a configuration profile installed on the device (or by policies configured by an Exchange server or similar product). IT departments may update these requirements periodically.

Setting a Passcode and Auto-Lock

A passcode is one of the most effective way to safeguard data on any portable device. Although it isn't going to guarantee that the mobile device won't get lost or stolen, it will prevent whoever finds the device from actually being able to use it without performing a complete restore operation, which will effectively wipe any of your content off the device (the exception is emergency 911 calls, which are always allowed on the iPhone).

> **CAUTION:** Passcode policies are effective in preventing casual thieves from obtaining access to your data, but determined data forensics experts will likely be able to use a number of forensic tools to eventually recover some data, which is one reason a passcode alone may not be enough security for some businesses and critical information. Remote wipe through MobileMe's Find My iPhone feature or an Exchange server (see Chapter 7) can help secure an iPhone, and should be used to help protect your device.

To set a passcode, select the Passcode Lock option (see Figure 2-15), and then type in a four-digit numeric code. You will be asked for this code to unlock the device. Multiple unlock attempts are allowed by an iPhone or iPod touch, but the after three initial attempts, you (or whoever is in possession of the device) will be forced to wait longer periods between attempts and will eventually be locked out after multiple tries (your company's IT department can vary the number of tries of failed lockouts allowed on your iPhone through a configuration profile or Exchange server rules).

Figure 2-15. *Setting a passcode*

After final lockout, the device will need to be restored using iTunes.

The Auto-Lock option goes along with the passcode lock for security in that it automatically locks a device after the specified time frame. As you can see in Figure 2-16, intervals of 1 to 5 minutes are supported, as is the option to never lock automatically.

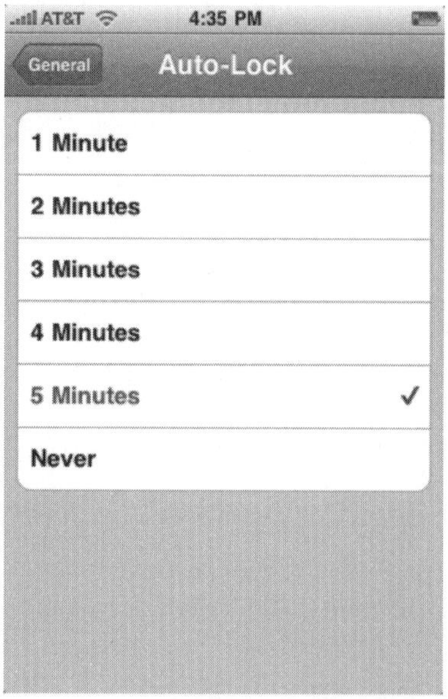

Figure 2-16. *Setting an auto-lock interval*

TIP: Auto-Lock isn't just about security. When a device is locked, the screen is disabled and running applications are paused (with the exception of the iPod app if music is playing). This makes it a great battery-saving feature as well.

Access Restrictions

You can configure access restrictions for the iPhone and iPod touch, which can function as part security feature and part parental controls. When access restrictions are enabled, you will be asked to enter another four-digit passcode in order to perform certain operations. As you can see in Figure 2-17, you can prevent web browsing with Safari, deny access to YouTube, prevent iTunes Store and App Store purchasing on the device, limit access to the camera, and force the disabling of Location Services.

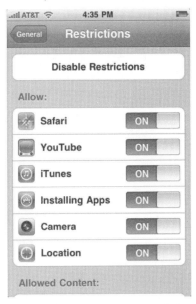

Figure 2-17. *Enabling access restrictions*

Many of these are restrictions that would legitimately present concerns for employees' iPhones. For example, a company is likely to prevent explicit content, YouTube, and purchases made on the device—both as a cost management feature as well as to limit the iPhone's use to business-oriented functions.

Restrictions can also set the type of content allowed on a device. There are options for allowing purchases from within applications and limiting access to the type of content that may be played. This limitation is determined using tags for content in the iTunes Store. For music, you can choose to limit content tagged as explicit. For movies and TV shows, you can choose allowed ratings (iTunes ratings are specific to the country in which the device is used and match the various governmental/industry standards for rating both TV shows and movies, such as the MPAA ratings system in the United States). For apps, the options include not allowing apps at all, and using the age-appropriate app-rating system that Apple has implemented in the App Store (age 4 and up, 9 and up, 12 and up, and 17 and up).

Interface Options

The next set of options allow you to define interface preferences for your device. As you can see in Figure 2-18, this includes a range of four options that define general device and phone behavior. Most people will probably use the default settings, but you may find your iPhone or iPod touch is easier to use with some changes.

Figure 2-18. *Options related to interface settings*

Home Button

The Home button options (Figure 2-19) allow you to control what happens when you double-click the Home button. For most people, the default Phone Favorites option makes sense, as it brings you directly to common calling features (if you're using the iPhone). But if you frequently play music or take snapshots, you may find it easier to set this to automatically launch the iPod or Camera applications.

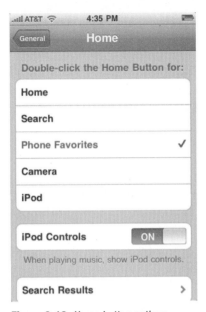

Figure 2-19. *Home button options*

You can also choose to have the iPod minicontrols display (Figure 2-20) if music is playing but you're working in other apps, as a quick way to pause or skip songs without leaving the current app.

Figure 2-20. *iPod minicontrols*

You can also configure what is displayed in search results on the Spotlight search screen. By default, search includes all the types of data shown in Figure 2-21. You can choose to omit some types of data from search results (e.g., you might want only business-related data to show up, so you could deselect Music, Podcasts, and Video) by tapping them to remove the check mark. You can also change the order in which search results appear. By default, they are displayed by type according to the order shown in Figure 2-21. If you want to change the order, tap the three-line icon to the right of the items in the list and drag to reorder the list.

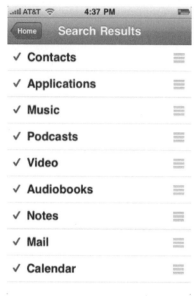

Figure 2-21. *Setting search results options*

Date & Time

Date & Time allows you to choose between displaying the time in 12-hour or 24-hour styles. It also allows you to set a device to automatically update the clock based on a carrier's time signal (commonly set with many phones and enabled by default).

Keyboard

The Keyboard options (Figure 2-22) allow you to enable the auto-correct feature (as discussed earlier in this chapter), auto-capitalization of new sentences, caps lock (in which case double-clicking the caps button on the keyboard will allow you to type capital letters without needing to press or hold the caps button), and the "." shortcut, in which a double-click of the spacebar will automatically insert a period.

Figure 2-22. *Keyboard options*

Finally, the International Keyboards option allows you to enable keyboards appropriate to a number of languages and alphabets. When international keyboards are enabled, a globe icon key is added. Tapping this key will cycle through the enabled keyboards in any application, with the name of the current keyboard language appearing on the spacebar as you cycle through them.

International Options

The International options (Figure 2-23) offer the ability to change the language that the iPhone or iPod touch displays to any one of several supported languages, and also offer another location for enabling international keyboards. When you change the language, you'll be returned to the home screen in the new language after a brief period as the language pack is loaded (to see this in action, be sure to pick a language you have an idea of navigating, since you'll need to get back to this option from the home screen to change it back). Finally, the International options allow you to specify formats for things such as date/time and phone/address details appropriate to any country where the iPhone or iPod touch is sold.

Figure 2-23. *International options*

> **NOTE:** International options only affect the display of an iPhone's interface. They do not offer the ability to change local carriers, which must be done using a SIM card. Even using an alternate SIM card may not allow you to switch carriers in many countries (including the United States), where carriers have exclusive relationships with Apple that allow them to tie the iPhones they sell to SIM cards for their networks.

Device Reset

The final option in the General settings is the Reset option. As you can see in Figure 2-24, there are a series of reset options. You can reset all settings across every application and option with or without erasing all content on the device (both of which can be common ways to troubleshoot problems, as well as to present a cleaned-up device to another person). You can also reset just network-related settings (again, useful for troubleshooting problems as well as removing preferred network choices and passwords).

Figure 2-24. *Reset options*

To get the iPhone back to a state that resembles its default look without erasing settings and contents, you also have the option of erasing any custom words that it has added to the auto-correct dictionary. You can also quickly restore the locations of icons on the home screen to their original locations (third-party apps will simply be grouped on pages after the built-in apps). Finally, you can reset Location Services alerts, requiring all applications to ask permission to use your location.

Summary

In this chapter, you learned the basics of working with the iPhone and iPod touch, as well as how to configure a number of basic options and settings. In Chapter 3, I'll talk about how to configure network and Internet access, and discuss what the options are for getting online at work, at home, and even in the middle of nowhere.

Getting Online

Understanding and Using EDGE, 3G, and Wi-Fi for Internet Access

As the *i* in *iPhone* implies, this is a device that is all about the Internet. In this chapter, you'll learn about the different ways the iPhone and iPod touch can connect to the Internet, and how to get online using each of them. You'll also learn about how to securely access a remote office network by configuring virtual private networking so that you can use business resources at any time from anywhere in the world.

Mobile Carrier Networks vs. Wi-Fi

The iPhone offers two primary choices for accessing the Internet: data connection through the mobile carrier, which uses the same connection that is used to place calls and send text messages, and Wi-Fi, which connects though a wireless network router in the same way that a laptop would in your home or office. Both options have their pros and cons. The iPod touch, however, only offers Wi-Fi connectivity.

Wi-Fi is usually a faster option because the areas of the radio spectrum used by Wi-Fi generally allow greater performance when transferring information, and because the connection to the Internet of a wireless router is generally faster than a data connection as well. However, Wi-Fi requires that you be within range of a wireless network. On the other hand, access through a carrier's network may be slower, but you can generally be assured that you will be able to access the Internet any place that you happen to be.

3G and EDGE Networking

Access to the Internet through a mobile carrier's network can be done using one of two technologies on the iPhone. EDGE networking (sometimes referred to as "2G networking" because it represented the second major generation of mobile data service) is an older technology. As I mentioned previously, EDGE networking is significantly slower than the second option, known as 3G (for "third generation") service.

Although EDGE is both older and slower, the fact that it is older means that it has been deployed across a much broader range of areas. It also requires less radio signal and therefore less battery power than 3G. By contrast, 3G can reach near–broadband Internet access speeds and is deployed in most major cities in the United States (and even more broadly in Europe and Asia). An original iPhone is limited to EDGE, but an iPhone 3G or 3GS will automatically use 3G service (unless you've disabled it, as discussed in the previous chapter) when possible, and switch to EDGE if 3G isn't available. In some remote locations, you may find that neither EDGE nor 3G infrastructure is available (in which case, you'll need a Wi-Fi network in order to get online).

> **TIP:** If you're traveling, you can check AT&T's web site (or that of another carrier) to determine where 3G coverage is available in advance. AT&T's coverage maps detail where general data coverage is available and where 3G coverage is available.

Generally, there is no need to configure your iPhone to use either EDGE or 3G networking. The iPhone will automatically detect and use either technology. The only configuration, as detailed in Chapter 2, is whether to enable 3G or to allow international data roaming.

Knowing When and How You're Connected

The iPhone will automatically choose the best Internet access available. You can tell how (or if) you're connected by the icon displayed in the status bar at the top of the iPhone's display between the carrier name/signal strength bars and the time. Figure 3-1 shows the icons for EDGE, 3G, and Wi-Fi, respectively, from left to right.

Figure 3-1. *The iPhone network icons*

Connecting to Wi-Fi

Wi-Fi networking isn't quite as automatic as EDGE/3G (though it does come close). By default, the iPhone and iPod touch will automatically detect Wi-Fi networks. When you attempt to access the Internet but are not connected via Wi-Fi, both devices will provide a list of available networks and ask if you want to join one of them, as you can see in Figure 3-2.

Figure 3-2. *Wi-Fi network detection*

In addition to the names of networks, you'll see an icon representing the relative signal strength of the network (the Wi-Fi icon in the status bar will also show the relative strength of a network that you are connected to), as well as a lock icon for any network that requires a password to join. Joining a network is as easy as tapping it in this list.

If the network is protected (both devices support a range of secure Wi-Fi protocols and will automatically select the most secure protocol available for a protected network), you'll be asked to enter a password to join it (the password is the same one you'd use for a laptop to join a network).

Once you've joined a network, the iPhone/iPod touch will remember it (and the password if one is needed), and will automatically connect to that network and use it whenever it is available. In some cases, such as in office, school, or public networks, you may find that the same network is available in multiple geographic locations. In these situations, the iPhone will still automatically connect to that network if available.

Managing Wi-Fi Networks and Options

The Wi-Fi option in the Settings app allows you to manage which Wi-Fi networks your device uses, as well as see which network, if any, you are currently connected to. Figure 3-3 shows the Settings app displaying the current network, while Figure 3-4 shows the Wi-Fi Networks options screen. From this screen, you can disable Wi-Fi entirely, view all available networks, select a network other than the one you are currently using, and disable the default automatic prompts to join detected networks (in which case, you'll need to use the Settings app to connect to any network).

Figure 3-3. *Settings app showing current Wi-Fi network*

Figure 3-4. *Wi-Fi networking options*

By selecting the small arrow icon next to each network, you can view additional details about the network. This screen, shown in Figure 3-5, can aid technicians and other IT staff in troubleshooting Wi-Fi connection problems. On this screen, you can also instruct the iPhone to stop automatically connecting to a network by clicking the Forget this Network button.

Figure 3-5. *Details about a Wi-Fi network*

Joining a Closed Network

Most Wi-Fi networks operate as "open" networks, meaning that they automatically advertise their presence to any computers or Wi-Fi–enabled devices. This allows you to simply select a network from the list of automatically detected networks. Some networks are "closed," meaning that they don't broadcast their presence, and a computer or device must be told the network name in order to locate it. The Other option at the bottom of the Choose a Network section (refer to Figure 3-4) allows you to join closed networks.

When you join a closed network, you will need to specify the name of the network, as well as the type of security encryption used by that network to protect the wireless transfer of data between it and your iPhone or iPod touch (see Figure 3-6). After providing this information and clicking the Join button on the iPhone keyboard, the iPhone will verify that the network exists and prompt you for a password (if it is a protected network, which will most likely be the case). The iPhone will then remember the closed network as well as any other networks you have joined.

Figure 3-6. *Joining a closed network*

Common Network Issues

Typically, the iPhone will switch between available networks with little problem. When in range of a known Wi-Fi network, it will automatically use it (or prompt you to choose one if it detects unknown networks). Otherwise, it will rely on 3G or EDGE networking.

Occasionally, however, there may be instances where the switching between networks can create some problems. One of these is if you join a Wi-Fi network that is not properly configured. Obviously, this isn't a problem with the device itself—but so long as it is configured to use the network, it will attempt to do so. The result will be that Internet access fails (as it likely would with a computer). In these situations, either turning off Wi-Fi (Figure 3-4) or telling the iPhone to forget the network (Figure 3-5) will cause the iPhone to ignore the offending network and rely on your mobile carrier for Internet access.

Another common problem occurs when your iPhone is configured to access internal resources on your company network (intranet sites, e-mail servers, etc.). Although these services can often be accessed from outside of a network, the naming schemes for the servers may vary depending on whether you are accessing them from inside or outside the network. This can cause an iPhone or iPod touch to be unable to access resources properly when you attempt to connect from outside (either from a Wi-Fi network or via 3G/EDGE). This problem occurs most commonly with accessing Microsoft Exchange servers, which are very dependent on network naming and addressing conventions. The solution to this type of problem may not be easily solvable by you as an end user, as it typically represents a network or server configuration issue. However, using a VPN connection (if supported by your company) can serve as a workaround.

Securing Communications

Over the past few years, Wi-Fi hotspots have become largely ubiquitous, either in the completely free variety (such as those found on many college campuses, libraries, or retail locations) or in the paid subscription variety (found in many hotels, airports, and coffee shop chains). Whether free or paid, public Wi-Fi networks offer an easy way for professionals on the go to gain high-speed Internet access. Even with the performance of 3G networking on the iPhone, Wi-Fi still often offers better performance, which can make using public networks very tempting, particularly if you're in a location where there is no 3G connectivity and/or the network is completely free.

There is, however, a bit of danger in using public Wi-Fi networks, because they rarely employ secure encryption between your device (be it an iPhone/iPod touch or a computer) and the wireless router managing access to the network. This means that any data sent or received could be easily snooped by other people using the same network. Even networks that require you to log in through a web browser still typically don't secure communications between the network's router and the devices connecting. If you join any network that doesn't show the secure lock icon, then communication between your iPhone or iPod touch and the router to which you're connecting is not secure.

This means that unless you or your company employs some additional layer of security, any communications to and from your device are inherently insecure and easily readable to anyone else using the same Wi-Fi network. This can include anything from e-mails (and e-mail passwords), to web surfing, to accessing private applications. This should be a concern for anyone, but particularly if you are connecting to confidential business resources. There are, however, a number of encryption technologies that can secure any connection, including those made from unprotected Wi-Fi networks.

SSL and Security Certificates

For e-mail and web communications, SSL (Secure Sockets Layer protocol) has been a long-used technology that is implemented by most e-mail servers and sensitive technology web sites. SSL relies on special identifiers known as *digital certificates* (occasionally also called *security certificates*).

Digital certificates provide two functions. First, they verify the identity of a server or computer. This allows your computer or iPhone to be certain that it is connecting to the real server and not to one designed to masquerade as it. Certificates can do this using an encrypted fingerprint that the server must match to prove its identity. A special server known as a *certificate authority* acts as a secure and trusted middleman to verify the identity using the server's digital certificate.

In a simple environment (such as a small office), a single certificate can be installed on a computer or device such as an iPhone or iPod touch that includes information about appropriate servers. This certificate will point to a private certificate authority managed by your IT staff.

In larger environments, such as the Internet, trusted third-party certificate authorities can act as middlemen in the verification process. Your iPhone may not know the fingerprint of your bank's web server, for example, but if your bank is registered with a public certificate authority such as VeriSign, and your iPhone knows to trust VeriSign, then your iPhone can rely on VeriSign to verify the identity of your bank. There are several such public authorities, and the iPhone (like Mac OS X and Windows) includes certificates for them, allowing you secure access to public SSL-enabled services without additional configuration.

The second function of digital certificates is to generate an *encryption key*. This is the secret code that is used to encrypt information that is exchanged between the server and computer or device. You can think of it as a very complex and secure version of the secret decoder rings that kids play with, except that although the secret code is created based on a mathematical formula or algorithm included in the certificate, it changes every time a computer and server initiate a connection with each other using SSL.

All this theory boils down to a couple of points for you as an iPhone or iPod touch user. If you are accessing a web site that needs to be secure, you should look for a lock icon in the Safari address bar. This tells you that your iPhone was able to verify the identity of the server using either a certificate installed on it or via a certificate authority. In this way, the iPhone is not much different from any web browser.

As a business user, however, there is another implication, in that your company most likely doesn't register its private servers with a public certificate authority. Instead, it likely uses its own internal certificate authority server, which your iPhone or iPod touch will not know about unless a certificate is installed on it. Certificates can be installed using configuration profiles on the iPhone and iPod touch. Your IT staff may have already done this before you receive your device. If not, they can provide the certificate to you as a configuration profile, which can either be e-mailed to you or hosted on a web site (for which they will provide the address). Whichever way you receive the profile, you will need to choose to install it as shown in Figure 3-7. Once installed, you can verify the certificate by accessing a secure internal web site and checking for the lock icon.

Figure 3-7. *Installing a certificate profile*

TIP: Configuration profiles can also be used to automatically configure several features of the iPhone and iPod touch, including e-mail server and account information. For more information on configuration profiles, see my article on the topic for Computerworld, at `http://ryanfaas.com/index.php/2008/07/31/how-to-configure-and-deploy-the-iphone-3g-for-business-part-1/`, or Apple's iPhone Enterprise Deployment Guide, at `http://manuals.info.apple.com/en_US/Enterprise_Deployment_Guide.pdf`.

A final point to consider about certificates is that they are often used for securing e-mail as well as web traffic (and can theoretically be used by other iPhone applications as well). While the public e-mail services supported by the iPhone and iPod touch (such as Gmail and Apple's MobileMe) rely automatically on secure communication using SSL and public certificate authorities, you may need to install company-specific certificates in order to secure communication with your internal mail server, which I cover in more detail in Chapters 6 and 7.

Making Secure Network Connections Using VPN

Another even more powerful option is *VPN (virtual private network)*. When a VPN connection is created, it uses encryption technologies to create a virtual connection between a device and a remote network using the Internet. Because the encryption technologies are so advanced, current VPN technologies allow this connection (typically referred to as a *tunnel*) to be as secure as if a device were physically connected to the network, instead of connecting through the normally unsecured Internet. Network communications are diverted through this virtual tunnel, and even though it passes through a public channel, it cannot be read.

VPN also has the advantage of making your device or computer appear and function on your company's network as though it were physically (not virtually) present on the network. This means that a VPN connection can give you access to resources that would otherwise be available only while connected to your own network, including internal-only web and e-mail services, as well as network applications and even shared printers and files hosted on a server.

The iPhone and iPod touch support the three most common VPN technologies (PPTP, L2TP, and Cisco's IPSec). They also support using passwords to establish your VPN connection or RSA SecurID tokens (keychain-sized devices that randomly generate new passwords every minute). This allows you to establish connections that are as secure as technically possible no matter where you are, and regardless of whether you are connected to the Internet via Wi-Fi or 3G/EDGE.

Configuring VPN will require a fair amount of information from your IT staff (and again, you may receive your iPhone with VPN already configured). The process is done in the General options of the Settings app—under the Network option (the same place where you enable 3G and/or International data roaming, as discussed in the last chapter), as shown in Figures 3-8, 3-9, and 3-10.

Figure 3-8. *The Network options under the General options in the Settings app*

Figure 3-9. *Selecting a VPN configuration and enabling/initiating a VPN connection*

Figure 3-10. *Adding/editing a VPN configuration*

When adding a VPN configuration, you will see tabs for each of the three VPN technologies that the iPhone and iPod touch supports. The exact details required will vary depending on the protocol used and the configuration of your company's VPN server, but each will require a description or name of the configuration, a VPN server address, and a user account name for the VPN server. Depending on the VPN configuration of your company's network, this may or may not be the same username that you use to access other services.

> **CAUTION:** If your VPN server only requires a password to connect (and not the use of RSA SecurIDs), you can store your password as part of the configuration. However, this introduces a grave security risk to your network because it means that if your device is lost or stolen, anyone in possession of it will be able to access internal network resources, including potentially confidential information.

Since the configuration details will vary widely from one organization to another, you will need to work with your IT staff to determine the exact details for any VPN configuration fields, such as Server, Secret (a passphrase shared by your device and the VPN server, and used to verify each other's identity and establish the encryption algorithm for each connection—which some servers may use instead of a digital certificate), and Encryption Level.

One feature of note, however, is the Send All Traffic option. If this is enabled, all Internet communication will be routed through the VPN server and your company's internal network. This can greatly enhance security and will make all Internet access appear to be coming from within your company network. It will also typically degrade performance when accessing non-company Internet sites and services.

When disabled, the VPN connection will still be used automatically when you attempt to access resources internal to your company's network, but not if you attempt to access public Internet resources (such as Google or other public web sites). In these cases, the Wi-Fi or mobile carrier connection will be used as it would if there were no VPN connection. This can decrease security (particularly on public Wi-Fi networks), but it will typically result in better performance for your device, as well as decrease network traffic on your company's VPN server. As a result, this is the more commonly used choice, but you may want to check with your IT staff to see which option is more appropriate to your company policies and VPN server capacity.

Once a VPN connection is configured, an option will be added to the General options of the Settings app. To establish a VPN connection, simply use the switch shown in Figure 3-11. To disconnect, which you should do to maintain the security integrity of your network whenever you are not accessing internal resources, simply use the same switch.

Figure 3-11. *VPN option in the Settings app*

> **TIP:** The iPhone supports on-demand VPN connection with some VPN technologies, meaning that you don't need to manually turn on your VPN connection because the iPhone will detect when you are connecting to an internal resource and connect automatically. Check with your IT department to find out if this is supported by your company's VPN server.

Bonjour: Saying Hello to Network Resources

The iPhone and iPod touch include support for Apple's Bonjour. Bonjour is a zero-configuration networking technology that allows computers and devices to automatically discover each other whenever they are connected to the same network. It is often used in home and office networks for computers to automatically locate shared files and printers. However, Bonjour can be implemented for a number of other uses. Common examples include allowing computers to discover shared iTunes libraries and automatically locate backup devices, and allowing ad hoc instant messaging (without the need for a messaging service like AIM or Google Talk).

> **NOTE:** Although Bonjour was developed by Apple, it is based on open source technology and is cross platform. Use of the technology on Windows, however, requires installation of a free add-on, available on Apple's web site, at http://support.apple.com/downloads/Bonjour_for_Windows.

The iPhone and iPod touch fully support Bonjour. Although there is limited out-of-the-box use for Bonjour with either device, many third-party applications make use of it to allow easy discovery of computer- and server-based technologies. Some examples—which I'll cover in later chapters—include the ability for the iPhone/iPod touch to print, be used as a storage device, or act as a remote for controlling presentations from Microsoft's PowerPoint or Apple's Keynote tools.

Since Bonjour is a zero-configuration technology, any applications that rely on it simply work and discover appropriate resources without any effort on your part. It is important to understand, however, that Bonjour works only for devices and computers on the same network as each other. This means that, unless you're using a VPN connection, you won't be able to rely on Bonjour to connect to resources in your office from your home Wi-Fi network or when connected to the Internet via 3G/EDGE. In some large enterprise networks, it may also mean that the resources that you can locate may vary depending on which location or network segment you are connected to.

Tethering Your iPhone

In iPhone OS 3.0, you can also use your iPhone's 3G/EDGE connection as an Internet access method for a computer. This process, known as tethering, allows your computer to direct any Internet access through the iPhone, over your mobile carrier's network, and to the Internet. Tethering can be done with a USB cable connecting your iPhone to your computer or by pairing your iPhone and computer using Bluetooth.

> **NOTE:** Not all iPhone carriers support tethering (and those that do may charge an additional fee for the service). As of this writing, AT&T has not yet announced plans to support tethering in the United States.

If your carrier supports tethering, you will see an option in the Network section of the General settings labeled Internet Tethering. If you enable this option and then connect to your computer using a USB cable (or by following the onscreen instructions for pairing over Bluetooth), the iPhone should be detected as a network port on your computer. Follow your computer's prompts for connecting using the iPhone-created port.

Summary

Now that you know how to get online with your iPhone or iPod touch, and understand the basics of the iPhone OS interface, it's time to find out how to use the device for typical business and personal purposes. In Part 2 of this book, we'll look at how to use each of the built-in apps and features, beginning in the next chapter with the Phone app.

Getting Down to Business
with the Built-In Apps

Chapter 4

Phone Home (Or Work, Clients, or Anyone Else)

Basic Calling, Visual Voicemail, Contact Management, and Easy Conferencing

With all the capabilities packed into the iPhone, it's easy to overlook one of its primary features (for both business and consumer use): it is a mobile phone. As basic and unexciting as that may sound, the iPhone's Phone application incorporates a number of useful features as well as a very original user interface that may take a little getting used to—especially if you've primarily used landline and traditional entry-level mobile phones. In this chapter, I'll walk you through the basics of the Phone application, how to manage calls, and how to use the iPhone's visual voicemail feature.

Meet the Phone Application

As I've said before, virtually every feature of the iPhone is implemented as an individual application, and the phone features are no exception. To make calls, view voicemails, and manage various calling features, you will work with the Phone app, which is by default the first icon in the iPhone's dock. Unlike most iPhone applications, which cannot run in the background while you're working on something else or while the iPhone is locked, processes associated with the Phone application are always running so that you can receive calls regardless of what you're doing, as well as to allow you to continue talking while performing other tasks.

> *I don't consider myself a tech head, but I have been a loyal Mac user since 1993. As it was, I had no problem making my first call, minutes after purchase.*
>
> John Cirrin, Nonprofit Board of Directors Member

The Five Tabs of the Phone App

As you can see in Figure 4-1, the Phone application has five tabs along the bottom of the screen. This interface approach allows the application to divvy up the various phone-related tasks and features without overwhelming you by presenting every feature on the screen at once. The same approach is used by a number of applications, most notably the iPod application (or the separate Music and Movies apps on the iPod touch), and Apple makes this interface available for third-party developers to help deliver a consistent feel across various apps.

Figure 4-1. *The Phone app*

The five tabs for the phone app are Favorites, Recents, Contacts, Keypad, and Voicemail.

Favorites

The Favorites tab (also show in Figure 4-1) acts like the speed dial feature on many traditional mobile and landline phones. It allows you to pick the most frequently dialed numbers from all the contacts stored on the iPhone and make them easily accessible without searching or browsing. To make a call to anyone in your Favorites list, simply tap their name. To view their complete contact information, tap the blue arrow to the right of their entry.

The Edit and Add buttons at the top of the list allow you to manage your favorites. Tapping Edit will display a red circle icon next to each entry (see Figure 4-2). Tapping that circle will display a Remove button to remove the person from your favorites (the double action required helps ensure you don't delete anyone accidentally). When you are done editing/deleting, click the Done button at the top of the editing display.

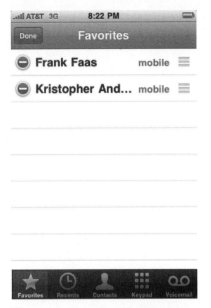

Figure 4-2. *Removing a Favorites entry*

When you click the Add button, you'll see your entire Contacts list displayed. You can select any contact to add them as a favorite. If a contact has multiple phone numbers (home, work, mobile, etc.), you'll be asked to choose which number to assign as a favorite, as shown in Figure 4-3 (you can assign multiple numbers for a contact as favorites, in which case you'll see multiple Favorites entries for that person, each indicating a type of phone number). Once a contact has been added as a favorite, they will appear in the Favorites list. If you view their actual contact information, you'll see a blue star next to whichever phone number(s) you've assigned as a favorite.

> **TIP:** You can also assign favorites directly from the Contacts browser/tab in the Phone application or in the Contacts application, which I'll cover later in this chapter and in Chapter 8, respectively.

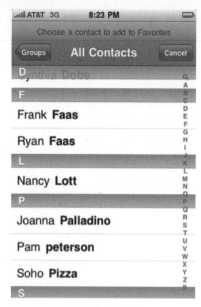

Figure 4-3. *Adding a favorite*

NOTE: Although favorites are based on your contacts (which sync to your computer), they are iPhone specific, and need to be managed on the iPhone itself. Likewise, your Favorites list is not synced along with contact information (though the data is backed up to a file by iTunes along with other iPhone-specific data, such as text messages, during sync).

Recents

The Recents tab, as you might expect, displays your recent call activity. As you can see in Figure 4-4, Recents is broken down into two tabs: one that displays all calls (incoming, outgoing, and missed) and one that displays only missed incoming calls. In both lists, missed calls are listed in red. For calls to or from numbers in your contacts, you will see the contact name. For others, you will see the number (or "Blocked" if the caller's number is blocked from caller ID services). Clicking an entry in the Recents list will place a call to that number.

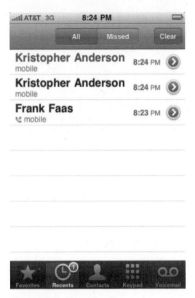

Figure 4-4. *Recent calls*

The Recents list (for both all calls and missed calls) will display the time of the call if it occurred on the same day, and the date if it occurred earlier. Clicking the blue arrow next to each entry will display the full contact information for a contact, as well as the time of the call (see Figure 4-5). If there is no contact associated with a number, you'll see the number (including any caller ID–supported location information) as well as the options to call back that number, send a text message to it, create a new contact for someone at that number, or add the number to existing information for one of your contacts.

Figure 4-5. *Details of a recent call*

Finally, you can use the Clear button at the top of the screen on the Recents tab to erase the call history from the iPhone (you will be asked to confirm that you do really want to delete all Recents entries).

> **NOTE:** As with favorites, call history data is not synced directly to contact information on your computer, but will be backed up to a file during the sync process.

Contacts

The Contacts tab (Figure 4-6) allows you to browse, search, and edit any contacts stored on your iPhone. If you've enabled syncing to your computer through iTunes (or over the air using MobileMe or Exchange), any edits you make on the iPhone will be synced to your computer and vice versa. The Contacts tab in the Phone application largely mirrors the functionality of the Contacts application.

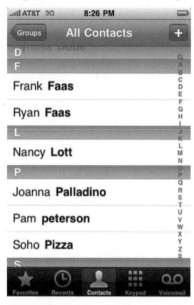

Figure 4-6. *The Contacts tab*

At the top of the Contacts list is the phone number of your iPhone, under which is a search field. The search field allows you to quickly locate a specific contact by searching for any fragment of their name or organization (if you've assigned organization/business names). Because the field is a live search, results are displayed with the first letter or two that you type and are refined as a you type more, making it easy to find a contact without having to type more than a few characters. In addition to searching, you can scroll and browse through your Contacts list, and you can use the alphabet displayed on the right-hand side to jump to specific areas of the alphabetized list.

All available contact details are listed when you select a contact, including name, business, phone numbers, assigned ringtones, e-mail and snail mail addresses, photo, birthday, and any notes (see Figure 4-7). If you are not using all the available details for a contact, only those that are assigned will be displayed.

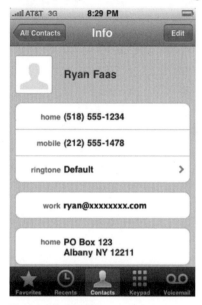

Figure 4-7. *Viewing a contact*

You can add/edit this information directly on the iPhone when editing a contact (by clicking the Edit button displayed at the top of a contact's information). When editing, you can not only change information in the existing fields for a contact (by simply tapping on the existing information or blank field), but also add additional fields. For fields such as additional phone numbers or e-mail addresses, you can simply click the Add button next to the fields (as shown in Figure 4-8), or you can add additional types of fields via the Add Field button at the bottom of the contact's information, for things such as birthday, company, phonetic spelling of names, nicknames, and notes (see Figure 4-9).

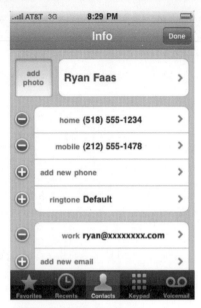

Figure 4-8. *Editing a contact*

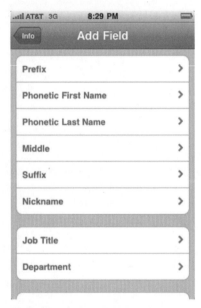

Figure 4-9. *Adding fields to a contact*

Adding Contact Photos

You can assign photos to contacts that will be displayed when the contact calls or when you call them. This is a great customization feature that also makes it easy to quickly determine who's calling you. Photos are synced to your computer along with all other contact data.

If you have assigned photos to contacts using Mac OS X's Address Book or Outlook, they will be synced to your iPhone. However, in most cases this will be a very scaled-down version of the photo, and it will display inline with the caller's name rather than full screen (as occurs if you assign a photo to a contact on the iPhone itself).

To add or edit a photo, click the photo (or placeholder image) next to the contact's name while editing. You will have the options to take a photo immediately with the built-in camera, choose a photo in the iPhone's photo library, or edit (zoom and crop only) the existing contact photo. You can also simply delete an existing photo. If you take a new photo or choose an existing photo, you will be able to zoom and crop the photo before setting it as the Contact's photo (see Figure 4-10).

Figure 4-10. *Editing a photo when assigning it*

Adding Contact Ringtones

You can assign ringtones to individual contacts. To do this, simply tap the Ringtone field while viewing or editing a contact. You will see a list of all available ringtones (those that come with the iPhone and any that you've added). Simply select a ringtone from this list.

Keypad

The Keypad tab of the Phone app provides you with a traditional phone keypad that can be used for dialing numbers not included in your contacts. As shown in Figure 14-11, the keypad looks like most traditional mobile phone keypads and includes a call button to initiate a call after dialing (much like the send button on most mobile phones), a delete/backspace button, and a button to add a number to a new or existing contact while dialing.

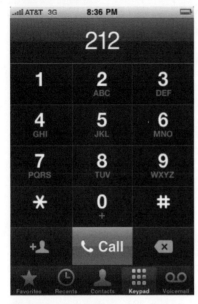

Figure 4-11. *The Phone app's keypad*

Visual Voicemail

One feature that the iPhone pioneered for mobile phones was the concept of visual voicemail. Rather than forcing users to dial into a voicemail system and navigate a phone tree of options and listen to each voicemail in succession, the iPhone's visual voicemail integrates with a carrier's voicemail system to display a list of a messages visually on the Voicemail tab of the Phone app. This not only makes accessing messages faster and easier in general, but also allows you to listen to specific messages at any given time.

As you can see in Figure 4-12, each message is displayed sequentially with the contact name (or phone number) and date (or time if the message was received the same day) on which the message was recorded. The look is very similar to the Phone app's Recents tab—right down to the ability to view the exact time of the message and full contact information via the blue arrow to the right of each entry.

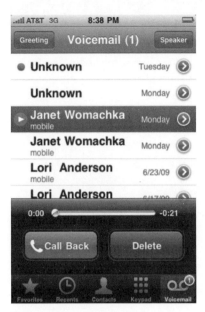

Figure 4-12. *Visual voicemail*

For new messages (those that you haven't yet listened to), simply tapping the entry in the list will play the voicemail. For messages that you have already listened to, a play icon will appear to the left of the message when tapped, allowing you to replay the message by tapping it.

A progress bar/slider displayed below the list of messages will let you know how long the message is and skip forward and backward while listening (much like when listening to a song in iTunes). Below the progress slider for each message are buttons to call back the contact/number from where the message was placed and to delete the message.

The Speaker button at the top of the screen allows you to toggle whether messages are played via speakerphone or at regular handset volume (which requires holding the iPhone to your ear to listen). The overall design of visual voicemail works well for listening to messages using the speakerphone option.

> **NOTE:** The first time you open the Voicemail tab, you will be prompted to enter a pin number for your voicemail. This will be stored by the iPhone for later use, and most carriers will allow it to be used to access your voicemail through a traditional phone tree system from other phones (refer to your carrier for details). Also, if you are roaming, you may find visual voicemail is unavailable—in which case the iPhone will display a notification above the message list with a button to call your voicemail through a traditional phone tree system.

Deleting Voicemails

Deleted messages are actually placed in a special Deleted Messages list (you can find this list by scrolling to the bottom of your message list). You can restore messages from the Deleted Messages list at any time (think of this as restoring files from the Windows Recycle Bin or Mac OS X Trash) by selecting them in the Deleted Messages list and clicking the Undelete button. Likewise, all messages in the Deleted Messages list can be permanently erased using the Clear All button.

> **TIP:** Visual voicemail stores messages as audio files on the iPhone itself (which are downloaded to the iPhone through a carrier's data connection)—meaning that they do take up file space (so periodically deleting them can be a good idea). This also means that you can listen to voicemails even when out of service range or while using Airplane mode. They also remain in the carrier's voicemail system until deleted from your visual voicemail, meaning that you can access them through whatever other mechanisms are available through your carrier (such as calling in from another phone line).

Setting a Greeting

You can record a voicemail greeting for your voicemail directly from the visual voicemail interface by tapping the Greeting button at the top of the display. When setting a greeting, you can choose a default greeting (the standard automated greeting of your carrier) or record a custom greeting. You can also directly review your current custom greeting and rerecord it using the Play and Record buttons.

Managing Calls

Now that you understand the basics of the Phone application, let's take a look at how to actually manage incoming and outgoing calls.

Answering an Incoming Call

When the iPhone receives a call, it will display the caller's contact name or phone number on the screen (as well as the contact's photo if one is a assigned), and will play either the default ringtone or a ringtone assigned to a contact. If you have headphones plugged in, the ringtone will play through them instead of the built-in speaker. Along with the incoming call information, a slider will be displayed to answer the call. Answering a call will leave whatever app you may be working in (and pause any music or video playing in the iPod app) and launch the Phone application to answer the call.

To silence a ringtone without answering a call, you can click the Sleep/Wake button once. The call will still ring silently until forwarded after the standard number of rings to your voicemail. You can also force a call to voicemail immediately by double-clicking the Sleep/Wake button.

If you receive a call while already on the phone, the iPhone will offer you the option of ignoring the incoming call (sending it to voicemail) or placing the current call on hold and answering the incoming call. When working with multiple calls, you will be able to swap between the various calls.

> **TIP:** The iPhone's headphones can also serve as a hands-free headset, as the button built into the right-hand earbud's cord includes a microphone. You can even answer an incoming call directly from the headphones by clicking this button when you hear the ringtone indicating an incoming call.

Placing a Call

There are actually a number of ways to place a call from the iPhone. These include using the Favorites list, browsing a contact (either in the Contacts tab of the Phone app or using the separate Contacts app) and selecting a phone number, manually dialing using the Keypad tab, and using the Call Back button from the visual voicemail list.

The iPhone also supports direct dialing from applications outside the Phone app because the iPhone can detect phone numbers. You can, for example, tap any phone number in a web page in Safari or in an e-mail, and the iPhone will ask if you want to call that number. Several third-party applications also offer various listing and additional contact management capabilities that can similarly dial a number directly.

In-Call Features

The iPhone offers number of in-call features that you can use. While on a call (either incoming or outgoing), you will see information about the call, as well as a series of buttons for managing these features.

- **Mute:** Mutes your voice on the call.
- **Keypad:** Provides access to a traditional phone keypad allowing you to navigate phone trees and menus.
- **Speaker:** Toggles speakerphone on and off.
- **Add Call:** Enables conference calling. Tapping this will allow you to dial additional numbers and merge them into the current call. There is no limit to the number of callers that can be added to a call using this feature, which can make the iPhone a hub for conference calls. This gives it a great leg up for conference calling over most mobile phones and many traditional phone systems.

I use my iPhone when I work at home—I take conference calls all the time and it's handy to conference other people and merge calls.

Nancy Lott, IT Project Manager

- **Hold:** Places the current call on hold. This also allows you to place additional calls (non-merged/conference calls), which you can swap between as required if you have received a second call while already on the phone.

- **Contacts:** Allows you to browse contacts while on the phone—helpful if you need to provide a phone number or address to whoever you're talking to.

- **End Call:** Ends the current call.

Working While on a Call

One nice feature of the iPhone is that you can work in any application while on a call. This allows you to continue web browsing, checking e-mail, entering data, or looking up information using any built-in or third-party applications. When combined with a hands-free headset (including the iPhone's headphones) or speakerphone, this can be a powerful option and a time-saver—particularly if you need to retrieve information or make notes for the person on a call.

> **NOTE:** If you are connected via EDGE network (as opposed to Wi-Fi or 3G), you cannot simultaneously access the Internet and talk on the phone.

To access other applications while on a call, simply press the Home button. You will be taken to the home screen where you'll be able to launch any needed application. While you are working in other applications (or viewing the home screen), a green bar will appear at the top of the display that will allow you to immediately return to the in-call display of the Phone app to access in-call features and/or end the call (see Figure 4-13).

Figure 4-13. *Working while on a call*

Setting Phone Options

While the Phone app itself manages the actual placing and managing of calls and call-related features such as visual voicemail, settings affecting the Phone app are managed in the Settings app. There are two areas of Settings that affect phone functionality: Sounds and Phone.

Sound Settings

The sound settings affect how the iPhone rings and provide audio notification for various calls and message alerts. The first option on the Sounds screen allows you to designate whether the iPhone will vibrate when silent mode is enabled (via the Silent/Vibrate switch on the side of the iPhone). When enabled, the iPhone will vibrate for all incoming calls, text messages, e-mails, and new voicemails. If turned off, you will receive no notification of these events while silent mode is turned on.

The remaining options apply when silent mode is turned off, and include the following:

- **Vibrate:** This option causes the iPhone to vibrate as well as provide audio feedback for incoming calls, text messages, e-mails, and new voicemails—very helpful if you carry your iPhone in a pocket where you may not hear such sounds (though vibrating does reduce battery life slightly).

- **Volume:** This slider designates the volume for ringtones and other alert sounds.

- **Ringtone:** This displays the current default ringtone (used for any callers for whom you have not assigned a custom ringtone, as described earlier)—tapping this will display a list of all ringtones on the iPhone and allow you to select one as the default (when you select one, a preview of it will be played).

- **New Text Message:** This displays the current sound used to alert you of new text messages and voicemails. Tapping this allows you to select one of several built-in alert tones (as with ringtones, you will hear a preview). If you work in a company that uses multiple iPhones, changing this tone can avoid everyone in a room checking their phones at the same time when the standard tri-tone ringtone is heard.

- **New Voicemail, New Mail, Sent Mail, Calendar Alerts, Lock Sounds, and Keyboard Clicks:** All of these items allow you to designate whether the iPhone should play the built-in sounds for each of these events.

Phone Settings

The Phone settings provide options common on most mobile phones and also display your iPhone's phone number. The options for the Phone settings include the following:

- **International Assist:** This will automatically add the appropriate international prefix for dialing contacts in your home country/region (1 in the case of the United States and Canada) when traveling abroad.

CAUTION: International roaming can rack up costs quickly. So, if you are traveling abroad, be sure to check with your carrier about how much it may cost.

- **Call Forwarding:** This enables forwarding of your incoming calls to any other phone number.

- **Call Waiting:** This enables/disables call waiting.

- **Show My Caller ID:** By default, the iPhone includes your phone number on outgoing calls via caller ID. If you want to prevent the people you call from seeing your iPhone's number, you can use this option to block it from appearing.

- **TTY:** This enables access to TTY phone services for the hearing impaired (check with your carrier for TTY options).

- **Change Voicemail PIN:** This allows you to change the PIN number for your voicemail. This is done visually by you entering the current PIN on a numeric keypad and then entering and verifying a new PIN.

- **SIM PIN:** This option allows you to require a PIN to access data on your iPhone's SIM card. Typically, the iPhone only stores carrier information on the SIM card, though some phones can store contacts on a SIM card as well. Using a SIM PIN requires the iPhone (or any other phone your SIM card is placed in) to access the PIN. In most cases, a carrier-designated PIN exists, but locking the SIM card using it is not enabled. Check with your carrier for details.

- **Carrier Services:** This last option displays carrier-specific phone services and provides buttons to immediately access them. For AT&T, this includes checking your bill and available minutes by phone and online, accessing directory assistance, paying your bill, and using AT&T's VoiceConnect service. Again, refer to your carrier for details about available services.

> **TIP:** AT&T offers an iPhone app that you can download to manage many features directly, in addition to the options listed here.

Summary

In this chapter, you learned how to use the iPhone for one of its primary functions—making calls. You also learned about how to use some of the iPhone-specific call features that allow you to work while on a call. In the next chapter, I'll cover how to use text and multimedia messaging services, as well as how these seemingly consumer-centric features can actually be applied effectively for business situations.

Chapter 5

Texting and Media Messaging for a Living

Not Just for Teens, the iPhone Turns Texting into a Serious Business Tool

The word *texting* often conjures up images of teens typing messages in the back of a classroom, but text and media messages can actually be very helpful for business users—particularly on the iPhone, where you can type messages using the onscreen keyboard instead of having to repeatedly type number buttons to choose each letter, as on a traditional mobile phone. In this chapter, I'll examine both how to use text and media (photo or video) messaging on the iPhone as well as how to use this technology in business settings.

What Are Text and Media Messages?

Text messages are short (160-character-or-less) messages that can be sent from one mobile phone to another. The technology behind text messaging, SMS (Short Message Service), has been around for quite some time and is supported by virtually all mobile phones worldwide, as well as by a number of Internet-based services.

Media messages are an offshoot of SMS technology, known as MMS (Multimedia Messaging Service). MMS allows photos or videos to be embedded in a message sent directly to another phone. The technology became popular when camera phones first shipped in the 2000s. MMS relies on a phone's data connection to actually exchange messages.

An early advantage of MMS was that the process was often simpler than manipulating photo/video uploads to a web service or even composing an e-mail with an attachment from a traditional mobile phone. Media messages also provided an easy solution for recipients, who might not have e-mail or web capabilities on their phones. With the abundance of smart phones today (including the iPhone), one can argue that those advantages have been somewhat negated, but there are still a lot of traditional mobile phones out in the world—keeping MMS as a common way of sending media between mobile users.

> **NOTE:** The iPhone has always supported text messages, but only the recent iPhone OS 3 release has introduced support for media messaging using MMS. However, earlier versions have always had the ability to share photos via e-mail. Also, MMS is not supported by all iPhone carriers—if your carrier doesn't support MMS, you will not see any of the MMS-related features on your phone.

> **CAUTION:** Remember to check your rate plan, as some plans charge for each text or media message while other plans may offer unlimited messaging or a limited number of free messages. Likewise, some carriers may charge for sending messages internationally or while roaming internationally.

The iPhone's Messages App

The iPhone's Messages application allows you to send and receive both text and media messages. Unlike many traditional mobile phones (including other smart phones), the iPhone groups messages that you exchange with other users as conversations—with each set of exchanges displaying in cartoon bubbles, much like Apple's iChat instant messaging application for Mac OS X (see Figure 5-1).

Figure 5-1. *Messages application*

Sending Text Messages

The process of sending a text message is extremely simple on the iPhone. Launch the Messages application. If you've sent or received messages, you'll see a list of contacts or phone numbers with whom you've exchanged messages by date, with the most recent messages at the top as well as the first two lines of the most recent message exchanges with each person (which may be the message you sent or received, depending on which is newest).

You can view the conversation of messages exchanged with each person simply by tapping the name of the contact (or phone number if you don't have the number associated with a contact on your iPhone). You can add a new message to the conversation by tapping the text field at the bottom of the screen (refer to Figure 5-1), which will display the onscreen keyboard and allow you to type your message. After that, click the Send button next to the text field. You'll see a progress bar indicating that the iPhone is sending the message to your carrier, and then your new message will appear in a new cartoon bubble of the conversation.

If you want to send a text message to someone not in your Messages list, you can click the Compose button at the top right of the screen, above the list. A new message screen will appear and you can type either a contact name or a phone number in the To: field (when entering a contact, the iPhone will autocomplete contact names as you type, allowing you to quickly select a contact without typing the entire name). You can also click the plus sign (+) button next to the To: field to search/browse your Contacts list. With the contact(s) selected, simply tap in the text field, type your message, and tap Send.

> **TIP:** You can use the plus sign button in the To: field to assign multiple recipients, each of whom will receive a copy of your message. If you do this, a group icon (which looks like a silhouette of two people's heads) will appear in the Messages list. You can then reuse the group by selecting that message in the list so that you don't have to reenter all the contacts. This is useful if you frequently send messages to the same group of individuals.

Sending Text Messages Directly from Contacts

Much like placing phone calls, you can actually initiate a text message from the Contacts application (as well as some third-party applications that support contact management), which includes a Send Text Message button for each contact assigned a phone number. This is particularly helpful if you are working with the global address list for an Exchange server, which allows you to look up contact information directly from the server without syncing it to your iPhone (I'll cover in Exchange in Chapter 9).

Sending Media Messages

Sending a media message via MMS is essentially the same as sending a text message. The only difference is that you will need to attach the photo or video to it. You can do this by clicking the Camera button when composing or replying to a message. The iPhone will then ask if you want to take a photo or record video using the built-in camera or use files already existing in the iPhone's library. If you choose to take a new photo or video, the Camera application will open, and you can use it to take the shot that will be attached. Otherwise, you will be able to navigate the library and select a photo or video to attach.

> **TIP:** You can also attach and send photos and video via MMS from the Photos application (just as you can attach and send them via e-mail). Refer to Chapter 10 for details.

Receiving Messages

There is really no special action needed to receive a text or media message on the iPhone. When a message is sent to your phone number, the iPhone will play a tone (refer to Chapter 4 for information on setting the tone for incoming messages using the Sounds settings) and will display the message and the sender as an alert on the screen. You can either choose to launch the Messages application and respond, or ignore the message and respond later. If you receive multiple messages, the alert will display just the number of messages, and you will need to launch Messages to view them. While you have unread messages, you will see a badge added to the Messages icon on your home screen displaying the number of unread messages.

Saving Media from Messages

If you receive photo or video messages, you may want to save the actual photo or video files for later use (and/or syncing to your computer). You can do this by clicking the photo or video. You will have the option to save it to your iPhone's library, where you will be able to browse, view, or even e-mail it as you would if you had taken it with your iPhone's built-in camera. When you sync your iPhone, it will be synced along with any other photos on your iPhone.

Deleting and Forwarding Messages

While text messages don't take up much file space on the iPhone, media messages can. Also, the iPhone is limited to a total of 1,000 text/media messages. Even without a space consideration, a large number of conversations listed in the Messages app can get out of control and make it difficult to locate particular messages or exchanges. You can click the Edit button at the top of the Messages list to delete individual conversations—much as you would contacts, as discussed in the last chapter—by clicking the red circle icon next to the conversation and then clicking the Delete button.

Deleting or Forwarding Individual Messages

In addition to deleting entire conversations, you can also delete individual messages from a conversation or forward individual messages. To do this, click the Edit button that is displayed while reading a conversation. Tap one or more messages in the conversation to select them. Then tap the Delete button or the Forward button at the bottom of the screen (see Figure 5-2).

If you choose to forward a message, Messages will prepopulate a new message with the forward. All you need to do is choose a recipient.

Figure 5-2. *Selecting individual messages to delete or forward*

TIP: Text and media messages are not synced to your computer, although they are included as part of the iTunes backup file created during sync. You can, however, use third-party desktop applications like MarkSpace's Missing Sync for iPhone (available for both Mac OS X and Windows) to view messages in this backup file on your computer.

REASONS TO TEXT FOR WORK

As I said at the beginning of this chapter, text messaging is generally considered a casual form of communication, particularly in United States. That doesn't mean that it is wholly inappropriate for business uses, however. The following are some ways to integrate text and media messaging business tools. Keep in mind, however, that because texting is often thought of in the same vein as instant messaging, it should be used mainly for internal communication rather than client contact (and should never serve as your first introduction to a client).

1. An alternative to e-mail and phone contact with coworkers: If you need to send brief notes to colleagues, particularly those working on traditional mobile phones, texting can be a great option. Even as a way of communicating with other iPhone or smart phone users, it can be helpful if you/they don't have an e-mail system that can deliver push e-mail (and thus instant notification of new messages), because texts can be received much more quickly than e-mail. This can also make text and media messaging a good quick way to communicate urgent information.

2. Coordinating impromptu meetings: Using shared calendaring tools (including those supported by the iPhone), e-mail, or phone/face-to-face contact are typically the best ways to schedule formal meetings, but for arranging quick get-togethers with colleagues or locating each other in crowded or noisy locations, texts can be a good option.

3. News and update services: Many news and industry sites (as well as most social networking sites) can be configured to send updates to your phone via SMS. While there may be iPhone applications that can also offer these features, the short and instant delivery of information by text can come in quite handy, particularly if you are traveling or in a location with limited data coverage or Wi-Fi access.

4. Posting to web services: Similar to getting news and information updates, you can post to many online services (social networking sites, some news agencies, and instant messaging tools among them) via text and media messaging. Again, there are typically iPhone applications or web interfaces for these features, but if you have limited or slow data coverage, texting can be a faster and easier alternative.

5. Tracking shipments: One of the most common reasons for using text messaging in business is the ability to receive tracking notifications from shipping companies like FedEx and UPS on the road, though these features are also available in other formats on the iPhone (including web sites, e-mail notifications, and custom tracking applications).

6. Sending customer updates: Depending on your industry, it may be appropriate to invite customers to sign up for text notices and updates about your products. You can use the iPhone as a way to issue these updates (conversely, it may be appropriate to sign up for such notifications from companies that you purchase from or work with), though if you plan to do a lot of serious text-based marketing, you'll probably want to investigate dedicated software or Internet-based services that specialize in the field.

7. Dealing with a downed e-mail and/or phone system: Hopefully, this isn't something you'll need to resort to very often, but if your company's e-mail server or phone system goes down, text messaging can be the quickest way to alert multiple people

(management, IT, and even customers) of the problem and to instruct them to use alternate communication methods (such as calling you on your iPhone).

TIP: The iPod touch doesn't have built-in text or media messaging support because both SMS and MMS are predominantly mobile phone technologies. Third-party apps like FreeSMS and ipTexter can add SMS capabilities to the iPod touch. Since the iPod touch doesn't connect to a carrier, messages are routed through a gateway server on the Internet (using Wi-Fi) that converts them from Internet data packets into messages that can be sent and received by mobile phones.

Summary

In this chapter, you learned not only how to send and view text and media messages on the iPhone, but you also learned some of the ways that this seemingly consumer-centric feature can be used as a business tool. In the next chapter, I'll cover one of the most commonly used business and messaging features of the iPhone: e-mail.

Chapter 6

E-mail

The Most Common Mobile Business Need Answered by the iPhone

One of the biggest needs a businessf user has for any mobile device is the ability to receive, search, and respond to e-mails quickly and easily at any time or place. With a simple-to-navigate Mail application and search capabilities, the iPhone more than fulfills these needs. In this chapter, I'll talk about the basic e-mail options, how to configure and use them, and how to organize your e-mail accounts so that you can get the most productivity bang for your buck on the iPhone.

Understanding iPhone E-mail Options

The iPhone offers built-in support for a number of public e-mail services (both free and paid), support for standard e-mail protocols, and support for Microsoft's Exchange Server and its ActiveSync protocol. Understanding the specific options and features offered by either public services, Internet provider services, or internal company-hosted e-mail services is a critical part to choosing the best option for you and your business.

Types of E-mail Accounts

When you first launch the Mail application on the iPhone or iPod touch, you'll be asked to configure an initial e-mail account. You can also later add more accounts using the Mail, Contacts, Calendars section of the Settings app (which I'll cover shortly).

As you can see in Figure 6-1, Apple provides you with a number of predefined types of accounts, including Microsoft Exchange, Apple's MobileMe (which, as mentioned in earlier chapters, offers not only e-mail with push notification but a host of other services as well), Google's Gmail, YahooMail, AOL, and Other. Although most of these types of accounts rely on a standard set of protocols to implement e-mail, Apple's approach very much simplifies the setup process, particularly with the public services of MobileMe,

Gmail, YahooMail, and AOL, because there is no need to enter server information—just user account details. In fact, all of these four types of accounts require just the same basic information shown in Figure 6-2.

Figure 6-1. *Choosing a new e-mail account type*

Figure 6-2. *Details needed for publicly available e-mail services*

Public vs. Private E-mail Accounts for Business

Public e-mail services can offer advantages to small businesses. They can typically be accessed easily from work, home, or on the road; they require less effort to set up and maintain, as they don't require any internal server (and often don't require a specialized backup strategy); they generally offer very effective spam filtering; and they are often integrated with other services or online communities. Although most such free and paid services are aimed at individuals, Google and Yahoo do provide some business-oriented features and add-on packages. Public services often also require less configuration of network firewall and security services—meaning that they may be attractive in larger businesses where IT policies may make it more difficult for individual users to attain mobile or out-of-office access.

On the other hand, these services have their downsides. They may not be as secure (particularly services that allow password resets only by a limited set of security questions that may be public knowledge for some users). They may not give a desired professional brand to your e-mails when working with clients or customers. And they may violate IT or personnel policies in larger organizations or even be blocked by network configurations.

Alternatively, the iPhone supports the standard common e-mail protocols (POP and IMAP for retrieving messages and SMTP for sending them) that will allow it to access virtually any e-mail system, including systems that are hosted internally by a company's IT department or hosted by an Internet service provider.

Push vs. Fetch E-mail Access

One of the major business features of e-mail access on the iPhone is its support for push notification of new messages. Push technology allows an e-mail server to notify your iPhone immediately when new messages arrive. If you need instant notification and access to your e-mails, this is a must-have technology.

Push access is a complex blend of technologies that rely on specific protocols—predominantly Microsoft's ActiveSync technology. As a result, not all e-mail servers or systems can provide push access. In those situations, the iPhone will rely on fetch access, in which it will periodically query the mail server to see if there are new messages (or manually when you choose to check your e-mail). Even if you are using a system that supports push access, you can choose to disable it and rely on fetch access to improve battery life.

Push access can be made available through both public and private e-mail services. Public services that include built-in access to push e-mail include Apple's MobileMe and YahooMail—both are aimed primarily at consumers. Gmail also offers push access by implementing ActiveSync (though setup for push notification via Gmail is done by configuring your Gmail account as a Microsoft Exchange account).

Private mail servers running Microsoft Exchange (or a mail server product that has licensed ActiveSync from Microsoft, such as Kerio MailServer and Zimbra Collaboration Suite) can also offer push access to e-mail on the iPhone. Similarly, hosted Exchange is an option for smaller businesses, in which an outside company (such as a consulting firm or Internet provider) hosts Exchange e-mail accounts that offer all the functionality of Exchange, including push notification, without the actual requirements of managing an Exchange server.

Over-the-Air Sync

In addition to push notification of new messages, MobileMe and Exchange accounts can provide over-the-air (OTA) sync of additional personal information. This can include sync of your contacts, calendars, and web browser bookmarks. The sync process is similar to that performed by iTunes except that it occurs wirelessly and will occur whenever updates have been made either on a computer or on your iPhone. We'll talk about how to configure MobileMe OTA syncing later in this chapter (as well as in the next two chapters where relevant), and OTA options for Exchange accounts in Chapter 9.

However, there are a couple of limitations to OTA sync that you should know about if you are considering it. First, you must choose whether to sync data through iTunes or OTA—the iPhone cannot use both. Similarly, you can only configure OTA sync for only a single MobileMe or Exchange account. This means that if you use OTA sync but have multiple e-mail accounts that support these features, you will need to choose which one will be used to sync data to the iPhone's contacts, calendar, and Safari applications.

Setting Up E-mail Accounts

Regardless of the type of e-mail accounts you're using, there are a number of ways to actually configure an e-mail account on the iPhone. The option you choose will depend on the type of e-mail account(s) that you're using and the computer to which you sync your iPhone. If you're using a company-provided iPhone or iPod touch, you may also find that your IT staff has preconfigured some or all facets of your e-mail account information for you.

Syncing Accounts via iTunes

The simplest way to set up an e-mail account on your iPhone is through iTunes. As I mentioned in Chapter 1, when you first sync your iPhone to your computer, you can choose what data is synced to it. Typically, you'll opt to sync calendar and contact information, but you can also opt to sync e-mail accounts (as shown in Figure 6-3). Any e-mail account configured for either Mac OS X's Mail application or Outlook/Outlook Express on a PC running Windows XP or Vista can be synced to the iPhone simply be selecting the check box for them in the Info pane of iTunes.

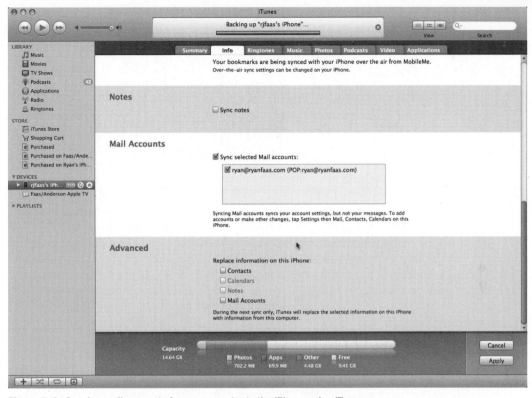

Figure 6-3. *Syncing mail accounts from a computer to the iPhone using iTunes*

If you select one or more e-mail accounts to sync through iTunes, all needed information about the e-mail server as well as your username and password will be synced to the iPhone. Once the sync operation is complete, you'll be able to simply launch the Mail application on the iPhone to check and send messages with no extra steps. Enabling syncing will also ensure that any changes to your account (such as an updated password) will be synced whenever you sync your iPhone.

NOTE: Syncing e-mail accounts only syncs your account information. It does not sync actual e-mails.

> **TIP:** As I noted in Chapter 1, you'll see the option on the Info pane in iTunes to sync or replace the e-mail account information on the iPhone. Normally, iTunes will sync such that the most recently updated data is kept on both the iPhone and the computer. However, if you've updated your password (or other changes have been made to an e-mail account), choosing to replace the information on the iPhone can ensure that accurate account details are placed on your iPhone. If you rely on syncing accounts and have e-mail access problems on your iPhone, this can be a helpful and simple way to resolve them.

Although syncing e-mail accounts is the simplest solution, it may not always be the best option. If you want to set up both work and personal e-mail accounts (which may not be configured on the same computer), you may want to configure one or more accounts manually on the iPhone rather than syncing to a particular computer. Also, if you rely on e-mail applications other than Mail or Outlook/Outlook Express, iTunes may not be able to sync your accounts for you. Finally, if you are using web-based or public e-mail services, you simply may not have a configuration within an appropriate e-mail application for iTunes to use.

Manual Account Setup for Public Service E-mails

As I mentioned at the beginning of the chapter, public service e-mails such as MobileMe and YahooMail are among the easiest types of accounts to manually configure on the iPhone and iPod touch. If you have chosen not to sync e-mail accounts via iTunes, then you will be asked to configure an e-mail account the first time that you launch Mail on the device. As noted earlier, to configure an account for MobileMe, Gmail, YahooMail, or AOL, you simply need to select the type of account and then enter the following information for the account:

- **Name:** The name that you want others to see in the From field of e-mails that you send.
- **Address:** Your e-mail address with the service provider. This is the full address to which people will send you messages—including both your username with the service (which will typically be your username to log into web-based e-mail) that appears before the @ symbol and the domain name of the provider that follows the @ symbol.
- **Password:** Your e-mail account password (which will be sent in secure form using SSL encryption for each of these services by default).

■ **Description:** A name for the account that Mail will use to differentiate mailboxes for each account (if you configure the iPhone to access multiple e-mail accounts)—by default, this will be populated with something like "My MobileMe Account," though you may want to change this if you will be configuring multiple accounts from the same provider.

Manual Setup of POP/IMAP Accounts

Most Internet service providers and many company e-mail servers make e-mail available to users via one of two protocols: the older POP (Post Office Protocol) and the slightly newer, though still very tried-and-true, IMAP (Internet Message Access Protocol). Typically, a mail server will support both protocols, though you may want to check with your provider or IT department to see if this is the case or if they have a policy of preferring one over the other. The iPhone and iPod touch support both protocols equally well (as do most e-mail clients for Mac OS X and Windows).

Understanding the Choice Between POP and IMAP

POP is a more lightweight protocol that simply transfers a copy of a message to your computer or mobile device. Once the e-mail is transferred, there is no more interaction with the server for incoming mail unless you choose to delete it from the server (which can be done at the time of download or at a specified time after the message is read). Because POP doesn't require continuous interaction with the server, certain tasks (like moving e-mails from one folder to another) may be faster than IMAP over slow connections, and all new messages are downloaded at one time. It may also be preferred by the provider because it places less load on the server to accomplish tasks.

One downside to POP is that while you can leave messages on the server after transferring them to an iPhone, computer, or other device (which is helpful if you check e-mail using multiple computers and/or devices), the messages on the server remain in their unorganized state. This means that you will need to manage messages separately on any device you use, which can add to the complexity and time requirements of keeping your mail organized.

By contrast, IMAP performs virtually all actions (marking messages read or unread, managing folders within mailboxes, and marking them for deletion) interactively with the server. This places a greater load on the server (and the connection between a computer or device with the server), but it means that any message you mark as read on your iPhone (or across multiple computers) will be marked as read when you access it from a computer. It also means that any folders you create to organize e-mails will be listed on any device or computer configured to access your e-mail account. This makes managing your e-mail on multiple computers and mobile devices like the iPhone a much simpler task.

Regardless of whether you configure an account as POP or IMAP, your iPhone or iPod touch will rely on SMTP (Simple Mail Transfer Protocol) to send outgoing messages.

SMTP is the primary protocol used by virtually all e-mail clients and servers to send messages across the Internet.

Setting Up a POP or IMAP Account

Regardless of whether you choose (or are asked to use) POP or IMAP, the first step in the process is to select Other as the type of e-mail account, as shown previously in Figure 6-1.

> **NOTE:** With iPhone OS 3.0, if you set up additional accounts, you can to choose whether each account should be strictly related to e-mail or whether it will be associated with a supported contacts server and/or calendar server (I'll cover these options in the next two chapters), as shown in Figure 6-4 (this screen is not typically displayed while setting up your first e-mail account on an iPhone).

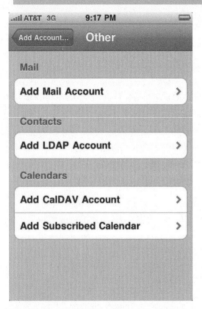

Figure 6-4. *Adding an Other account*

To set up e-mail, you'll need to tap the Add Mail Account option. This will display a screen very similar to the one for setting up public e-mail services, as you can see in Figure 6-5. However, when you save this information by tapping the Save button in the upper-right corner, you will then need to enter additional information about the e-mail server (some details about the server may be autodiscovered by the iPhone, but many will need to be completed manually).

Figure 6-5. *Adding basic e-mail information for a POP/IMAP account*

In Figure 6-6, you can see the server and account details for a new POP/IMAP account. There are two tabs—one for POP and one for IMAP (you should only work with the tab for the protocol you will be using)—that describe the server address, user account name, and similar details. Refer to your Internet provider or IT department's guidelines for what information should be entered. Also note that either screen will also include fields for outgoing (SMTP) mail server details that must be entered as well—these will generally (though not always) be the same as the incoming server information. When completed, click the Save button in the upper right of the screen.

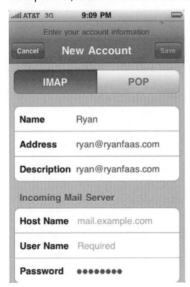

Figure 6-6. *Setting up server details for a new account*

CAUTION: Many e-mail servers require you to provide user account information to send outgoing e-mails (such as a username and password, which typically mirror those required to receive e-mail). This helps prevent spam from being sent through outgoing e-mail servers— again, check with your provider or IT department guidelines and enter this information in the SMTP server section at the bottom of either the POP or IMAP tab. If a server requires such information and you don't enter it (or don't enter it properly), you may find that you are unable to send e-mails from your device.

Adding Additional Accounts

The iPhone and iPod touch can support multiple e-mail accounts. After configuring a single account or syncing one or more accounts via iTunes, you can configure additional e-mail accounts by launching the Settings app, selecting the Mail, Contacts, Calendars option, and selecting the Add Account option, which will bring up the new account screen (shown previously in Figure 6-1).

Changing Mail Options After Setup

You can also make adjustments to existing e-mail accounts after they're initially set up using the Mail, Contacts, Calendars option in the Settings app, as well as adjust the behavior of the Mail application. As noted previously, each of the accounts that you configure can be selected and adjusted. The exact options for accounts will vary somewhat depending on the type of account. Figure 6-7 shows examples of the options available for public e-mail and IMAP/POP accounts.

Figure 6-7. *Changing options for existing mail accounts*

As you can see, the majority of the options for editing accounts mirror the initial setup options. Typically, the option you will need to change after that first setup will be your password if/when it changes on the e-mail system for the account, which can be done simply by tapping the password field and entering a new password.

SMTP and Other Advanced Options

That said, this screen does allow editing of SMTP options, which allow you to specify multiple servers through which outgoing e-mail can be sent, as well as advanced options for mailbox behavior and SSL encryption. Typically, you will not need (or want) to adjust these for public e-mail services, as doing so could render the account inaccessible. However, for in-house e-mail accounts and those hosted by an Internet provider, you might need to use these features (refer to your IT department or provider for details on how to configure these options, as they can vary widely from on server configuration to another).

Deleting an Account

You can also delete an account from your iPhone or iPod touch using the Delete Account option at the bottom of each account's options screen. This will delete both the account data and any messages. This can be done if you no longer need or have access to an account, or as a troubleshooting step if you cannot properly access an account (which would be followed by adding the account again manually or via iTunes sync).

Setting the Fetch Interval and/or Disabling Push Notifications

By default, MobileMe and YahooMail accounts are configured to support push notifications. As I mentioned in Chapter 2, you can use the Settings app to turn off push notification to save battery life using the Fetch New Data option (shown in Figure 6-8). If you do choose to disable push notification of new e-mail, you can choose a fetch interval. This is the interval at which your iPhone (or iPod touch) will check in with the appropriate e-mail server(s) for new messages.

Even if you are not using an e-mail server that supports push notifications of new e-mails, you can configure the fetch interval here, which will apply to all accounts that do not support push notification, as well as to accounts that do if you opt to disable push. Also, as I mentioned earlier, you can use the Advanced option (Figure 6-9) here to configure specific accounts to use Manual as an option to indicate that the iPhone should only check for new e-mail when you launch the Mail application (regardless of the fetch interval, Mail will check for new messages on launch).

Figure 6-8. *Fetch New Data options*

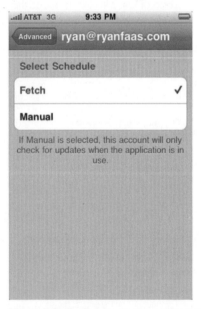

Figure 6-9. *Configuring an account for manual e-mail/data checking*

OTA Access Options for MobileMe

If you are configuring a MobileMe account, you can configure it for OTA sync as well as for push notification. This capability is not implemented by default if you sync MobileMe e-mail accounts through iTunes. To configure it, first use the MobileMe Preferences pane in Mac OS X System Preferences (Figure 6-10), or use the MobileMe control panel applet for Windows (Figure 6-11), which can be downloaded from www.apple.com/mobileme/setup/pc/, to enable syncing of your bookmarks, calendars, and contacts to Apple's MobileMe servers (which will also allow you to sync across multiple computers and view/edit your data through the MobileMe web site, at www.me.com). You will need to enter your MobileMe account information on the Account tab, and then choose what data you want to sync to MobileMe using the Sync tab (shown in Figures 6-10 and 6-11).

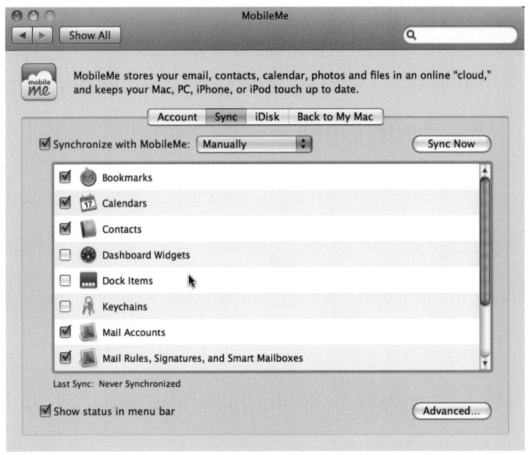

Figure 6-10. *MobileMe System Preferences pane in Mac OS X*

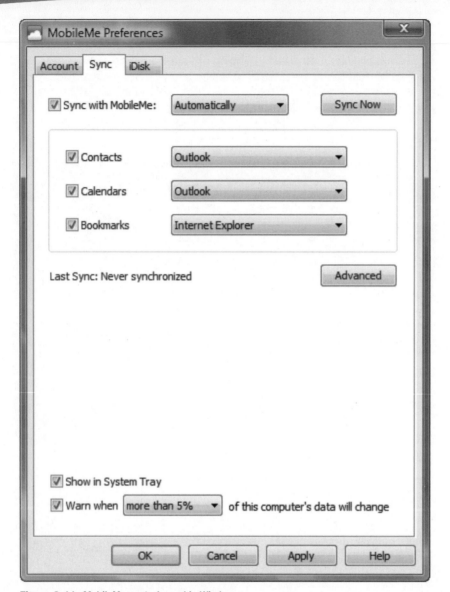

Figure 6-11. *MobileMe control panel in Windows*

Next, set up your MobileMe account on your iPhone (either manually or by syncing with iTunes). Select your MobileMe account in the Mail, Contacts, Calendars option in the iPhone's Settings app (see Figure 6-12—note that this option is more extensive than for other account types), click the switches for syncing the options that you want to sync to the computer wirelessly, and then click the Save button.

Figure 6-12. *Options for MobileMe accounts*

CAUTION: Syncing via MobileMe may erase any data that had been previously synced through iTunes. So be sure to perform a sync via iTunes if you had previously updated contacts, calendar items, or bookmarks on your device.

TIP: By default, the iPhone and iPod touch will sync OTA data via push, as will your computer. This means that any change you make to synced data on any computer or any iPhone or iPod touch will typically sync immediately (provided all the devices and computers are turned on and connected to the Internet). However, if you disable push notification on the iPhone or iPod touch, sync will happen on the fetch interval that you specify. Similarly, you can set each computer you use to sync via push (referred to as Automatically) or via a schedule from the Synchronize with MobileMe pop-up menu (shown at the top of the sync tab in either the MobileMe pane in System Preferences for Mac OS X or the Sync tab for the MobileMe control panel applet in Windows (see Figures 6-8 and 6-9 again).

Find My iPhone or iPod Touch

A final feature available when setting up OTA access for a MobileMe account is the "find my device" option. This feature is implemented by Apple and allows you to report an iPhone or iPod touch (and a Mac running Mac OS X Snow Leopard) as lost or stolen via the MobileMe web site. This will send a notification to the device (using push notification if you have it enabled) that will instruct it to use location services such as GPS, cell tower triangulation, or Skyhook's database of Wi-Fi hotspots to identify its current location. This should help in retrieving the device or reporting a theft to the police.

General Mail Options

In addition to configuring e-mail accounts, the Mail, Contacts, Calendars option in the Settings app allows you to configure general behavior of the Mail, Contacts, and Calendar applications. As you can see in Figure 6-13, the options that affect Mail are grouped together (just as various other options are logically grouped in other parts of the Settings app) into two sections: one for receiving and viewing e-mails, and one for sending e-mails.

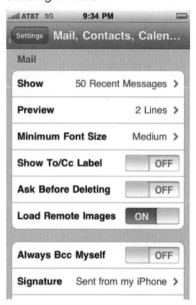

Figure 6-13. *Mail options in the Mail, Contacts, Calendars section of the Settings app*

The following list describes the settings in these two sections:

- **Show:** This option allows you to choose how many messages (read and unread) are downloaded and displayed in each mailbox on the iPhone at a given time. The default option is 25, but you can set this to 50, 100, or 200 messages.

- **Preview:** This determines the size of the message preview seen in a mailbox, which can be anywhere from one to five lines of text (which is displayed in addition to sender, subject, and date received).

- **Minimum Font Size:** This controls the size of text in e-mails. Options include small, medium (the default), large, extra large, and giant.

- **Show To/Cc Label:** This includes the To and CC fields in the display of new messages (in addition to sender and subject). This can be useful if you need to quickly see who all the recipients of a message were.

- **Ask Before Deleting:** This activates a safeguard feature in which the iPhone will ask you for confirmation when you delete a message.

- **Load Remote Images:** This tells Mail whether or not to load images that are part of an HTML or rich text e-mail but are not actually attached files. Turning this feature off can make such e-mails load faster. It can also help prevent accidental access to malicious web content in spam messages.

- **Always BCC Myself:** With this feature enabled, a copy of any e-mail you send will be sent to your e-mail account using blind carbon copy (such that other recipients won't know it was also sent to you). This is a good feature if you routinely send important messages from your iPhone that you need to later reference on your computer. Since some e-mail systems will maintain copies of outgoing messages on the server for later review, this feature may or may not be something that you need.

- **Signature:** This is an e-mail signature line that is added to every outgoing message. By default, it is set to "Sent from my iPhone," but it can be changed to anything you want. One limitation is that the iPhone offers only one signature that is used, regardless of how many different e-mail accounts you configure. So, if you use a signature, you may want to give some thought to what might be appropriate personally and professionally.

- **Default Account:** This is the primary e-mail account that will be selected for new messages if they are created outside of Mail (such as e-mailing a picture directly from the Photos application or clicking an e-mail link on a web page).

Sending and Receiving E-mail

Now that we've covered the options for setting up Mail, let's get to the real action of sending and receiving messages. Unless you've chosen the option to check for new messages manually, your iPhone will either automatically check for new messages based on your fetch interval or always be on the alert for new messages via push. When mail arrives, the iPhone will alert you with a tone and/or vibration (depending on your sound settings, as discussed in Chapter 4), and a badge icon with the number of unread messages will appear on the Mail icon on the home screen. Mail will also manually check for new messages each time you launch it.

Launching Mail

Like any iPhone application, launching Mail is as easy as tapping its icon. It can also be launched from other apps—for example, you can tap the e-mail address for one of your contacts or click an e-mail link on a web page. You can also launch Mail from applications that allow you to e-mail files, such as the Photos application. If you've configured multiple e-mail accounts, you'll see an Accounts list like the one in Figure 6-14. Tapping each account will take you to the list of mailboxes for that account (Figure 6-15). If you have only a single e-mail account set up, then when you launch Mail, you'll immediately see its mailboxes (Figure 6-15) without seeing an Accounts list.

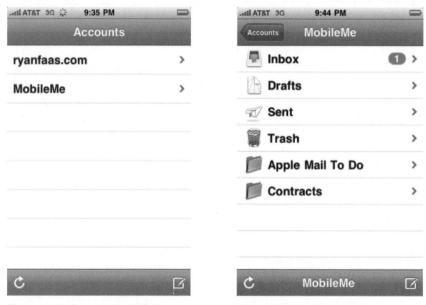

Figure 6-14. *Accounts list in Mail*   **Figure 6-15.** *Mailboxes for an account*

Navigating Mailboxes

Getting around in Mail follows the same intuitive approach of many iPhone applications. As you tap an item in the list (such as a particular account), you will begin to drill down through mailbox folders, and then into actual messages. You will always see a gray bar at the top of the screen that tells you what you are currently looking at, and an arrow-shaped button with the name of the account or mailbox directly above it, allowing you to navigate back level by level all the way to the Accounts list.

Reading Messages

As you begin drilling down from the Accounts list to an actual mailbox, you'll notice a couple of things. First, you'll be able to see the number of unread messages for each account or within each mailbox of an account, because this is displayed as part of the list (as shown in Figure 6-16).

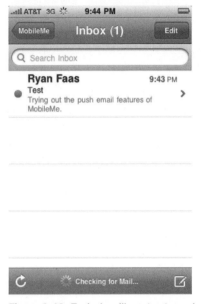

Figure 6-16. *Typical mailbox structure, showing unread message count*

The exact structure of mailboxes that you see on the iPhone might vary from one account to another. The organization is actually imposed by your mail server. Public e-mail services, Exchange servers, and IMAP servers all allow you to create multiple mailboxes (either using an e-mail client on your computer, such as Outlook or Mac OS X's Mail, or via a web interface such as Gmail and YahooMail). So, if you've created folders for organizing your e-mail on your computer, the iPhone will display that same set of mailbox folders, and allow you to view messages in each one and move messages from one folder to another.

> **NOTE:** Typically, all new messages will appear in the Inbox folder on the iPhone, but if your mail service supports automated rules, you may be able to filter e-mail into specific mailboxes based on subject, sender, or other factors.

A final navigational element is the gray bar at the bottom of the screen that you see when you're inside a mailbox. This includes some general information about the current mailbox, including when it was last updated (successfully checked for mail) and the status when receiving or sending messages. It also includes a Refresh button (on the left) for manually checking for new mail and a Compose button (on the right) for composing a new outgoing message.

To actually read an e-mail, simply tap the message in the Messages list. The message will be displayed. You'll be able to use the up/down arrow buttons to skip forward and backward sequentially through the messages in the mailbox without going back to the list. The iPhone's Mail app conserves screen space by not showing the detailed headers for each (such as the To and CC fields), but you can tap the details section in the header to display all of this information, as shown in Figure 6-17.

Figure 6-17. *Message showing all header details*

At the bottom bar of each message are five buttons. The Refresh and Compose buttons mentioned earlier still remain on the left and right edges, but three additional buttons appear between them: Move to Folder, Delete, and Forward/Reply (from left to right). Each of these does exactly what its name implies: allows you to organize your mail by moving the current message to another folder, deletes the message immediately, and either forwards the message to someone else or replies to it. When you tap the Forward/Reply button, Mail will ask which you want to do. It will then create a new message either replying to the original sender or allowing you to enter recipients (if you are forwarding the message).

Managing E-mail

You can manage messages (deleting them or organizing them by moving them into different folders) either while viewing individual messages (using the Delete and Move to Folder buttons, respectively) or in large batches, which can often be faster and easier. When you get down to an actual mailbox folder (such as the one in Figure 6-18), you'll also find an Edit button. Tapping this button allows you select multiple messages to either delete them or move them to another folder (Figure 6-19). This allows you to maintain some organization of your mail.

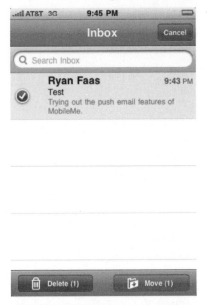

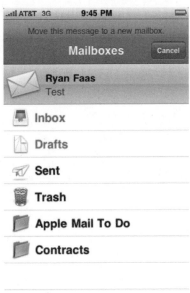

Figure 6-18. *Selecting messages to delete or move*

Figure 6-19. *Completing the move of messages to a different folder (the same dialog is used for one message and multiple messages)*

You can also delete individual messages by swiping your finger across the message, which will display a Delete button (Figure 6-20). Tapping elsewhere on the screen will cause the Delete button to disappear without deleting the message.

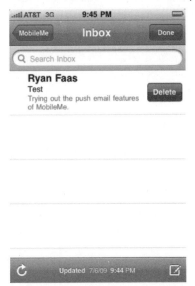

Figure 6-20. *Deleting an individual message*

TIP: You can't create folders for mailboxes on the iPhone directly. You must do that using your computer's e-mail application or web-based e-mail system. However, as long as you are not using POP to access your e-mail from your computer, all folders that you create should be server-based and available on the iPhone.

TIP: The iPhone's drill-down navigation for e-mail accounts and mailbox folders is intuitive and works well. However, if you have multiple accounts or accounts that have layers of folders nested within one another, navigating around can get cumbersome. For that reason, it can be helpful to streamline mailbox folder hierarchies and/or rely on just one or two e-mail accounts for use with your iPhone.

If you do use a limited number of accounts, most e-mail services allow you to configure rules for forwarding e-mails automatically, which can ensure that you get them. Another advantage to this approach is that you can forward all you e-mail to an account that supports push notification of new messages and one that offers particularly strong junk mail filtering, such as Apple's MobileMe or YahooMail.

Working with Attachments

The iPhone supports e-mail attachments. This means that you can view photos, audio/video files, and a range of document types—including text, Microsoft Office, iWork, and PDF documents. In the case of images, you'll see that they display right along with the message itself. For other document types, you'll see an icon that you can tap to view the document (such as the ones in Figure 6-21).

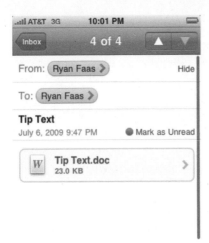

Figure 6-21. *Other file types attached to an e-mail*

Tapping the icon will open the file in a read-only viewer. For documents, the viewer will resemble that shown in Figure 6-22, and you'll be able to scroll and zoom as you would any other item on the iPhone. For media files, you'll see a playback viewer similar to the one shown in Figure 6-23.

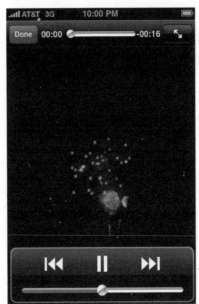

Figure 6-22. Document viewer

Figure 6-23. Media viewer

> **NOTE:** If an attachment hasn't fully downloaded, you'll see a spinning gear icon, and progress details will be displayed while the attachment is transferred (which is often the case if you are connecting to the Internet through a mobile carrier's network rather than Wi-Fi). Once the attachment has downloaded, it will open.

Although Mail will allow you to view attachments, it will not directly let you save attachments other than photos. To save a photo from an e-mail to your iPhone's photo library, tap the photo itself, and then select from one of the options shown in Figure 6-24.

Figure 6-24. *Options for saving/working with photo attachments*

Sending Mail

I've already mentioned the Compose button in Mail, which is the primary way to send a new message. Simply tap the Compose button (which is always available no matter where you are in Mail), and you'll see a new blank message like the one in Figure 6-25. A similar blank message will be created when you click the Forward/Reply button when viewing a message—the exception being that the text of the original message, subject line, and (if you're replying) recipient will already be identified.

To compose a new e-mail, tap in the To field and begin typing the name or address of the first recipient. As you type, Mail will offer autocomplete options to match individuals from your contacts or e-mail addresses with which you've previously exchanged e-mail (see Figure 6-25). When an autocomplete suggestion matches the person you want to send an e-mail to, simply tap their name or address (or continue typing if Mail doesn't provide a match). To add more recipients or browse your Contacts list and select someone rather than typing, tap the plus icon next to the To field. You can also add CC and BCC recipients in the same manner.

Figure 6-25. *Mail recipient autocomplete*

If you have multiple e-mail accounts configured on your iPhone, you can tap the From field and select between them. If you compose a new e-mail while browsing the mailbox folders of an account, that account will be used as the initial From address. If you compose a new message from the Accounts list view or via another application, whichever account is designated as your default account in the Settings app will be used.

Tap in the Subject field to enter a subject (or modify an existing subject, in the case of forwards and replies). Then tap in the body of the e-mail and type your message. When you're done, tap the Send button in the gray bar above the body of the e-mail (or click the Cancel button if you change your mind).

When you send an e-mail, you'll see a progress bar along the bottom of the screen as it sends, and, provided you haven't disabled the sound, you'll here a whoosh noise as soon as the e-mail is sent. That's about all there is to it.

TIP: You don't need to wait for a message to send before beginning other tasks, particularly if you're sending a message with a photo or video attached to it (or forwarding one with another attachment), which might take a little time. You'll still hear the sent mail sound to let you know when the message has been sent. However, you can only send one e-mail at a time, so while you can compose another message while one is sending, you won't be able to actually send it until the first finishes.

Sending Mail from Other Apps

As I mentioned, many applications can trigger a new e-mail. If you tap a contact's e-mail address in the Contacts or Phone app, for example, Mail will launch and compose a new message with that address in the To field. The same will happen when tapping an e-mail link in a web page. Similarly, when viewing items in your photo library, you will have the option of sending them as e-mail attachments (I'll cover this in more detail in Chapter 10). In fact, many third-party applications, as well as those provided by Apple, can automatically generate new messages. Often, these can be great time-savers since they typically autopopulate parts of the e-mail (such as recipients) for you.

WEB-BASED MAIL SERVICES

Mail is the primary e-mail application for the iPhone, but it isn't the only option. Various web and Internet providers offer web-based e-mail applications (including MobileMe, Gmail, and YahooMail). Most web-based e-mail services also provide the option of a stripped-down mobile interface for mobile phones. While these aren't always the best option, they do offer advantages in that they are somewhat more secure (since no actual mail is ever stored on your iPhone) and may provide integration with web-based address books or online collaborative suites. Google's range of tools may be the most typical example of this range of features—in fact, Google offers a free Google application for the iPhone (which I'll cover later in this book) that offers direct access to many of it's web-based technologies.

Summary

This chapter focused on one of the core business features of any smart phone. In the next chapter, we'll focus on another core application for business users: Calendar. We'll discuss both how to use the Calendar application as an individual professional and how to integrate with various shared calendaring services so that you can schedule meetings and events with other users both within and beyond your own company.

Chapter 7

Calendar

Keeping Track of Your Schedule and Those of Your Colleagues

Calendaring is a crucial function for any business device. Equally important is the ability to integrate your calendars with a computer or Internet/network collaboration tools that let you track schedules, organize meetings, plan events around other people's busy days, and track company or regional events automatically. The iPhone's calendar offers all of these abilities and makes them easy to use, as you'll see throughout this chapter.

Getting Around in the Calendar

One of the nicest features about the iPhone's Calendar app is that it is both simple and very functional. It is one of the ways in which the iPhone's multitouch interface makes something normally associated with a pen and paper tool much simpler than many computer-based solutions.

Calendar List

As you can see in Figure 7-1, the first screen of the Calendar app is a list of all the calendars that exist on your iPhone. The iPhone (like most computer-based calendaring solutions) allows you to have multiple separate calendars for discrete uses—perhaps one for each project or client and one for home, or one associated with different departments or even different jobs.

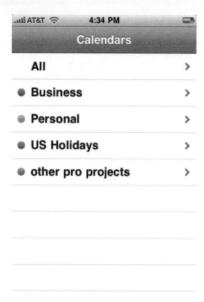

Figure 7-1. *Calendar list*

Because the iPhone can interact with several different calendar systems, calendars included in this list are based on the computer or over-the-air (OTA) calendar systems through which the iPhone syncs calendar data (I'll cover syncing later in the chapter). This means that you can have a number of different calendars, including ones that you create, as well as shared calendars to which you subscribe. Even if you opt not to use multiple calendars, a single default calendar will be displayed here.

> **TIP:** Different calendars will display with a different colored dot next to them (as will events associated with each calendar). When you create calendars, they are assigned a color, though you can manage the color/calendar combinations if they are synced to your computer or via MobileMe—refer to documentation for either iCal or Outlook for details.

You can choose to view individual calendars from the list by tapping them. You can also tap All for a combined view of events in all of your calendars. Viewing all calendars gives a very broad view of upcoming events, but if you have particularly active calendars, it may be easier and/or faster to locate your events in a specific calendar.

Calendar Displays

Whether you are looking at an individual calendar or all calendars at once, the view options will be largely the same. There are three view options: List (Figure 7-2), Day (Figure 7-4), and Month (Figure 7-5). Which ones you use most will largely be a question of personal preference and how busy your schedule tends to be.

As you can see in each of the screenshots, there are common elements to all of the views. There is always a Today button at the lower left that takes you to today's date in the current view, the buttons to switch between all three views, the standard search bar for locating events across all calendars (which features live search with auto-complete), a back button to take you to the calendars list at the top left, and an Add Event button at the top right.

List View

List view is the most task-oriented of the three calendar views. As you can see in Figure 7-2, List view simply shows a list of all events in the selected calendar (or in all calendars) with breaks for each day. You can scroll backward and forward from the current date, though when you first open List view, it will center on the current day (which you can return to quickly using the Today button).

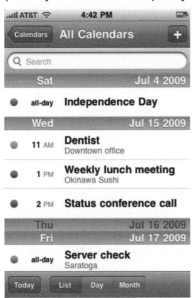

Figure 7-2. *Calendar's List view*

Although List view is convenient, it doesn't display full details about each event (just the date, color dot for the calendar of each event, and location if available). Tapping an event will display full details for the event, as shown in Figure 7-3). You can return to List view using the back button at the upper left (which will display the date of the event), and edit entries using the Edit button (I'll cover adding and editing events right after the remaining views options).

Figure 7-3. *Event details*

Day View

While List view looks almost like a notepad or an agenda of upcoming events, Day view (Figure 7-4) resembles a traditional paper-based daily planner (which can make it very handy if you're used to working with such planners). Individual events are displayed as colored blocks (with the colors corresponding to each calendar) that mark out the times of the event. Full-day events appear in a bar across the top of the screen. As with List view, only the event name and location are displayed, but tapping on an event allows you to view and edit all details.

Figure 7-4. *Day view*

Month View

Month view is the view most like a wall or desk calendar. As you can see in Figure 7-5, it shows an entire month with simple dots in the square of each date when you have an event scheduled. Tapping a date will display the event(s) for that day in a list (which can be scrolled) below the calendar itself, complete with calendar dot, time, and location (if included). As with the other views, tapping an event allows you to view and edit details.

Figure 7-5. *Month view*

If you have particularly heavy calendars, this may seem the most cumbersome view since relatively few details are immediately available. However, if you have a lighter workload, or events that are mostly all day in nature, this can be a useful view because it is so broad. It also works well if you organize your schedule using multiple separate calendars.

Adding/Editing Events

You can add or edit events on your iPhone relatively easily. When you make changes to an existing event or add a new one, those changes will be synced with the calendar on your computer during the next sync operation. This is a two-way sync. So, in addition to events added on your iPhone, any new events or changes made on your computer will be added to your iPhone. In addition to manually adding events and syncing new events from your computer, you can add events by responding to event invitations (either on your computer, which will add them to the iPhone during sync, or directly on the iPhone).

Manually Adding and Editing Events

To add a new event, click the Add Event button displayed in the upper right of the all three calendar views. In the Add Event dialog (Figure 7-6), tap each set of event details to enter them. As you can see, there are a number of different types of details that you can enter for an event, including the title/name of the event displayed in the calendar, a location, the start and end times (when setting these times, you'll also have the option of specifying that an event is an all-day event, as shown in Figure 7-7), whether the event is a repeating event (and how often it repeats), whether your iPhone will display an alert prior to the event, and any notes about the event.

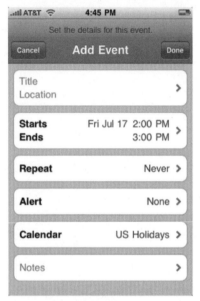

Figure 7-6. *Adding an event*

Figure 7-7. *Setting an event's time frame*

On nice feature about setting an alert is that alerts are synced to your computer along with all of the other data about each event. This means that if you set an alert, it will be displayed on both your iPhone and your computer. On the iPhone, alerts are displayed much like text messages. On your computer, you may be notified of an alert via a pop-up dialog and/or by a sound, depending on the iCal, Entourage, or Outlook settings on your computer. You also have a fairly wide range of choices in terms of when an alert is displayed, as you can see in Figure 7-8.

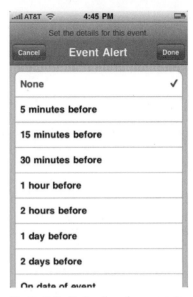

Figure 7-8. *Alert options for an event*

NOTE: You are not required to use all the available fields for event details. You're only truly required to add an event title and start/end time, and select which calendar the event will be placed in.

TIP: The Notes field for an event can be particularly helpful because you can include notes and URLs, and even copy and paste details about an event from an e-mail or web page into the event itself. This makes it easy to refer back to information without having to dig through a series of e-mails or external notes.

Editing Existing Events

The process of editing an existing event is virtually identical to that of adding a new event. There are a couple of differences between the Add Event dialog (shown previously in Figure 7-6) and the Edit dialog (shown in Figure 7-9). The most notable is that the Edit dialog includes a button to delete the event. Also, the Edit dialog doesn't allow you to change the calendar with which an event is associated, as this can only be done on the iPhone when creating an event (though some calendar tools on your computer may allow you to do this after the fact).

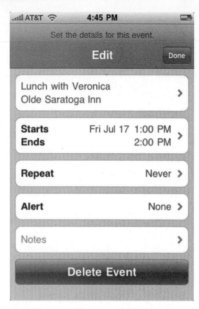

Figure 7-9. *Editing an existing event*

Responding to Invitations

Many calendaring solutions allow users to send each other event invitations. These invitations typically rely on a special type of file called an iCalendar or ICS file. This is an industry standard file type for exchanging calendar information that is most typically sent by e-mail. The reliance on e-mail and industry standards allows iCalendar invitations to function with a wide range of calendaring tools.

Both iCal in Mac OS X and Outlook in Windows support these files, as do other common tools like Novell Groupware, Mozilla Thunderbird, and even Google Calendar. The iPhone can also support invitation files. Should one arrive by e-mail, you can tap it in an e-mail, and the iPhone will launch Calendar and automatically create an event based on it. You can then edit the event as you would any other. Similarly, any invitation you receive and accept on your computer (if you are using iCal or Outlook) will be synced to your iPhone.

> **NOTE:** Some calendaring systems, such as Microsoft Exchange, support more complex event invitation processes. At this time, Exchange is the only full-blown such service supported by the iPhone, and I'll cover it in Chapter 9.

CAUTION: In some instances, when event dates/times are updated on the iPhone, you may experience sync issues between the details of the event of your iPhone and on your computer. This is most common when events with multiple attendees are rescheduled. If this happens, you may see a sync error dialog on your computer asking you which set of data (the version on your computer or on your iPhone) you want use. Double-check which is the most current and choose that. In severe cases, you may need to use the option on the Info tab in iTunes to replace all data on your iPhone with that stored on your computer to resolve the problem (but make sure the event data on your computer is the correct version first).

Calendar Settings Options

There are a handful of options for the Calendar application in the Settings app under the Mail, Contacts, Calendars section (you'll have to scroll down past the Mail and Contacts settings).

These options include the following:

- **New Invitation Alerts:** Enables support for Calendar, notifying you if it receives invitations via Microsoft Exchange or a similar calendaring system.

- **Sync:** Determines how far back the iPhone should sync events for earlier dates (the default is one month, but you can also select two weeks, three months, six months, or all events). By not syncing older events, you can allow the iPhone to sync faster and also free up space. However, you may wish to maintain a history of earlier events on the iPhone.

- **Time Zone Support:** When this is enabled, events will always be displayed in a fixed time zone rather than in local time. This means that if you enable Time Zone Support and set it for Eastern time, your events will display in Eastern time even if you're using the iPhone in a different time zone. You can enable/disable this at any time and select any time zone, as shown in Figure 7-10.

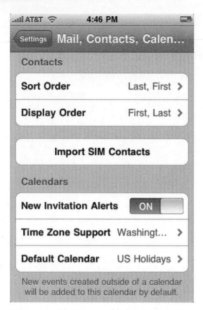

Figure 7-10. *Configuring Time Zone Support*

The What, Where, and How of Syncing

There are a number of ways to sync calendar data between your iPhone or iPod touch and your computer. The simplest of these is a basic sync with data that is stored in iCal on Mac OS X or Outlook on Windows using iTunes and the USB cable that comes with the device. Beyond basic sync, there is the ability to sync data over the air with one or more computers using MobileMe, the option to directly interact with server-based calendars hosted by Microsoft Exchange or an alternate server that relies on the CalDAV protocol (such as Mac OS X Server), and the ability to sync or subscribe to other public calendar servers such as Google Calender.

Basic iTunes Sync

The simplest way to sync calendar information and events to your iPhone is through a basic sync with iTunes. As I mentioned in Chapter 1, a basic sync allows you select one or more iCal or Outlook applications. The process is very easy. Simply connect your iPhone to your computer, select it in the iTunes sidebar, and then use the Info tab to select which calendars you want to sync (see Figure 7-11).

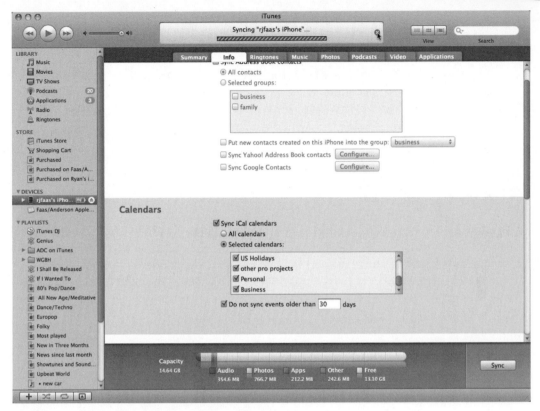

Figure 7-11. *Choosing which calendars to sync in iTunes*

NOTE: The iPhone currently supports only Outlook 2003 and Outlook 2007 calendars on Windows only. It does not support the Windows Calendar tool in Vista.

With a basic sync configured, your iPhone will sync calendar data through iTunes as part of every sync operation (by default, this means every time the iPhone is connected). Under typical circumstances, the sync process will occur with no intervention. However, if you have events that you have modified on both your iPhone and your computer between syncs, iTunes will ask you which version you want to keep (the other version will be discarded). This is one reason that frequent sync operations are a good idea if you are relying on manual syncing. Any additional management of calendars and events will be done in iCal or Outlook just as it would be done normally.

MobileMe OTA Sync

If you configure OTA sync for a MobileMe account as I described in the last chapter, you can sync your iCal or Outlook calendars via MobileMe. You can also access and edit them using MobileMe's online web calendar application (this is a great option for ultimate access to your data if you are self-employed). There is no need for additional setup of MobileMe syncing beyond what I described in the last chapter.

> *My favorite part of MobileMe is the ability that it gives me to keep the key parts of my life (calendars and contacts) synced across all my devices (iMac at home, MacBook Pro for work, MacBook Pro for personal use, my iPhone, and my iPod touch. Yes, I have one of each).*
>
> Cynthia Dobe, Educational IT Director

CalDAV Sync

CalDAV is an open source calendaring standard based on the HTTP web protocol that has emerged in the past couple of years. It allows you to have an account on a central calendar server that can be accessed via a wide range of calendar applications. With iPhone OS 3, Apple has introduced support for CalDAV servers—most notably its own Mac OS X Server.

CalDAV servers allow for wireless sync of calendar data (much as MobileMe does). Although the CalDAV standard (and desktop applications that support it, such as Apple's iCal or Mozilla Thunderbird) supports shared calendaring, including the ability to send event invitations directly through the server (as opposed to ICS files attached to e-mails) and the ability to view the availability of other users when scheduling an event, these features are not supported on the iPhone at this time. For iPhone users, CalDAV is simply a method, like MobileMe, that allows you to sync events on your iPhone to a central calendaring server. Other devices or desktop calendar applications configured to access your CalDAV server account can also sync to the server, giving you one-stop access to your calendar no matter where or how you are accessing it. In some CalDAV server implementations, such as Mac OS X Server, a web-based calendar is also supported.

Configuring a CalDAV Account

The process of configuring a CalDAV user account on the iPhone is largely similar to that of setting up a POP/IMAP e-mail account. Select the Mail, Contacts, Calendars option in the Settings App, select Add Account, and then select Other as the account type (refer to the last chapter for details). On the Other dialog (shown in Figure 7-12), select Add CalDAV account.

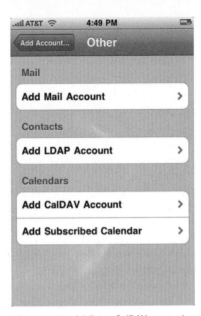

Figure 7-12. *Adding a CalDAV account*

Next, enter the server and user account information (username/password) and a description in the CalDAV configuration screen shown in Figure 7-13. Refer to your IT department for the exact information required.

Figure 7-13. *CalDAV account information*

The iPhone will then attempt to query the server and verify your account information. If successful, the iPhone will then configure your account and add any existing calendars and event data into Calendar. If your server supports push notifications, updates will occur whenever your make them using a CalDAV client that has been configured to access your account. Otherwise, they will use your default fetch interval.

You can later modify your account in much the same way that you can an e-mail account, by selecting it in the Mail, Contacts, Calendars option of the Settings app. As you can see in Figure 7-14, this allows you to alter your account information and/or password, and disable and delete the account. If needed, you can also alter whether the iPhone should use SSL encryption when accessing the account, the port used for communication, and the address of your actual calendar data (refer to your IT department for details).

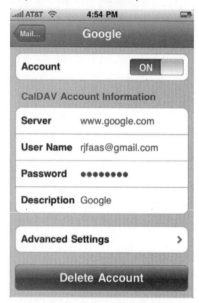

Figure 7-14. *Modifying a CalDAV account*

GOOGLE CALENDAR AND CALDAV

Google's suite of online tools includes a calendar (as well as the free Gmail mail service and a number of other web-based tools). Google Calendar is a useful tool for self-employed professionals because it can provide an online calendar similar to that provided by MobileMe or CalDAV. Although originally solely a web-based solution, Google has opened the calendar portion of its service up to be able to sync with both mobile devices and with desktop applications including iCal, Outlook, and Mozilla Thunderbird.

Google actually provides two primary methods of syncing Google Calendar events with the iPhone. One is using the CalDAV protocol and the other is using Microsoft's ActiveSync, with which Google's server appears to the iPhone as an Exchange server (I'll discuss Exchange in greater detail in Chapter 9). CalDAV offers one main advantage over ActiveSync with Google Calendar in that you can only sync an iPhone with a single Exchange account (meaning if you have already synced your iPhone to your company's Exchange server, you cannot also sync it using ActiveSync to Google Calendar).

On the flip side, using ActiveSync provides the ability to sync contacts with Gmail as well as events with Google Calendar. It also enables push notifications between Google's services and the iPhone for updates to contacts and events. This can make using ActiveSync a tempting prospect if you don't need to sync with a company Exchange server. ActiveSync also allows sync of multiple calendars created using a Google Calendar account while CalDAV provides access to only your primary calendar.

If you do opt to use CalDAV to sync Google calendars, you can follow the same instructions detailed in this chapter for a private company-operated CalDAV server. Simply enter `www.gooogle.com` as the server name and your full Gmail account information (e.g., `username@gmail.com`) when configuring the account. The iPhone will automatically detect the rest of the needed information.

For more information on using Google Calendar with the iPhone via CalDAV, see `http://justanotheriphoneblog.com/wordpress/general/google-calendar-speaks-caldav-to-the-iphone`.

Subscribing to ICS Calendars Online

I mentioned the iCalendar file standard earlier in the chapter as a way to exchange event invitations via e-mail. While this is one of its most useful benefits because it allows you to schedule events with users of other calendaring tools as well as in environments where no shared calendaring solution exists, it isn't the only use of the technology.

Most calendaring tools that support iCalendar include the ability to publish exported calendar data in ICS files. Typically, these are published to a web site (either on a company's intranet or publicly on the Internet). Users of other calendar tools that support the standard can then subscribe to the hosted file. The iPhone supports such subscriptions (though it cannot publish calendars as ICS files—refer to instructions for your calendaring tool of choice for details on how to publish a calendar).

Like using ICS files for event invitations, subscribing to published ICS calendars can be a solution for loading calendar data from public sources as well as from private users when no advanced calendaring solution exists. One common use for ICS is for a business to publish a list of public events or for a department to publish upcoming events. This can also be used to locate publicly published calendars for things like local or regional holidays, school closings, and community events.

> **TIP:** Two excellent sources for examples of public ICS calendars are `http://ical share.com` and `http://www.icalworld.com` (where, as a professional, you may even want to consider posting your company's public events).

Adding an ICS Subscription

The process of subscribing to a ICS file is very similar to the process of adding a CalDAV account. Begin by creating a new account using the Mail, Contacts, Calendars option in the Settings app and selecting Other as the account type. Instead of selecting the option to add a CalDAV account, select the option to add a subscribed calendar.

As you can see in Figure 7-15, the basic information required is simply the URL of the ICS file. After entering this and tapping the Next button at the upper right, the iPhone will attempt to access the server hosting the file.

Figure 7-15. *Subscribing to a calendar*

You will then be asked to provide more detailed information (Figure 7-16), such as to verify the server, enter a description, and provide a username and password (if needed to access the server hosting the file). If a username and password are needed, you can opt to require the use of SSL encryption when communicating with the server. Finally, you will have the option of deciding whether you want to include alarm notifications with the calendar or not.

Figure 7-16. *Details about a subscribed calendar*

Once setup is complete, the iPhone will download the information from the ICS file and add the related events as a separate calendar that will be updated according to your fetch interval. You will be able to view and edit the calendar like any other. However, any edits you make will exist only on your iPhone and will not be synced back to the server.

As with a CalDAV account, you can later edit a subscribed calendar by selecting it in the Mail, Contacts, Calendars settings option. As you can see in Figure 7-17, you can edit all the options, delete the subscription, and disable updates of the calendar.

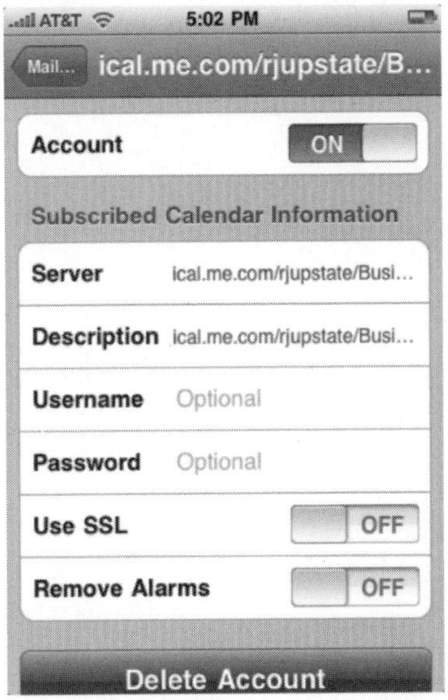

Figure 7-17. *Updating a subscirbed ICS calendar*

NOTE: If you subscribe to a calendar, the subscription will be synced back to your computer on next sync and/or via OTA syncing.

NOTE: If you subscribe to multiple ICS calendars or make use of CalDAV servers, the calendar list will look slightly different than shown earlier in Figure 7-1. As you can see in Figure 7-18, the list is separated by the various types of calendars that are being displayed (though you can still view events from all calendars, regardless of type, using the All Calendars option at the top of the list).

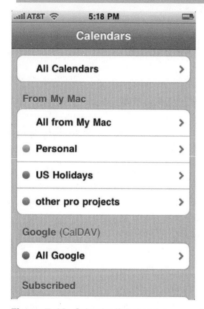

Figure 7-18. *Calendar list showing synced, CalDAV server, and subscribed calendars*

Summary

In this chapter, you learned to set up and navigate the iPhone's calendar application. In the next chapter, I'll introduce the Contacts app, including basic setup and use as well as syncing of Contacts data. Then in Chapter 9, we'll take a look at how e-mail, contacts, and calendaring are approached from the unique perspective of an Exchange server environment.

Chapter 8

Contacts

Part Organizer, Part Phone Book, Contacts Helps Keep You in Touch

When it comes to business, nothing is more important than being able to communicate with another person, be it a customer/client, colleague, supervisor, employee, or even the occasional family member or friend. But contact doesn't just mean the ability to call, e-mail, or text someone. It often also means the ability to understand who they are, where the work, and what their needs are.

In this chapter, we'll explore the Contacts app that comes with the iPhone and iPod touch. Much of the actual functionality of the Contacts app is similar (and in some cases identical) to the Contacts tab in the Phone app, which we already looked at in Chapter 4. So, this chapter will focus less on every particular feature and more on the differences between the two apps, though I'll take some time to look at how to manage contacts as well.

Syncing Contacts

I've already covered the basics of syncing contacts along with other personal data in earlier chapters. To recap, the primary method for syncing contact data is through iTunes, as discussed in Chapter 1. When syncing from iTunes, you can choose to sync contacts from supported applications on Mac OS X (Apple's Address Book and Microsoft's Entourage) or Windows (Outlook, Outlook Express/Windows Address Book, or Windows Vista Contacts). If you configure a MobileMe account, contacts will be synced over the air whenever you make changes using either a computer, iPhone, or iPod touch associated with a MobileMe account or using the MobileMe web interface.

In addition, iTunes allows you to sync contacts directly with address books for YahooMail and Google's Gmail (see Figure 8-1). For Mac OS X users, there is also the option to configure the syncing between Address Book and the appropriate services, which can be done from the General Tab of the Address Book preferences (shown in Figure 8-2), which is accessed from the Address Book menu in the menu bar.

> **TIP:** If you create contacts on your iPhone, they will be automatically synced with your computer (or over the air via MobileMe). You can specify that all new contacts are placed in a particular contact group (as also indicated in Figure 8-1).

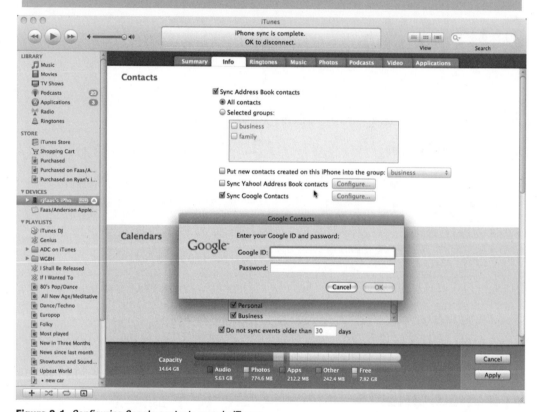

Figure 8-1. *Configuring Google contacts sync in iTunes*

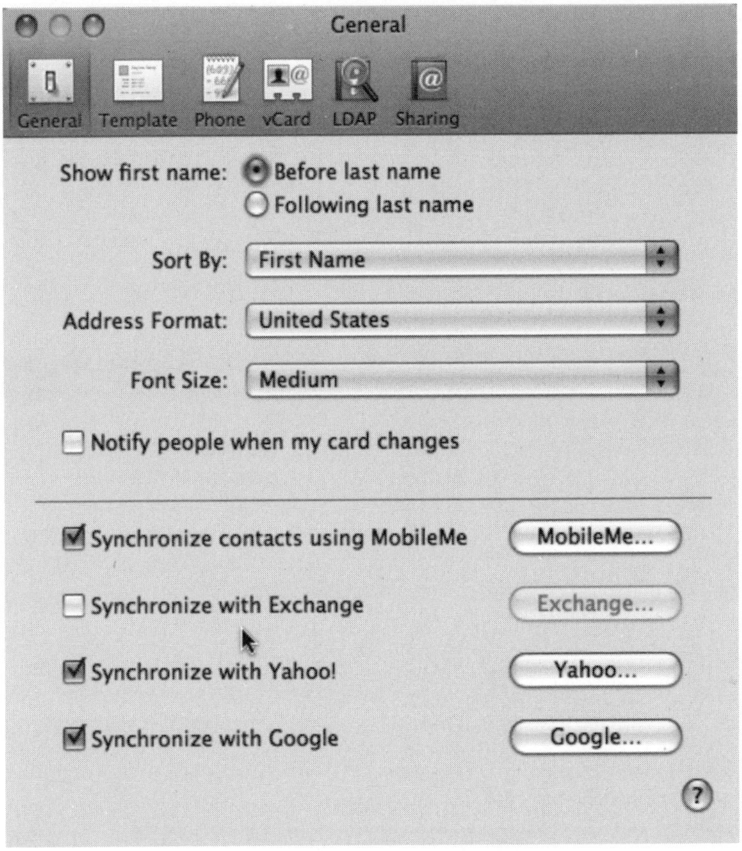

Figure 8-2. *Configuring Google/Yahoo contacts sync in Address Book for Mac OS X*

TIP: If you use Yahoo Messenger or GoogleTalk as an instant messaging solution, syncing your contacts with either Yahoo or Google will also automatically populate any instant messaging tools that you use with any of your contacts that also use these services. There are a number of IM applications for the iPhone that support both of these solutions, as well as AOL Instant Messenger, Skype, MSN/Windows Live, ICQ, and the open source Jabber. Depending on the app(s) that you choose, you may find that several can also rely on IM information if it is included for your contacts.

> **TIP:** Some car makers offer iPod/iPhone integration with their stereo, GPS, and in-dash calling features. For those that support the iPhone, it is possible to sync your contacts to the in-dash system for use with the car's built-in GPS and calling capabilities. If your car (or after-market stereo) offers iPhone integration, refer to its documentation to find out the exact level of integration and instructions.

Contacts and Social Networking Sites

Social networking sites offer professionals a way to connect with each other, share information, collaborate, and promote services and products. Most social networking sites provide native iPhone applications that allow you to view and post updates and messages directly from the iPhone (several of which I'll cover in Part 3 of this book). However, many social networking sites can also act as a repository for contact information—either duplicating the information in your computer/iPhone contacts or providing a source for contact information with additional potential colleagues and/or clients.

Managing the integration of your contacts with social networking sites can be a cumbersome process. However, the free service Plaxo offers the ability to sync contacts across multiple social networking sites, including MySpace, Facebook, and LinkedIn. Plaxo can also sync contacts from these sites with both Yahoo and Google address books and, through the use of downloadable tools, with Mac OS X's Address Book and Outlook.

For more information about Plaxo, visit `www.plaxo.com`.

The Contacts App

As I said, the Contacts app is very similar to the Contacts tab in the Phone app. In fact, in the original iPhone software release, there was no separate Contacts application, and Contacts as we know it today was based on that tab. This will make this section partly review for you, as I'll be giving an overview of the Contacts app and how it has brought some additional capabilities and usefulness beyond the Phone app.

Searching and Browsing Contacts

As with the Contacts tab in the Phone application, the Contacts app allows you to easily browse or search for specific contacts. As you can see in Figure 8-3, the app's primary interface is an alphabetical list of your contacts. You can scroll through them and jump to specific portions of the list by tapping the appropriate letter along the right side of the screen.

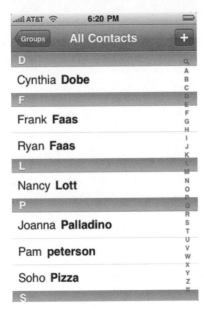

Figure 8-3. *Contacts app*

As in other apps, a live search bar at the top of the screen allows you to search for specific contacts. Simply tap the box and begin typing all or part of a person's name (first or last) or company, and you will see all matching results as you type, as shown in Figure 8-4.

> **TIP:** Being able to perform a search based on a company name (as well as an individual's name) is a particularly nice feature if you frequently work with many people from a single company. However, in order to generate company name search results, you'll have to have included company names for contacts—either when creating contacts on your iPhone itself or on your computer.

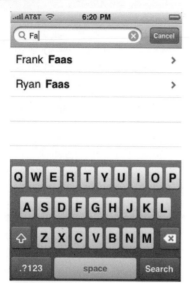

Figure 8-4. *Live search for contacts*

One particularly nice feature about live search in Contacts is that you can select a contact in the list and view his or her information, but the search is still active—meaning that if you view a contact's details (Figure 8-5) and then use the All Contacts button at the top of the screen to return to your list, you'll actually be returned to the current search. This is particularly helpful if you are trying to locate a specific individual at a company (but may not remember the exact name) and/or have many contacts with similar names. Returning to the full list of contacts or initiating a new search is as easy as tapping the Cancel button next to the search box (or tapping the X button on the right side of the search box to clear anything you've previously typed and begin again).

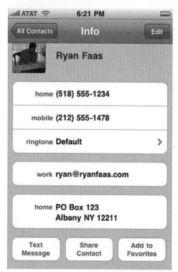

Figure 8-5. *Viewing a contact*

Setting Browsing Options

I'll revisit the idea of viewing and working with contact data for individuals in a second. First, I want to cover a couple of options available when it comes to the order in which contacts are displayed. You can choose to display and sort contacts in a couple of different ways, both of which are configured in the Mail, Contacts, Calendars option in the Settings app.

As shown in Figure 8-6, you can choose the sort order and display order for contacts. The sort order defines how a list of contacts is sorted and can be either by last name (and then by first name if there are multiple people with the same last name) or by first name (and then by last name if there are multiple people with the same first name). The first of these is the default and most common choice because sorting by last name is a standard business practice.

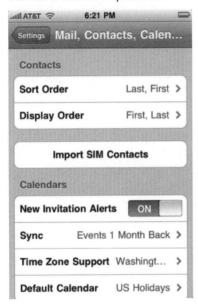

Figure 8-6. *Choosing sort and display orders*

The display order is the way in which contacts are displayed (not in which they are sorted). Again, you can choose to have last name/first name (which is common in business) or first name/last name (which may be more easily readable). One nice feature is that you since you can set these independently, you can still sort your contacts by the standard last name/first name approach, but actually see them in the more readable format.

> **NOTE:** Regardless of the combination of sort and display orders you choose, they will apply to all contact lists, including the All Contacts list, live searches, and any contact groups you create (see the next section). They will also apply to both the Contacts app and the Contacts tab in the Phone app.

Using Contact Groups

Contact groups are a useful feature for anyone with even a moderate amount of contacts. They allow you to organize your contacts into smaller and more easily manageable groups—such as family members, other personal contacts (doctors offices, friends, etc.), specific clients or customers, and departments or offices.

Both Mac OS X's Address Book and Outlook provide the ability to create contact groups. And if you create them, they will be synced automatically to your iPhone (this occurs automatically during sync regardless of whether you sync contacts through iTunes or over the air using MobileMe or an Exchange Server). If you use MobileMe, you can also create contact groups through the MobileMe web interface.

> **NOTE** Although the iPhone supports contact groups and they can be very helpful from an organizational perspective, you cannot create or edit the groups directly on the iPhone; they must be created on your computer or using MobileMe's web interface.

You can view contacts by group by tapping the Groups button in the All Contacts list (refer to Figure 8-3) at the top left of the screen. This displays a list of all groups (see Figure 8-7) that you can browse. As you can see in Figure 8-8, each group displays as a list just like the All Contacts list. You can use the Groups button at the upper left to return to your list of groups, from which you can also select the All Contacts list.

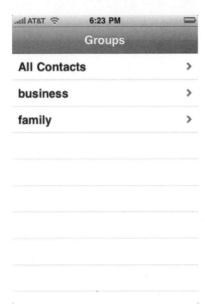

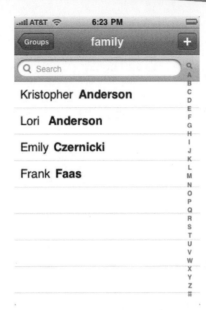

Figure 8-7. *Browsing contact groups*

Figure 8-8. *Viewing a contact group*

NOTE When you are browsing a contact group, you can still use the search bar for a live search, but the search results will only include contacts in the group.

Viewing, Editing, and Using Contacts

I covered much of the details of how to view and edit contact data in Chapter 4. As you may have noticed in the earlier figures in this chapter, the details available for a contact in the Contacts app are exactly the same as those in the Phone app. Since you're already aware of how to view, edit, and take actions (e-mail, text, or call) from a contact, I won't repeat.

However, I will make a few additional points before we move on to the next chapter. First, I'll cover sharing contacts with other users and importing contacts directly from others via vCard files. Then we'll move on to working with contact servers and finally importing and exporting contacts from a SIM card.

Sharing Contacts As vCards

vCards are small files (with a `.vcf` extension) that are designed to hold and share contact information. Much like iCalendar files were introduced to allow users to share event data with each other regardless of the type of calendar tool, the vCard format is designed to allow any e-mail or contact management application to share contact information. As such, vCards are essentially virtual business cards, which is where they get their name.

Virtually all e-mail and contact management tools support vCards, as do most mobile devices (including the iPhone). vCards can be generated by most such programs (including Mac OS X's Address Book and Outlook) simply by selecting the contacts and dragging them to a folder. A single vCard file can contain contact details for a single person or multiple people.

vCard files are very flexible because they can contain multiple contacts and are supported by almost any e-mail or contact management tool. You can often import new contacts into any tool from a vCard file simply by opening the file or dragging it onto a contact manager icon on a desktop computer. This versatility makes them helpful for both sharing data and for moving contact information from one tool to another, even if the tools themselves are not compatible—a feature that can be useful if you have been using a contact management tool (such as Thunderbird) that cannot directly sync to the iPhone.

If you receive a VCF file as an e-mail attachment, you can open the file on the iPhone and it will create one or more new contacts, complete with all details included in the original contact used to create the file. Similarly, you can share information about a contact stored on the iPhone (including yourself) quickly and easily with others by tapping the Share this Contact button on a contact's screen (see Figure 8-9), which will generate a vCard file and attach it to a new blank e-mail.

Figure 8-9. *Sharing a contact*

TIP This feature makes it easy to share contact information in a standard format with other users, clients, and contacts that you are trying to cultivate. The fact that you can immediately do it on the go is a great way of presenting a virtual business card with all your details to someone at first meeting; simply ask for their e-mail address and you can ensure that they receive all your information by sharing the contact information for yourself on your iPhone (though it's always still a good idea to use a traditional physical business cards as well).

Contacts Servers

Another way for businesses to share contact information internally is through the use of contacts servers. These are servers that store personal and/or shared contacts available to users within a company's network. The iPhone supports this technology in a handful of different ways. I'll cover two of these (web/wiki-based servers and LDAP servers) in this chapter. Another way, which involves Exchange Server's Global Address List, will be covered in the next chapter, along with details about Exchange functionality.

Web-Based Servers and Wiki

Web-based databases containing contacts that can be searched and are hosted on a company's private intranet/web site are common ways to make shared contacts available using a web server. This is the simplest solution for many companies because such a site can be powered through a wide range of technologies and accessed by many different types of computers and devices. If your company uses such a site, you would access it using the mobile version of Safari just as you would from any computer or device.

Some solutions are static contact lists (updated by specific individuals within a company) while others are dynamic solutions that offer the ability for any user to update either their own information or other people's details. Increasingly, products such as these are tied into wiki solutions (web sites that can be dynamically and easily edited, but that also keep a history of changes made by users—Wikipedia being the most well-known example). Several such products exist, including Apple's own solution included with Mac OS X Server.

LDAP Servers

LDAP is a highly adaptable database technology. It is the basis for most modern computing systems that allow users to have a single account that can be accessed from any workstation and/or application. It also allows a flexible and largely platform-neutral way to look up information about users, groups, computers, and even resources such as conference rooms. Because of its broad lookup abilities, LDAP has increasingly become a common open standard for looking up contact information.

The iPhone supports the use of LDAP servers as a repository of shared contacts (though it does so for lookup purposes only, rather than as a mechanism for editing shared contacts). Adding an LDAP server to the iPhone allows you to look up information about users throughout a company provided that contact details are included in the user account information (check with your IT department to find out if this an option).

> **NOTE** Although LDAP is broadly supported and likely implemented to some degree in most medium and large environments, exactly how IT departments choose to implement and utilize it (and whether they even allow access to it) can vary widely. You should check with your IT department before assuming you will be able to use LDAP servers for contact searches.

Adding an LDAP Server

The process of adding an LDAP server configuration to the iPhone is very similar to that of adding a POP/IMAP e-mail or CalDAV calendaring account, which I discussed in the last two chapters. As with those account types, the initial steps are to launch the Settings app; choose Mail, Contacts, Calendars; choose the Add Account option; and choose Other as the account type (refer to Chapter 6 for detailed instructions).

Once at the Other screen, shown in Figure 8-10, choose the Add LDAP Account option. On the LDAP screen (shown in Figure 8-11), enter the details about the server, including the server name, a username and password (if they are required), and a description. Refer to your IT department for details about the server and username/password requirements.

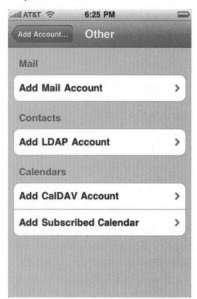

Figure 8-10. *Adding an LDAP account*

Figure 8-11. *Entering LDAP server details*

Once you add the server, the iPhone will attempt to access it securely using SSL. If SSL encryption fails, it will provide the option to connect without SSL. Based on the server name and information retrieved from the server during initial access, the iPhone will attempt to configure the server for contact searches (in most cases, additional information known as the *search base*, which instructs the iPhone how to locate contacts within the database, will also be needed—you should refer to your IT department for details), and it will appear as an account in the Mail, Contacts, Calendars section of the Settings app (see Figure 8-12).

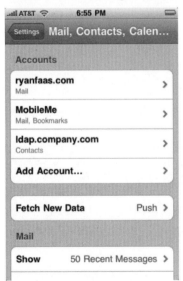

Figure 8-12. *LDAP server account in Settings app*

As with a CalDAV account, you will be able to make adjustments after the fact if server settings or your username/password change (see Figure 8-13). You may also need to manually add search variables specific to your company's server configuration if the iPhone cannot automatically detect them or if you experience problems. Since these details can vary widely from one environment to the next, you will need to work with your IT department to find out if you have any specific needs and how to enter them.

Figure 8-13. *Editing an LDAP account*

Looking Up LDAP Contacts

The process of using contacts stored on a LDAP server is actually quite simple. The Contacts search box will automatically search contacts on an LDAP server as well as contacts stored locally on your iPhone without any additional action on your part. Similarly, when you begin typing a contact into Mail, the iPhone will query the LDAP server, if available, and offer auto-complete matches to contacts stored in the LDAP server along with those stored on the iPhone. You cannot directly browse the contacts stored on an LDAP server.

> **NOTE** Although Apple has done a good job in building LDAP support into the iPhone, the $3.99 LDAPeople application available from the App Store is a more flexible option that allows you to browse, edit, and copy contacts from the LDAP server to your phone (allowing them to be used even when your iPhone cannot access the LDAP server).

Importing SIM Contacts

The option to import SIM contacts in the Mail, Contacts, Calendars section is also worth noting (refer back to Figure 8-6). As I mentioned in Chapter 4, many cell phones offer the ability to store contact details (typically name and phone number only) on a SIM card. This allows users of mobile phones to transfer not only their phone number, carrier details, and account information, but also contacts from one phone to another.

Though the iPhone is focused on syncing data through a computer or OTA solution for such functionality, it can also import contacts from an existing SIM card. Depending on your carrier and the mobile phone or device you may have had previously, this can be a way of getting previous phone contacts into the iPhone's Contacts app (and thus onto your computer as well). Refer to your carrier or previous mobile phone's instructions for details on how to store information from that phone/device onto a SIM card (the process can vary widely from one phone/device to another).

To import any existing contacts from a SIM card, simply tap the Import SIM Contacts button in the Settings app. The iPhone will scan the contents of your SIM card (as shown in Figure 8-14) and add any contacts it finds. There is nothing to distinguish a contact imported from a SIM card from one synced to or created on the iPhone. Also, you can edit details about these contacts like any other contact.

Figure 8-14. *Importing contacts from a SIM card*

NOTE: Although the iPhone can import SIM contacts, it does not support storing/exporting contact data to the SIM card.

Summary

Over the past few chapters, you've learned about the iPhone's core business tools, how to use them, and how to sync data with both your computer and various Internet- and server-based resources. You've also seen how to use these technologies in shared business spaces. In the next chapter, I'll cover how to expand upon these in enterprise environments based around Microsoft's Exchange Server.

Chapter 9

Microsoft Exchange and ActiveSync

Extending the iPhone's Capability for Collaboration with Microsoft Exchange Server

Microsoft's Exchange Server is the most common collaboration suite in business and offers a wide range of tools and features that you can access using a variety of software packages (such as Outlook on Windows PCs or varying combinations of Entourage, Mail, Address Book, and iCal on Mac OS X), as well as from mobile devices, including the iPhone. Exchange provides e-mail, personal and shared contacts, advanced multiuser calendars, public folders for collaborating on documents, and task managers. All of these make Exchange a powerful business suite. The iPhone pairs well with Exchange Server 2003 and 2007 to offer mobile access to some of Exchange's core business features (e-mail, personal and shared contacts, and advanced calendaring).

In this chapter, you'll learn how to configure your iPhone to access an Exchange server account, how to work with both personal contacts and the Exchange Global Address list, and how the iPhone's calendar app integrates with shared and group calendaring hosted by an Exchange server. I'll also cover how to manage mobile features specific to the iPhone from Outlook Web Access, including the ability to remotely erase all your content should your iPhone ever be lost or stolen.

Configuring an Exchange Account

Configuring an Exchange account on the iPhone is largely similar to configuring any other e-mail account. Apple's implementation of Microsoft's ActiveSync protocol includes some of the protocol's autodiscovery features, so setup is generally very simple.

As with other types of e-mail accounts, the process for configuring an Exchange account on the iPhone begins in the Mail, Contacts, Calendars option in the Settings app. First, select Add Account, and then select Microsoft Exchange as the account type. You will then be asked to provide information about your server and account (Figure 9-1).

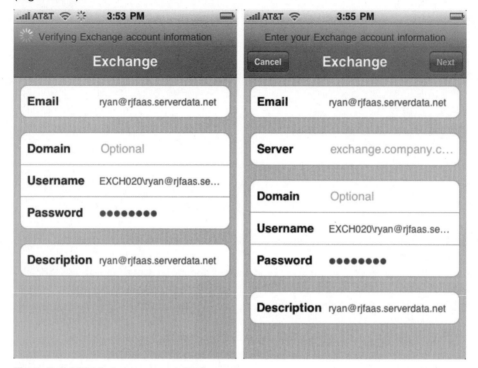

Figure 9-1. *Initial Exchange account detail screens*

The exact account information required will obviously vary from one organization to another, and you will need to work with your IT staff to determine exactly what information to enter. This is particularly true of the server address (one organization may have multiple servers providing different facets of Exchange functionality). Typically, your username and domain are the same that you would use to log into a Windows PC at your office.

Once you enter the information, the iPhone will query the server to verify that it is accessible and that your account information is correct. At this point, Exchange will also add information about your iPhone to your Exchange account that will allow the server to be able to identify your iPhone. This is an important step as this association is what allows Exchange to remotely wipe your iPhone if it is ever lost or stolen (which I'll cover later in the chapter).

This process also configures your iPhone to use any security policies being enforced by the Exchange server. Exchange security policies typically relate to locking your iPhone at specified periods of inactivity and requiring a passcode to unlock the phone. If a passcode is enforced, you may be required to change it after a specified period of time (such as every month or every 90 days), and it may require an alphanumeric passcode (one that includes numbers and letters instead of just numbers) that has a specific length or complexity.

> **TIP:** Any Exchange security policies will override any settings on your iPhone and you will not be able to bypass them. So, it's a good idea to ask about the use of such policies when setting up your iPhone to work with your Exchange server so that you're aware of them.

Once the iPhone has verified your account, you'll be asked what information you want to sync over the air using it (Figure 9-2). Similar to MobileMe, you can choose to sync mail, contacts, and calendar data, and if you do over-the-air (OTA) sync, then all such details will be synced to you iPhone through the Exchange server, not through a cable-sync in iTunes.

> **CAUTION:** When you choose to sync contacts and calendars using Exchange, the iPhone will ask whether you want to delete or keep any existing data. If you choose to delete but haven't synced your existing contacts, then any changes will be lost.

> **NOTE:** You can only configure a single Exchange account on an iPhone. You can, however, still configure non-Exchange accounts on the iPhone, including a MobileMe account.

Figure 9-2. *Exchange options available during account setup*

Post-Setup Exchange Account Options

After you've set up an Exchange account, you'll be able to adjust the options you selected during initial configuration using the Mail, Contacts, Calendars option in the Settings app—much as you can other e-mail accounts. As with other accounts, Exchange accounts will appear in the list of available accounts (Figure 9-3), and you can tap the account to modify it.

Figure 9-3. *Available accounts*

As you can see in Figure 9-4, you'll also have the option of choosing how many days worth of mail to sync. By default, the iPhone will only sync three days of e-mail (though you can search previous messages from your mail server using the same e-mail search features that you would use for other e-mail servers, as described in Chapter 6). This is one area where Exchange accounts are different than other accounts—which download messages but only save up to a specific number of them (up to a maximum of 200). Because Exchange syncs interactively, Exchange accounts rely on a date range to determine how many messages are stored to your iPhone.

Syncing less mail can save space, but syncing more can give you immediate access to messages (particularly if you'll be traveling and won't have access to Wi-Fi or your carrier's network, such as when flying). As shown in Figure 9-5, there are a range of options for how much mail to sync, including unlimited (i.e., every e-mail you haven't deleted). The amount you choose should be dictated by how much e-mail you receive, how much you keep, and how often you need immediate access to older messages.

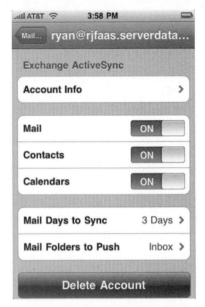

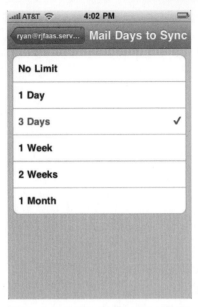

Figure 9-4. *Options for an Exchange account*   **Figure 9-5.** *Options for how much mail to sync*

CAUTION: If you disable syncing of mail, contacts, or calendars to your iPhone after setup, any existing data on your iPhone that was synced from the server will be erased. The same is true if you delete an account.

Choosing What Gets Pushed and What Gets Fetched

You also have an option to determine which mail folders trigger push notifications. Unlike other e-mail systems that offer push notification of new messages delivered to your inbox, Exchange can be configured to send notification of new messages delivered to other folders created within your account. This is because Exchange supports complex delivery rules that allow you have the server automatically sort incoming mail (and respond to it) in different ways—based on sender, subject, and other criteria.

This is a powerful organizing tool, but because the rules are done by the server (and not your e-mail client itself), it means that you may have messages that are placed in specific mailbox or folders without ever arriving in your inbox. So, this option allows you to add other mailboxes as well so that you're notified about messages delivered to them immediately.

NOTE: Regardless of whether you choose to have push notification of folders other than your inbox, the iPhone will still sync these folders using your fetch interval, or manually if you navigate to them in Mail.

> **TIP:** By settings rules to deliver messages to other folders and not including those folders as ones to generate push notification, you can avoid getting immediate notifications for messages that you don't need to read or respond to immediately.

Changing Account Information

The Account Information option allows you to modify all the general Exchange account details (as shown in Figure 9-6). Typically, the only option you may need to use here is that for changing your account password. Any other changes will be the result of changes to your Exchange environment, and your IT staff should inform you about those (or make them for you).

Figure 9-6. *Modifying account information*

Using Exchange-Specific Features

The most notable Exchange feature for the iPhone is the ability for push notification of new e-mail messages. Like MobileMe, Exchange also offers OTA sync of contacts and calendar data. Generally, these features function similarly to the more general iPhone features described over the past few chapters. E-mail for an Exchange account is displayed and can be organized in the same ways, contacts are searchable in the same manner, and OTA sync happens much as it does with MobileMe (which is to say without major effort on your part).

That said, Exchange does bring with it some additional features that aren't present for other accounts. To make the most of Exchange, you'll want to know how to use (and get the most use out of) these features.

Exchange Contacts and the Global Address List

Contacts in Exchange come in two varieties: personal contacts that are associated only with your account and contacts stored in the Exchange Global Address List (GAL). Personal contacts are ones that you create in Outlook, Outlook Web Access, or another tool like Mail or Entourage for Mac OS X. These contacts are synced to your iPhone much as they would be if you were syncing using iTunes or MobileMe.

The GAL is a searchable listing of all users in an Exchange environment, as well as additional shared contact entries. It can also include distribution groups, or mailing lists, where a single address can be used to send messages to a selection of users (such as entire departments or people associated with specific projects). For large companies, the GAL is a powerful tool because it makes it easy to contact, e-mail, or send an event invitation to anyone in the organization or any commonly used outside contacts. It also saves individual users from having to manage large identical or similar collections of contacts.

Accessing the GAL

The iPhone offers full support for searching the GAL in an Exchange environment—a very powerful and practical feature. You can access the GAL either from the Contacts app or from Mail. In Contacts, navigate to the list of available contact groups as described in the last chapter.

As shown in Figure 9-7, this will screen will look a bit different when you have configured an Exchange account. It will list personal contacts synced from your Exchange account as a group (Contacts) and will have an item for the GAL (the name will include the description of your account). To search the GAL, select the appropriate item.

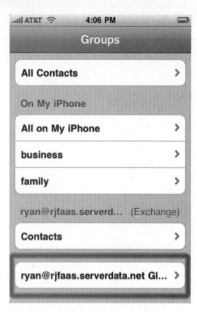

Figure 9-7. *Navigating to the GAL*

If you have both Exchange and MobileMe accounts configured on the iPhone, this screen will look like Figure 9-8, as it will also include contacts and groups synced from MobileMe, as well as from Exchange and the GAL.

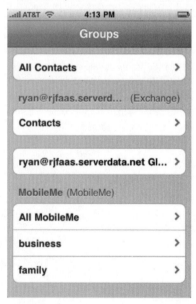

Figure 9-8. *Contacts groups with both Exchange and MobileMe accounts*

As shown in Figure 9-9, the GAL is largely like any other contact search option on the iPhone. One difference is that the GAL must be searched—it cannot be browsed (which is good, considering in some businesses the contents could be quite massive).

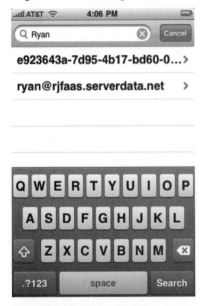

Figure 9-9. *Searching the GAL*

As with other search fields, this is a live search from which you can select a matching contact at any point (though because it is a server-based search, it may be a bit slower depending on the connection between your iPhone and the Exchange server). Selecting a matching contact brings up a contact screen that is pretty much identical to any stored on the iPhone itself, and that can be used to send e-mails, make calls, and send text or media messages. It can also be shared as a vCard.

The GAL and Mail

The GAL is also available when you are composing an e-mail using an Exchange account. In this case, the GAL is searched automatically along with other contacts when you begin typing in the To, CC, or BCC fields. Results will appear along with other contacts (though again, they might be slower to appear, depending on your server connection). You can also tap the Add button, as you can with other types of e-mail accounts, and navigate to the GAL search just as you would from within the Contacts app.

Exchange Calendaring Options

Being a collaboration suite, Exchange includes built-in shared calendar capabilities. For the most part, these capabilities function for Exchange accounts as they do for calendars synced using iTunes or MobileMe. The view options for Exchange calendars are much the same as for synced calendars (or CalDAV- and iCalendar-subscribed calendars) except that, as you can see in Figure 9-10, Exchange calendars are grouped together in the list of available calendars (and like contacts, they use your description of the account as part of the name of that grouping).

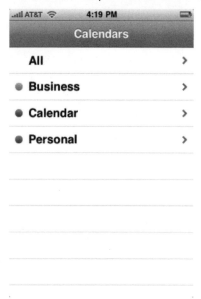

Figure 9-10. *Exchange calendars listed in Calendar*

Event Invitations

Exchange supports the use of event invitations that are sent directly through the Exchange server (unlike iCalendar invitations sent via e-mail). The iPhone supports receiving invitations as well as sending invitations from the Calendar application. As you can see in Figure 9-11, when you have configured an Exchange account for your iPhone, there's an additional button to the lower right of the Calendar display that is used to display your list of event invitations. You can tap any invitation in the list to display details about the event, and to respond regarding whether you will attend (Figure 9-12).

Figure 9-11. *Calendar with Exchange account configured*

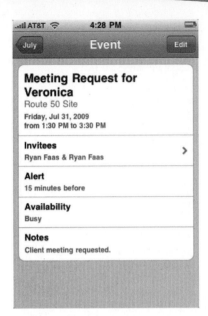

Figure 9-12. *Event invitation*

Unanswered invitations will show up as events on your calendar, but instead of being represented by a dot, they'll be represented by a dot with a line through them. Invitations that you've sent or accepted, on the other hand, will appear like any other event. You can also respond to invitations directly by tapping them to view details and indicate a response. (The event selected in Figures 9-11 and 9-12 illustrates an event invitation.)

Inviting Other Users to an Event

You can also send event invitations to other Exchange users when creating events on your iPhone. As you can see in Figure 9-13, the dialog for creating or editing an event will include an Invitees item after you've configured an Exchange account. Tapping this will bring up a dialog similar to that of an e-mail or text message, which you can use to add invitees (see Figure 9-14). As when sending an e-mail in Exchange, adding an invitee provides a live search of your contacts and the GAL, and you can use the Add button to view and/or browse contacts as well.

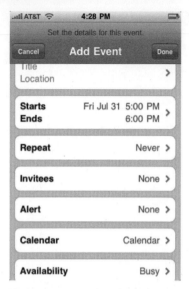

Figure 9-13. *Additional Exchange event options*

Figure 9-14. *Adding an invitee*

Specifying Availability

Another calendaring feature of Exchange is the ability to indicate times when you are free for meetings or events and times you aren't. This information can be viewed by others in Outlook, iCal, and other Exchange clients when they attempt to invite you to an event. The Availability option allows you to specify how other people will see your availability listed for an event that you create on your calendar. As you can see in Figure

9-15, you can select from different options to indicate whether you are free during that time frame or not.

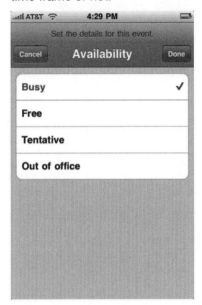

Figure 9-15. *Setting availability for an event on the iPhone*

Remote Wipe of a Lost/Stolen iPhone

One of the final major features that Exchange adds to the iPhone is the ability to remotely wipe all data from the device if it is lost or stolen. This is a powerful feature and one that can be considered a must if you will be storing any confidential data on it. This feature can be activated by the IT staff who manage your Exchange server or by yourself through Outlook Web Access.

To remotely wipe a lost/stolen iPhone using Outlook Web Access, log into your account through a web browser (refer to your IT or Exchange provider guidelines for details). Click the options button in the upper left of the Outlook Web Access window, and then select the Mobile Devices option in the sidebar to the left. At this point, you will see any mobile devices associated with your Exchange account. You can select your iPhone or iPod touch in the list and click the Wipe All Data from Device link. Outlook Web Access will warn you about the consequences (Figure 9-16 illustrates both how to access mobile devices and the warning shown when you send the remote wipe command).

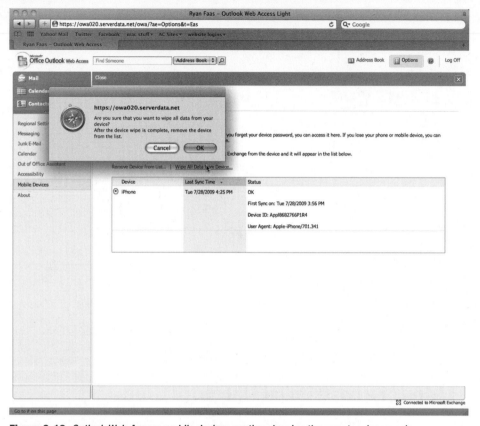

Figure 9-16. *Outlook Web Access mobile devices section showing the remote wipe warning*

Once you have issued the wipe command, you will see the status of the command displayed in Outlook Web Access, and you will receive an e-mail when the wipe has been completed. Exchange will send a push notification to the device immediately after you issue the command. If your iPhone is powered on and connected to the Internet (either via Wi-Fi, 3G, or EDGE networking), it will lock itself out and begin the wipe, erasing all content (including personal data, settings, music and video, and installed third-party applications), after which it will restart and appear as a brand-new device.

> **TIP:** While an a wipe command is pending, you can return to Outlook Web Access and cancel the command by selecting the device and clicking Cancel Wipe, which will replace the Wipe All Data from Device link. Once the command has reached an iPhone and the wipe begun, however, it cannot be canceled.

If an iPhone is powered off or without Internet connectivity (such as while in Airplane mode), it will receive and process the wipe command immediately on being turned on and making an Internet connection. If you have disabled push notifications, the iPhone will receive and process the wipe command at its next fetch interval.

Once a device has been successfully wiped, you should return to Outlook Web Access and again select Options and then Mobile Devices. Then select the device and click Remove Device from List, as this will remove any association between the iPhone and your Exchange account. You can then configure a replacement iPhone as described earlier in the chapter (or even your original one should you find/recover it).

> **CAUTION:** A remote wipe will erase all content on an iPhone and is effective against preventing casual thieves or someone who accidentally finds the device from accessing your content (though computer forensic tools might still be able to locate data).

ACCESSING GOOGLE SERVICES USING ACTIVESYNC

Google has begun offering OTA sync and push notification of the company's free Gmail contacts and Google Calendar services with the iPhone in a service known as **Google Sync**. Powering these capabilities is the same ActiveSync technology that enables the iPhone to communicate with Exchange servers. As a result, the setup process and operation are essentially the same as any other Exchange server, as discussed throughout this chapter.

When setting up Google Sync, you will configure your iPhone to access your Gmail account using the Exchange option for a new account rather than Gmail option. Then you will set up the account using your full Gmail address as the username and your Gmail password (leave the domain field blank). When asked for a server name/address, enter m.google.com. You can then choose to sync contacts and calendars to your iPhone (you can sync up to 25 calendars).

It is important to note that Google Sync is still in beta testing as of this writing, and that it has some known limitations as compared to syncing to an actual Exchange server. The service currently doesn't reflect attendee status, and it syncs only limited pieces of information for each contact.

For additional information on using Google Sync, including the current status and limitations of the service, see www.google.com/support/mobile/bin/answer.py?hl=en&answer=139635.

HOSTED EXCHANGE SERVICES

Exchange is a very complex server technology that can be difficult and expensive for small businesses to set up and maintain. For many small businesses and individual professionals, hosted Exchange services are a better solution. With hosted Exchange, you rely on an outside company to configure and maintain an Exchange server for you. This provides all the collaborative and mobility benefits of Exchange without any of the technical hassles, and can be a good solution for small organizations or individuals. Also, the specific focus on providing Exchange services virtually guarantees broader experience and better user and device support options. There are a number of such companies out there with a variety of service packages and price points—many of which have extensively tested their services with the iPhone and other mobile devices.

ALTERNATIVES TO EXCHANGE

Some options for larger organizations looking to lower the costs of deploying Exchange (and simplify the process somewhat, particularly when integrating with non-Microsoft server environments) are similar collaborative suites developed by companies that have licensed the ActiveSync protocol from Microsoft. From an iPhone and client perspective, these products function largely as though they were accessing an Exchange server. The following list identifies some of the most common options. For more information on these options, visit http://ryanfaas.com/index.php/2008/11/21/seven-ways-to-push-mail-to-the-iphone-without-exchange/.

1. Kerio MailServer: Kerio MailServer offers features similar to Exchange's, including mail, centralized contacts, calendars, notes, tasks, and public folders using both ActiveSync and other protocols such as CalDAV and LDAP (discussed in the previous two chapters). See www.kerio.com/mailserver.

2. Zimbra Collaboration Suite: This is a full-featured e-mail and groupware product available at a variety of price points for different needs that relies on client-installed tools to sync data to computers and an additional server-based package to support mobile devices including the iPhone (see www.zimbra.com/products/).

3. Zarafa and Z-Push: Zarafa is available in both open source and commercial variations designed for Outlook or web use by computers. Z-Push is the add-on component that allows syncing with mobile devices including the iPhone (see www.zarafaserver.de/).

4. CommuniGate Pro: This is a full-featured messaging and groupware product that integrates support for e-mail, instant messaging, centralized contacts, calendar, task management, and VoIP phone services. It supports a wide range of client protocols for messaging and collaborative tools that can be accessed natively from Outlook, Thunderbird, and Apple's Mail and iCal, as well as ActiveSync for iPhone and other mobile devices (see https://www.communigate.com/).

5. NotifyLink: NotifyLink is designed to act as a bridge between an existing non-ActiveSync mail or collaboration server and mobile devices, allowing them to receive push notifications using ActiveSync (see www.notifycorp.com/).

Summary

The past few chapters have focused on core office tasks and collaboration (in this one, you learned about the advanced collaboration tools offered by pairing the iPhone with Microsoft Exchange). The next few chapters will focus on teaching you how to take the remaining built-in iPhone applications and put them to work for you—including some, such as the iPod and YouTube, that may have business uses despite their largely consumer focus.

Chapter 10

Photos and Video

Using the iPhone's Camera for Quickly
Recording Information

In this chapter, we'll examine the camera and photo library capabilities of the iPhone (and in the case of the iPhone 3GS, its video capabilities). Although a camera may not seem like a useful tool in many professions, the ability to quickly capture visual information (or even evidence in some situations) can often be easier than transcribing written content (such as from a dry-erase board) or writing a description of a person or place. The iPhone's ability to share snapshots makes it easy to take these photo records and make use of them in any number of different ways. This chapter will also look at the iPhone's photo library, which can contain any number of high-resolution images synced from your computer that can be used as reference tools or visual aids during meetings or trainings (particularly impromptu meetings).

Shooting Photos and Video with Camera

The iPhone's Camera app may be the simplest of iPhone apps to use. As you can see in Figure 10-1, the app consists almost entirely of the view from the camera as if the entire screen were a giant viewfinder. This makes it pretty easy line up a shot and be certain what each shot will look like before you take it.

Figure 10-1. *Camera app*

At the bottom edge of the screen is a small toolbar that includes a shutter button in the middle. To take a photo, simply line up the shot and tap the shutter button. You'll notice that an animated shutter effect plays across the face of the display.

Once you've take a photo, you'll see a small thumbnail of it appear to the left of the shutter button (or to one side if you're holding the iPhone in landscape orientation). You may also notice that both the camera icon on the shutter button and the thumbnail of the most recently snapped photo rotate to match the orientation of the iPhone and even display appropriately if the iPhone is held upside down.

That's essentially all there is to taking a snapshot. You can tap the thumbnail of the most recent photo to view the Camera Roll album (which contains any photos you take with the iPhone) in the Photos application, which I'll cover in the next part of this chapter.

SHOOTING VIDEO WITH THE IPHONE 3GS

If you have an iPhone 3GS, you might notice that there's an additional item in the Camera toolbar (as shown in the following image). To the right of the shutter button, you'll see a small switch. This switch allows you to toggle between taking still photos and taking video.

To shoot video, simply tap the switch to use video mode. The shutter button will change to a red record button that you tap to start recording and then tap again to stop recording. The iPhone 3GS will record both sound and video, and you can shoot video in both portrait and landscape orientation. Once you finish recording, your video will be stored in the Camera Roll album along with photos, and a thumbnail of the first frame of the footage will be displayed (that thumbnail will also be displayed in the Camera toolbar, just like a photo).

FOCUSING ON THE IPHONE 3GS

The iPhone 3GS also includes the autofocus and tap-to-focus features. Autofocus is enabled automatically and functions like the autofocus feature on any digital camera, setting the focus of the image on the center object. Tap-to-focus allows you to set the focus of the image on anything in the shot (such as a person's face, a building in the distance, or a close-up or background object). The Camera app will automatically adjust the various image settings including focus, white balance, and exposure to highlight whatever you want to focus on, giving you very easy-to-use but powerful control over how images are shot. To use this feature, simply tap the area you want to focus on before tapping the shutter button. You can use tap-to-focus when shooting still photos or videos.

NOTE: The iPhone automatically geocodes photos, embedding the coordinates where the photo was taken using either GPS (or other, less accurate, location services if GPS isn't available). When paired with tools that can access this data, like Apple's iPhoto for Mac OS X or the Flickr image sharing website, the location information is automatically included with each photo. This can be a fun feature, but it also makes it easy to accurately map locations (such as real estate) and provide location and time/date evidence of when and where a photo was taken.

Viewing Images in Your Photo Library

You can view your photos on the iPhone using the Photos application. Photos contains your iPhone's entire photo library, including the Camera Roll album, which stores photos and video you take with the iPhone's built-in camera, as well as any albums that you have chosen to sync from your computer using iTunes. As shown in Figure 10-2, the library is organized as a simple list of albums.

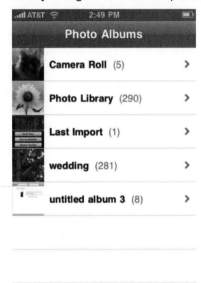

Figure 10-2. *The list of albums in Photos*

The Camera Roll album will always be listed first in the Photos, making it easy to locate (we'll cover the Camera Roll in detail later in this chapter). The second album listed will always be the Photo Library album, which contains all the photos on your iPhone (both those taken with the iPhone's camera and those synced to the iPhone). Any other albums you sync will be listed based on the age of the most recent photo in the album (so an album with an image from last week will appear above one that contains only pictures from last month).

When you tap a photo album, you'll see thumbnails of all the images it contains, as shown in Figure 10-3. The oldest photos in the album will be listed at the top of the album and the most recent at the bottom.

Figure 10-3. *Viewing the contents of an album*

Viewing and Working with Photos

To view a photo at full size, simply tap while browsing an album. When a photo is viewed at full size, such as in Figure 10-4, you can use multitouch to zoom in or out and to pan around a photo that you've zoomed in on.

Figure 10-4. *Viewing a photo*

Also notice that there's a translucent toolbar at the bottom of the photo when it is first displayed, some details (the position of the photo and number of photos in the album), and a button displaying the name of the album at the top of the display—tapping this button will bring you back to the album view. These disappear after a few seconds, but you can display them again simply by tapping the iPhone's screen.

The toolbar includes buttons for performing photo-related tasks, as well as back and forward arrow buttons to move to the previous or next photo in the album. You can also move back and forth through the album using multitouch by flicking you finger quickly to left or right of the screen.

Photo Tasks

Tapping the photo tasks button (the leftmost button in the toolbar displayed beneath a photo—see Figure 10-4) brings up a dialog that allows you to do a number of things with the photo, as shown in Figure 10-5. You can choose to e-mail the photo (which will launch Mail, create a new blank message, and add the photo as an attachment). You can upload the photo to the online gallery associated with your MobileMe account (you'll be asked to choose a title for the photo, enter a description, and choose from your existing MobileMe albums, as shown in Figure 10-6). You can assign the photo as a contact's image (you'll see a standard Contacts browser from which you choose a contact to assign the photo to; you'll also have the option to scale and zoom the photo, as discussed in Chapter 4). And finally, you can set the image as your iPhone's wallpaper, as shown in Figure 10-7.

Figure 10-5. Photo tasks dialog

Figure 10-6. *Uploading a photo to MobileMe*

Figure 10-7. *Setting a photo as your wallpaper*

TIP: You can also set the iPhone's wallpaper by using the Wallpaper option in the Settings app (which will also allow you to pick from your photo albums as well as Apple's prepackaged wallpaper images, as shown in Figure 10-8.

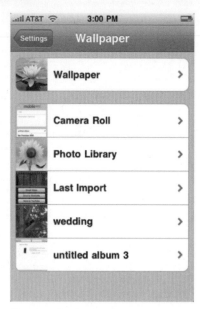

Figure 10-8. *Setting the wallpaper using the Settings app*

If you upload a photo to MobileMe, you'll see a progress bar during the upload (after you specify details about the image). When the upload has completed, you'll have the option of viewing the photo in your gallery using Safari or notifying other people that you've published it via e-mail.

Working with Multiple Photos

You can also work with multiple photos at one time from the album view. The album view also includes a translucent toolbar (as well as a bar at the top displaying the album name and a button that you can click to return to the album list). There are two buttons in the album toolbar: a play button in the center that will play a slideshow according the options you configure for Photos in the Settings app (which I'll cover shortly) and a tasks button.

The tasks button in an album view allows you to select multiple photos in the album and display buttons to share or copy those photos using the buttons that appear at the bottom of the display (see Figure 10-9). There's also a button at the top of the display to cancel multiple photo selection.

Figure 10-9. *Selecting multiple photos*

If you tap Share, you'll be asked if you want to share the photos via e-mail. If you tap Email, the iPhone will create a new blank e-mail and attach all the selected photos. If you tap Copy, all the selected images will be copied to the iPhone's clipboard and can then be pasted into another application that supports copy and pasting of image data.

Slideshows

You can view a slideshow of a selected photo album by tapping the play slideshow button in the middle of the toolbar along the bottom of the photo album. The slideshow will begin playing with all photos in the album according the settings you choose in the Photo option in the Settings app. You can pause a slideshow by simply tapping the screen, at which point, Photos will treat the current image as if you were viewing a still image (you'll need to go back to the album to restart the slideshow).

> **TIP:** When paired with an Apple Universal Dock and the appropriate cables (or some third-party accessories), you can display video from an iPhone on a television screen or monitor that accepts appropriate inputs. This can make the iPhone a useful tool for displaying a slideshow, setting the mood for an event, and even playing video. For additional information, see the following article from Apple's Knowledge Base: http://support.apple.com/kb/HT1454.

Slideshow Settings

Options related to slideshows are the only ones available in the Photos section of the Settings app. As you can see in Figure 10-10, these settings offer you the length of time each photo is displayed, a choice of five basic transitions between slides (Cube, Dissolve, Ripple, Wipe Across, and Wipe Down), and the options to automatically repeat a slideshow as a loop or shuffle the slide order.

Figure 10-10. *Basic slideshow options*

The Camera Roll

Now that we've covered the basics of taking pictures and viewing photos on your iPhone, let's talk about where these two feature sets come together: the Camera Roll (Figure 10-11). For the most part, the Camera Roll works like any other album in Photos, except that it isn't a static album synced from your computer, because it is populated with images (and video, in the case of the iPhone 3GS) taken with the Camera app. This means there are a couple of differences between the Camera Roll and any other album, because it can be organized and edited.

Figure 10-11. *The Camera Roll*

The most obvious difference for the Camera Roll compared to other albums is that you can delete photos from it. If you use the tasks button to select photos (as you can with other albums), a Delete button will join the Copy and Share buttons (as shown in Figure 10-12).

Figure 10-12. *Selecting Camera Roll photos for deletion*

When you actually tap the Delete button, you'll be asked if you really want to delete the selected photo(s).

Deleting from the Image or Slideshow View

The Camera Roll's mass-select-and-delete feature is new in iPhone OS 3, and it's quite a time-saver because you can quickly scan, select, and delete photos that didn't come out well without having to view each photo. However, you can also delete a photo while viewing it at full size. Notice in Figure 10-13 that when a photo in the Camera Roll is viewed at full size, a trash icon will appear at the lower right (the same will happen in a paused slideshow). Similar to deleting photos from the Camera Roll itself, you'll be asked to confirm your choice.

Figure 10-13. *Photo in the Camera Roll (note the trash icon in the lower-right corner)*

CAUTION: There is no undo for deleting photos from the Camera Roll.

TRIMMING VIDEO ON THE IPHONE 3GS

Trimming video is a simple aspect of video editing in which you cut content from the beginning or end of a clip to shorten and maintain focus on a subject. The Camera Roll app in the iPhone 3GS allows both viewing recorded video clips and trimming clips.

To view a clip, simply tap the clip's thumbnail as though it were a still image. You'll see a full-screen version of the clip (similar to a still image, but with a large play button, as shown in the following image:

Once you tap a video clip to play it, you'll see a toolbar very much like the one at the bottom of a still image. This includes the familiar tasks button that allows you to e-mail the video, upload it to MobileMe or YouTube, or send it via MMS, if supported by your carrier (see the following image). It also includes forward and back buttons for viewing other images and video clips in the Camera Roll, and a trash icon to delete the entire video (again, with a delete confirmation).

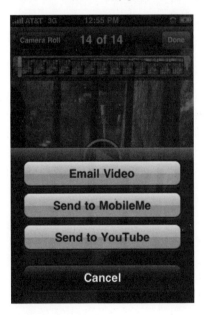

While the video is playing, a control bar along the top allows you to select video to trim (refer to the following image). You make a selection by dragging along either edge of the timeline. When a segment is selected, holding your finger on the selection enlarges the segment's timeline for more accurate adjustment. When a clip segment is selected, tapping the play button will play only that segment, but will not remove other portions of the video. When you've adjusted your clip to just the content that you need/want to save, tapping the Trim button will remove any other content and save the changes.

Taking Screenshots

There may be times when you need to take an image of what's on your iPhone's screen. Called *screenshots*, these images have all manner of uses ranging from recording the exact content of a web page, to providing details to your IT department during remote troubleshooting, to sharing a particular configuration of an application or settings, to recording a portion of an app's display that can't be copied or printed (or, as in the case of this book, to assist in explaining iPhone features to others).

Taking a screenshot is simple with the iPhone. Just press the Home and Sleep/Wake buttons at the same time. You'll see a white flash and hear a camera shutter click. A copy of the screen's content will then be stored as a picture file in the Camera Roll (from where it can be viewed and will be synced to your computer just like a photo).

> **NOTE:** Remember, as I've mentioned in earlier chapters when talking about photos in e-mail and media messages (and as I'll point out in the next chapter while discussing web sites), you can save images from each of these sources into the Camera Roll for later use by holding our finger on them for a couple of seconds and using the appropriate option from each app's pop-up dialog.

Copying Photos to Your Computer

In Part 1 of this book, I covered syncing images from your computer to your iPhone. iTunes supports managing this sync for you, and can do so whether you are using iPhoto or Aperture on Mac OS X, or Photoshop Album or Photoshop Elements on Windows. You can also sync to a folder containing images.

This process is a little bit different than the process of copying images from the iPhone to your computer. Whether you are using a Mac or a PC, iTunes does not actually sync photos contained in the Camera Roll. In fact, your computer will simply treat the Camera Roll as a digital camera.

This means that if you are using Mac OS X, iPhoto or Aperture will launch and allow you to view images, and copy them into the your image library. If you are using Windows, you can use tools like Photoshop Elements to manage the camera, or you can simply allow Windows to autodetect the iPhone as a camera device and copy photos from it into your My Pictures folder automatically.

> **NOTE:** Most photo tools offer the option of erasing digital camera memory after copying photos to a computer. This will erase only the Camera Roll photos if used with the iPhone. However, you may want to leave photos in the Camera Roll for later viewing. A better approach, however, is use your photo editor of choice to create new albums for imported photos (or add them to existing albums/folders) and sync them back as regular photo albums to your iPhone through iTunes.

> **NOTE:** iPhone 3GS videos can be imported by iPhoto, Windows, and most third-party Windows digital camera/media tools. However, they cannot be added to photo albums that iTunes can sync back to the iPhone 3GS photo library. Therefore, you may wish to maintain copies of videos on your device or share them using a service like YouTube or MobileMe.

> **TIP:** Many social networking apps (such as Facebook and the array of third-party Twitter apps available for the iPhone) allow you to take and share photos from directly within the third-party app without needing to open the Camera or Photos apps. Figure 10-14 illustrates how to do this using the Twitter app Tweetie. In most such apps, the camera option will be displayed as a camera icon when creating a new post (as in Figure 10-14), and will offer you the option to either select and upload a new photo from your photo library (including the Camera Roll and any synced photos) or take a photo right from within the app itself.

Figure 10-14. *Posting a photo to Twitter with the Tweetie app*

> **TIP:** Although the iPhone's Photos application and camera mainly handle taking photos, a number of different third-party apps can also add fairly sophisticated photo-editing capabilities (I'll cover some of these in Part 3 of this book).

Summary

In this chapter, you started branching out from the basic business functions of the iPhone into some of its broader capabilities. We'll continue that exploration in the next few chapters, beginning with the built-in Apple Safari web browser.

Chapter 11

Web Browsing with Mobile Safari

Using Apple's Safari Browser to Get the Full Web Experience No Matter Where You Are

Web browsers have been available on mobile phones for about a decade, but they have typically been stripped-down browsers that didn't display web pages anywhere near what they would look like on a computer. For the iPhone, Apple designed a mobile version of its Safari browser that renders pages using the same engine as the desktop version of Safari. And because multitouch makes it easy to pinch and zoom, pages don't need to be reformatted to fit the iPhone's smaller screen. In this chapter, I'll walk you through using Safari to surf the Web and discuss the various settings available to tailor and secure your web experience to your needs.

Navigating Safari

Overall, Safari on the iPhone looks and works pretty much like any web browser. As you can see in Figure 11-1, the interface includes the typical browser components like the address bar (where you type in a web site URL) and search bar (which by default searches Google, but can be set to search using Yahoo, as I'll cover later in this chapter) along the top. At the right of the address bar is Safari's reload button, which you can tap if you need to reload a currently displayed page.

Figure 11-1. *Safari*

When you tap either the address bar or search bar, you'll see the iPhone's keyboard display (Figures 11-2 and 11-3), which you can use to either enter the URL of a web site or a search string. When typing a URL, you'll see a small circle with an X icon at the right of the text field that will clear the field of any current address and allow you to begin typing.

Figure 11-2. *Entering a URL in the address bar*

Figure 11-3. *Entering a search query*

> **TIP:** The keyboard displayed when entering a URL in the address bar includes a ".com" shortcut key that saves you from having to type the .com part of an address. However, if you tap and hold your finger on this key for a few seconds, a pop-up with other common domain name components (.net, .edu, and .org) will appear.

Along the bottom is a toolbar with other common features. To the left there are back and forward for navigating recently viewed pages. The other buttons relate to working with bookmarks and multiple web pages.

Working with Bookmarks

The next two buttons on the toolbar allow you to add, view, and manage bookmarked web sites. The + button in the middle allows you to perform one of three actions (as shown in Figure 11-4): add the current page as bookmark in Safari, create an icon for the page that is displayed on your home screen, or send an e-mail including the address of the page.

Figure 11-4. *Choices for the + button*

Adding a page to the home screen as an icon can be useful to provide quick access to commonly used web sites. When a page is added as an icon, you can simply tap the icon and Safari will automatically open the web site in a new page. Although this can be used for any web site, it is most common for web-based applications, particularly those designed for use with the iPhone, as I'll talk about more in Chapter 15. Web-based applications (often called web apps) are particularly helpful for businesses that want to develop tools, such as databases, project/task managers, and even expense/HR systems that can be made available to workers anywhere in the world and using any computing or mobile device platform, including the iPhone.

The fourth button displays Safari's bookmarks (Figure 11-5), allowing you open any bookmarked site. Bookmarks also includes a folder named History, which acts much like the history menu on traditional web browsers and can be used to review or revisit pages you've looked at previously.

Figure 11-5. *Bookmarks*

Managing Bookmarks

As with most web browsers on a computer, the iPhone supports organizing groups of bookmarks into folders, deleting older bookmarks, and editing the name or URL of a bookmark. All of these features are available by tapping the Edit button in the lower-left corner of the Bookmarks screen.

As you can see in Figure 11-6, editing bookmarks is done in an interface similar to that used to delete and organize messages in Mail. As with deleting individual messages, you can delete bookmarks by tapping the red circle icon next to a bookmark, which will reveal a Delete button.

Figure 11-6. *Editing/deleting bookmarks*

You can also edit the name of the bookmark or the URL it points to simply by tapping it. As you can see in Figure 11-7, this displays a screen with fields for the name (by default, bookmarks rely on the `title` tag of web page to populate this, but you may later find that a shorter or more descriptive name is helpful for easily locating a particular bookmark), the URL (this you typically only to need to change if the address of the actual page or site changes), and the folder where the bookmark is stored.

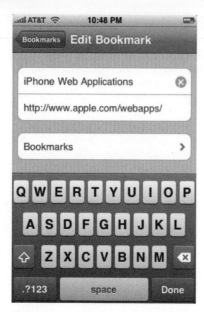

Figure 11-7. *Editing an individual bookmark*

You can move a bookmark from one folder to another by tapping its current folder on the edit screen. This will bring up a list of all bookmark folders, organized in a hierarchy if you have folders within folders, similar to the one in Figure 11-8. To move a bookmark, just select the folder you want to move it into.

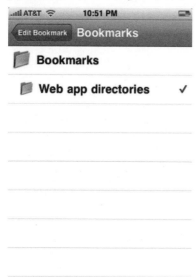

Figure 11-8. *Choosing where to move a bookmark or folder*

You can also create new folders by tapping the new folder button on the edit screen while rearranging/deleting bookmarks (refer to Figure 11-4). This will bring up a screen that allows you to name the folder and choose which folder to place it in (Figure 11-9). As with bookmarks, you can edit folders by tapping them from the Edit Bookmark screen.

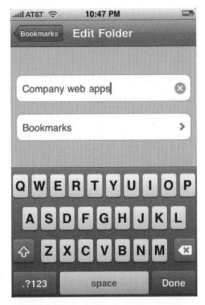

Figure 11-9. *Creating/editing a folder*

Finally, you can also rearrange the order in which bookmarks and folders are listed. To do this, tap and drag on the square three-bar icon to the right of a bookmark or folder (refer back to Figure 11-6).

> **TIP:** If you sync bookmarks between your iPhone and computer (using either iTunes or MobileMe), changes you make using your computer's web browser will be copied to your iPhone and vice versa. You may find it easier to organize bookmarks using your computer (particularly if you have a large hierarchy of folders). When organizing your bookmarks on your computer, keep in mind how they will appear on your iPhone to make navigating them quick and easy. If you have multiple web browsers installed on a computer, sync will only occur with the browser specified in iTunes or your MobileMe preferences (typically Internet Explorer on Windows and Safari on Mac OS X).

Bookmarks and Auto-Complete

The address bar in Safari, like most desktop web browsers, features an auto-complete feature. If you begin typing a URL, the auto-complete feature will suggest the URLs of matching bookmarks. This can make a quick and easy alternative way of working with bookmarks because you don't need to browse through them. Figure 11-10 shows this feature in action.

Figure 11-10. *Bookmark auto-complete suggestions*

Viewing Multiple Pages

Much like a computer can have multiple web pages open in separate web browser windows or tabs, Safari on the iPhone can display up to eight pages simultaneously (though Safari may become unstable if you actively try to load multiple pages at one time, particularly if one or more of the pages are large or graphics intensive). Since applications on the iPhone, including Safari, don't display in windows the way that applications do on a computer, Apple included the final button in the Safari toolbar to manage multiple pages.

If you have multiple pages, clicking this button, which resembles a pair of overlapping squares, will display thumbnail versions of each page (see Figure 11-11) and allow you to scroll across them by flicking your finger left or right. Each page, like each home screen on the iPhone, is also represented by a small dot, and you can tap a specific dot if you know which one represents which page.

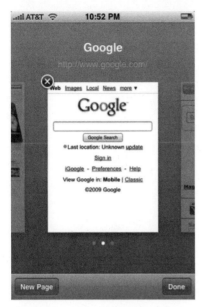

Figure 11-11. *Viewing multiple pages (notice that page name and URL are displayed above each thumbnail)*

You can return to a selected page simply by tapping the thumbnail and close a page by clicking the red circle with an X icon above it. You can always tell how many pages are actively open because the button in the toolbar will include the number of active pages if more than one is open.

Opening Multiple Pages

Multiple pages can be opened by Safari in a handful of ways. The first and most obvious is the New Page button available when viewing or selecting from existing pages (see Figure 11-11 again). This button will create a blank new page and immediately make it the active page, allowing you to type in an address, select a bookmark, or perform a search.

When you open a link in Safari, you can also choose to open it in a new page—which can be helpful if you want to open the link but not lose your place on the current page. To do this, simply tap the link and hold your finger down for a few seconds. You'll see the dialog shown in Figure 11-12 asking you whether you want to open the link in the same page, open it in a new page, or copy the URL of the link (which you can then paste into another application like an e-mail message).

Figure 11-12. *Options for opening a link*

Multiple pages may also be opened automatically. If a web site is designed to open a link in a new window on a computer or open a pop-up window, Safari will open the link in a new page. New pages are also opened when a web page is opened by another application—such as if you click a link in an e-mail. This occurs so that any existing pages you were reading or working with are not closed in favor of the link that is being opened.

Working with Images

The iPhone can work with images on a web page in a couple of ways. First, if you want to zoom an image quickly and easily to full screen, you can double-tap the image and Safari will center the image and zoom the display around it (you can do this by pinching and zooming yourself, but this can sometimes be quicker). The drawback is that if you do this with an image that is also a link, you'll actually end up opening the link.

You can also copy and save images. To do either, simply tap and hold your finger on the image for a few seconds. You'll see the dialog in Figure 11-13, which allows you to copy the image (and later paste it into another application) or save the image to your iPhone's photo library. This can be a great way of adding images to your iPhone for later use. Images are saved to the iPhone's Camera Roll, meaning that they will also be synced to your computer along with any photos on your iPhone (either to your Pictures folder or the application specified in iTunes to copy photos to—refer to the previous chapter for details).

Figure 11-13. *Copying/saving an image*

Tips for Getting Around Web Pages Quickly and Easily

So far, I've talked about the basic features of Safari, which are similar to most desktop web browsers. This makes general use of Safari very easy, but here are a few navigation tips that are a little less obvious that can make your web experience a little faster and easier on the iPhone.

- Double-tapping for scroll and zoom: I've already touched on this with regard to photos, but double-tapping also functions with text, and if you double-tap a piece of text or a column (if a page displays in multiple columns), Safari will recenter the page on that section and zoom in on it (generally to a quite readable size).

- Tapping once to stop scrolling: If you're scrolling through a particularly long web site, you can flick your finger several times to keep the iPhone scrolling. When the portion you want comes on the screen, tap the screen once to pause the scroll.

Changing Safari's Settings

Now that you've learned the basics of getting around in Safari, let's move on to the various ways you can configure Safari's settings to suit your needs. Like most iPhone applications, this is handled by the Settings app. And, as you can see in Figure 11-14, Safari has its own section in Settings. As shown in Figure 11-15, Safari's settings options are broadly divided into sections, the first two of which relate to more general settings while the later ones deal with web browser security options.

Figure 11-14. *Safari options in the Settings app*

Figure 11-15. *Safari options*

General Settings

The first option concerns which search engine is used by Safari's search bar. As I mentioned earlier, the default option is Google, but you can also select Yahoo (as of this writing, these are the only two options).

The second option is AutoFill. AutoFill enables Safari to automatically fill in common types of data in forms on web pages so that you don't need to type as much. Safari supports the use of AutoFill for your contact information (name, address, etc.) or for remembering usernames and passwords that you enter to access password-protected sites.

As you can see in Figure 11-16, you can enable each type of AutoFill separately. If you enable AutoFill for contact information, you will use the My Info field to select the contact information you want to use. You can choose to base AutoFill around any individual stored in Contacts, though you will most likely choose yourself.

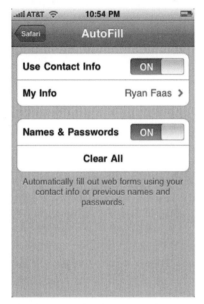

Figure 11-16. *Configuring AutoFill*

There is not much configuration needed if you choose to use AutoFill for usernames and passwords. Simply enable the feature and Safari will begin recording the usernames and passwords as you enter them for various sites. You can also use the Clear All button to erase the usernames and passwords.

CAUTION: AutoFill's ability to remember passwords for sites you commonly access can be tempting, but it can also present a big security risk if your iPhone is lost or stolen, because anyone who can access Safari on your iPhone will have access to any accounts you've logged into using Safari. Therefore, you might choose not to enable this feature if you routinely access sites that display confidential or personal information.

Security Settings

While AutoFill has some security implications, there are other Safari options that specifically address securing your web usage on the iPhone. The Security settings cover a fairly broad range of areas, many of which are similar to security settings available for any web browser. Figure 11-17 shows the available security-related settings.

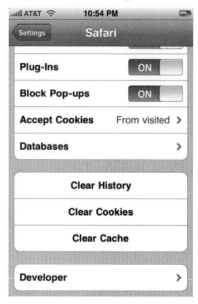

Figure 11-17. *Security settings*

Fraud Warning

Fraud Warning is a relatively new web technology. It relies on Google's database of web sites tagged as potentially being fraudulent—this includes sites known or suspected of being coded with malware that can infect or compromise the security of a computer or device, as well as sites often linked to phishing schemes. In a phishing scheme, a site is designed to mimic a legitimate site, but in reality when you enter your user credentials or personal information, that information is recorded and can be used to impersonate you on an actual web site (some of the most common phishing schemes involve mimicking banking or other financial sites—PayPal being one of the most often targeted).

When Fraud Warning is enabled, the iPhone will alert you if you attempt to access a site known or suspected of being used in these ways. You can still opt to visit the site, but you should do so only with caution and/or after verifying that you are accessing the correct URL of a web site.

JavaScript

This option allows you to disable the running of JavaScript embedded in a web page. JavaScript is often used to generate dynamic web content and some web animations. However, because the scripts themselves execute like code, they can be used as a vector of attack against a computer or device. Disabling JavaScript will increase the security of your iPhone, but may result in some pages not being displayed properly. If you have sensitive information on your iPhone, you should consider disabling JavaScript (if in doubt, check with your IT department), but for most situations, typical users can leave JavaScript enabled in order to ensure a better browsing experience.

Plug-Ins

Like browsers on computers, the iPhone can rely on plug-ins to Safari to render some web content (typically video content). However, as with JavaScript, plug-ins can be used as an attack vector and, if not properly built, can cause instability in Safari (or potentially with the iPhone itself). Disabling them can make it impossible to view some forms of web content, but can increase security, stability, and performance.

> **NOTE:** As of this writing, there has been limited development of Safari plug-ins for the iPhone. Some third parties have been actively pursuing plug-in development to allow both viewing of additional video content and saving varying types of files.

Block Pop-Ups

This feature enables Safari's built-in pop-up blocker. When enabled, pop-up windows (or more accurately, pop-up pages on the iPhone) will not be opened. This increases security, but more practically provides relief from multiple pages (pop-ups) being opened with ads while you browse the Web. Some sites, however, may be designed to function properly only by using pop-ups.

Accept Cookies

This option determines whether Safari will accept cookies from web sites. Cookies are small pieces of data that can be set by a web site, stored by a web browser, and then returned to the web server. Typically, cookies are used to track information that you enter in a web-based form as you move from one page to another (such as while using a shopping cart feature of an online store).

However, cookies can also be used to track sites that you visit, and many sites and advertisers use cookies to determine browsing habits. They can also be set by malicious sites to determine other information about you and your online habits. For these reasons, you might choose to avoid cookies altogether or delete cookies regularly (see the next section).

As you can see in Figure 11-18, the iPhone offers three options when it comes to cookies: accepting all cookies (Always), accepting cookies only from sites that you explicitly visit (From visited) (meaning that cookies must be served by the same site as the one you are viewing), and never accepting cookies (Never). Accepting cookies only from sites you visit is the default option for the iPhone, and it is generally a very good middle ground and a sensible choice for most business users, as many web-based applications (such as banking and e-commerce sites) require cookies to function. At the same time, limiting the cookies you accept only to sites that you explicitly visit can protect you from some malicious tracking cookies.

Figure 11-18. *Accept Cookies options*

Clearing History, Cookies, and Cache Files

The last major section of Safari's options in the Settings app are the options to clear the browser's history, clear all cookies, and clear cache files. All of them have some security and performance implications.

Clear History does just what its name implies: it removes the history file of previously viewed sites. This will prevent someone from easily viewing sites that you've previously visited. However, it is worth noting that since the Safari history is backed up to your computer (along with other data, such as your call history and text/media messages), it might still be possible to view the history if someone had access to your computer and the appropriate tools or knowledge to look inside your iPhone's previous backup.

Likewise, Clear Cookies does just what it says. It erases all cookies that have been set. This can mean that some web content and settings for certain web sites may be erased if they are set using cookies. This can be a good troubleshooting and security tool if you are worried about malicious cookies having been set on your iPhone.

Cache files are local copies of web pages and/or images that are stored temporarily on your iPhone. As with any computer, Safari uses cache files to quickly load or reload pages and images without having to repeatedly download them. Clearing cache files can sometimes improve general performance and can be a companion to clearing your browser history. Also, because cache files can sometimes become corrupted, this can be a good troubleshooting step if you are having trouble accessing a web site or with Safari performing slowly or erratically in general.

> **NOTE:** There is a final option in the Safari options, called Developer. This enables the developer debugging console, which can be used by web designers to troubleshoot problems if they are designing and testing their pages for use with the iPhone. It is not covered here because it is not a feature intended for most general or business iPhone users. Designers interested in the debugging console or developing web content specifically intended for the iPhone can find out more from Apple's iPhone developer site, at `http://developer.apple.com/iphone`.

Summary

In this chapter, you learned how to browse the Web using Safari on the iPhone. You also learned how the Web can be used as an interactive tool for working remotely (a topic that I'll revisit in Part 3 of this book when we talk about third-party apps for the iPhone) and how to configure Safari's settings. In the next chapter, we'll continue our tour of built-in iPhone apps with one of the best tools for business users on the road: Maps.

Chapter 12

Getting Around Using Maps

Getting Directions, and Finding People and Businesses Across Town, Across the Country, or Clear Across the World

Whether your job requires you to travel between client locations in your own city or if it requires you to travel throughout your state or region or internationally, the Maps application can quickly and easily become the best travel tool you've ever used. Tied into both Google Maps and the iPhone's location services (including its GPS capabilities), you can not only find exactly where you are at any given minute and how to get to a specific address from your current location (either on foot, by car, or using the local mass transit system), you can identify any type of nearby business and get details about it, such as location, contact information, hours of operation, and web address. As if that wasn't enough, Maps can also give you real-time traffic alerts and show your progress as you navigate your way to your destination. On the iPhone 3GS, a built-in digital compass not only allows you to see where you are and get directions, but to automatically orient your map and view according to the direction you're facing.

All of these capabilities make Maps an indispensible tool for anyone on the go, but particularly for business workers who need to make it to meetings, find and locate new clients, and make travel arrangements. They can also help you research a new city or area for choosing hotels, restaurants, and business facilities, and other key services that you may need to make your trip a success. In this chapter, you'll learn all about the Maps application, how to use it, and how to tie its capabilities into your daily life and make them work for your needs.

Maps Basics

The Maps application is designed to be intuitive as well as powerful, though when you first launch it and see a giant map of the entire country (as you can see in Figure 12-1), it may seem a little intimidating. However, learning the basics is pretty simple, and if you've ever used Google Maps (which Maps relies on for its map data, satellite images, and location searches), you'll find that although the interface is somewhat different, the overall feature set is pretty similar.

Figure 12-1. *The Maps application on initial launch*

Finding Out Where You Are

The first challenge to using the Maps application is to get a display of something a little more granular and helpful than almost an entire continent. The easiest way to do that is through the locate me button. This button, which looks like a set of crosshairs, is the leftmost button in the toolbar at the bottom of the Maps display.

When you tap the locate me button, Maps will use the iPhone's various location services to pinpoint your location to the best of the iPhone's capabilities. As I mentioned early on in this book, the iPhone 3G can use GPS, cell tower triangulation, and Skyhook's database of known Wi-Fi hotspots to determine its location while, the original iPhone can rely on cell towers and Skyhook (and the iPod touch only Skyhook).

While the iPhone is determining your location, you will see a bouncing blue circle that becomes narrower and narrower as the iPhone pinpoints your location. During this time, which may take anywhere from a couple of seconds to a few minutes depending on the available data and your Internet connection, you'll also see the map zoom in on your actual location. Both of these are illustrated in Figure 12-2.

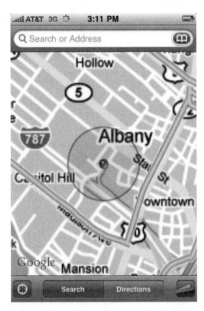

Figure 12-2. *Maps display while the iPhone determines location*

If the iPhone is able to determine a precise location, you'll see the blue circle resolve into a blue dot. As you move and the iPhone updates your location, you may see blue rings appear around the dot to reflect the updating of position information. If the iPhone cannot get a precise fix on your location, you'll see a blue ring around the best approximation that it can manage (as in Figures 12-3 and 12-4).

Figure 12-3. *Maps displaying a precise location*

Figure 12-4. *Maps display for approximate location (note that this is the same location as Figure 12-3)*

Working with the Map Display

Once Maps has determined and displayed your location, you can begin working with the map itself. As with photos or web pages, you can use pinch multitouch gestures to zoom the map in and out. You can also tap and drag to scroll and view areas outside the current map, and as with web content, you double-tap any part of the map to recenter and zoom in on a specific area.

As you work with Maps, you'll notice that many traditional roadmap features are used. Parks and public lands are displayed in green. College campuses are tinted an orange/yellow, hospitals and emergency services are tinted red, and bodies of water appear blue. You'll also notice that one-way roads include arrow directions to indicate the direction traffic is allowed to travel and that major surface streets are colored yellow while highways are colored orange to denote their higher capacity nature than side streets, which remain an off-white. You'll also notice that in most cases, highway exit numbers are identified as well.

Searching for Nearby Businesses and Contacts

The ability to find your location and view a detailed map is helpful, but it doesn't provide a lot of information about how to get from point A to point B. It also doesn't help you locate nearby businesses, resources, or people. For those capabilities, you'll use the search bar at the top of the Maps display. One of the great features about the search capabilities in Maps is that they are very flexible and can be used in a few different ways.

Searching for an Address

The simplest way to use search in Maps is to locate a specific address. As
you might expect, you can simply type in an address and tap Search (see
Figure 12-5). As with the Google Maps web site, you can search for addresses very
broadly or granularly, but will get the best results if you enter a complete address
(number, street, city, state/province, and ZIP/postal code).

Figure 12-5. *Searching for a specific address*

Once you've entered an address, Maps will locate it and center and zoom the display to
that address, identifying it with a red map pin (see Figure 12-6). You can locate
addresses nearby you or clear across the world. The map display will function with
remote addresses just as it does when you work with your own location as a source.

Figure 12-6. *Specific address pinned in Maps*

Searching for a Specific Business

You can also use the search bar to locate a specific business, even if you don't know the address. In this case, simply type in the name of the business. If the business exists in Google Maps (which in many cases it will if it exists in the Yellow Pages), Maps will recenter the display and drop a red map pin at its location (Figure 12-7).

Figure 12-7. *Specific business pinned in Maps*

If you've already determined your location and multiple businesses match your query (such as multiple outlets of a chain store), Maps will pin only those that are nearest to you (Figure 12-8). If you want to find a specific location, you can try adding part of the address to the search query.

Figure 12-8. *Multiple businesses pinned in Maps*

If Maps cannot determine a specific business because your query is too vague or you mistype a name, you may be presented with some of the potential choices and asked to select one (Figure 12-9). This is particularly common if you are searching for businesses in remote areas rather than near your current location.

Figure 12-9. *Selecting from potential matches*

Searching by General Category

In addition to searching for specific businesses, you can search by a general category or type of business. For example, you could search for any post offices or copy centers near your current location. You can be very general or specific in the search queries for types of businesses or institutions. Obviously, the more general you are, the more results you'll see. When searching by a category rather than a specific name, you'll see multiple red map pins identifying each of businesses of that type, as shown in Figure 12-10.

Figure 12-10. *Maps showing multiple businesses of a given category*

Getting More Information About Businesses That You Find

In addition to simply locating businesses, Maps can provide you with additional information about them. If you click the arrow icon next to a business name, you'll see whatever additional information is available about that business from Google displayed similarly to a Contact (see Figure 12-11 for an example). This will always include the detailed street address and often the phone number and a web site for the business as well (both of which can be tapped to either call or view in Safari, respectively).

Figure 12-11. *Viewing business details*

In addition to viewing details about a business, you can also use this display to accomplish some other tasks (though you may need to scroll down to see them, as shown in Figure 12-12), including directions to or from the business (which I'll cover in the next section). You can also create a contact for the business based on the phone number and address located by Maps (a useful tool for recording business that may be potential customers or sales leads), share the location via e-mail (the e-mail includes both a Google Maps link that will open in Maps on an iPhone or in a web browser on a computer, and a vCard for the business, as shown in Figure 12-13), and save the location as a bookmark in Maps.

Figure 12-12. *Tasks for a business in Maps*

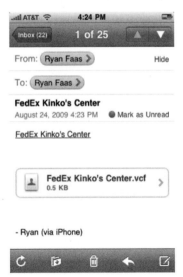

Figure 12-13. *Location e-mail generated by Maps*

Locating Contacts and Viewing Bookmarks and Recent Locations in Maps

To the right edge of the location bar is a button that has an icon that resembles the bookmark icon in Safari. Tapping this button will allow you to see the locations of any one of your contacts, as well as to view locations that you have bookmarked in Maps and a list of recently viewed locations or directions that you have searched (the last two of which act very similarly to bookmarks and history in Safari).

When you first tap this button, you'll see a screen similar to the one shown in Figure 12-14. As you can see, there are three tabs along the bottom of the screen, allowing you to choose to view Maps bookmarks, recent searches, and Contacts (despite being the third tab, Contacts is the default option).

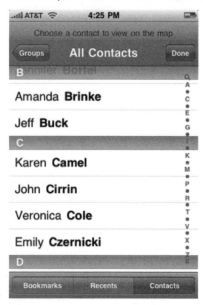

Figure 12-14. *Contacts search in Maps*

As in most of the other uses of Contacts on the iPhone, you can browse or search for any contact from this screen. Provided the contact has address information, Maps will locate the contact, center the map view on that address, and drop a red map pin on the location.

Similarly, you can use the Bookmarks and Recents tabs to view a list of bookmarked locations (Figure 12-15) or recent search results (Figure 12-16). When you are viewing the recent locations search list, you can clear the list (much like clearing Safari's history) by tapping the Clear button.

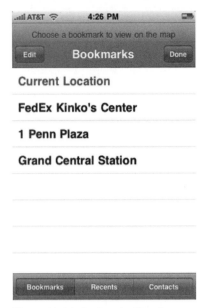

Figure 12-15. *Bookmarked location*

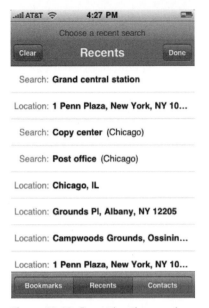

Figure 12-16. *Recent location searches*

As with bookmarks in Safari (and shown in Figure 12-17), you can edit and reorder your location bookmarks by clicking the Edit button. Your editing options are limited to adjusting the order of bookmarks (unlike Safari, Maps doesn't support organizing bookmarks in folders), and you can only edit the name of a location (Figure 12-18). As with Safari bookmarks, you can delete a location bookmark by tapping the red circle icon and then tapping the delete key that appears.

Figure 12-17. *Editing/organizing bookmarks*

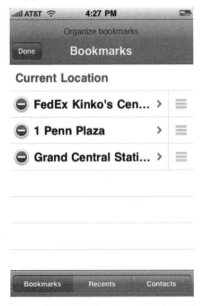

Figure 12-18. *Editing the name of a bookmark*

Getting Directions

Finding different locations isn't the full meat of what Google Maps is capable of offering (either on the Web or through Maps on the iPhone). One of the most frequently used features is the ability to get directions from one location. Maps offers this capability in spades, and perhaps at no time is it more useful than if you've taken a wrong turn or when you're lost.

Directions From a Search, Contact, or Bookmark

There are two principal ways to get directions in Maps. The first, which I've already touched on, is from the details view about a location that you've already mapped. This can include a contact that you've located, a bookmark, or a search result. As you can see in Figure 12-12, two of the options for tasks associated with a mapped location are to get directions either to or from that location.

If you tap either the Directions To Here or the Directions From Here button, a directions search box like the one shown in Figure 12-19 will be displayed. If you tap Directions To Here, the End (or destination) field will be prepopulated with the location's address. If you tap Directions From Here, the Start field will be prepopulated with the address.

Figure 12-19. *Directions search dialog*

If you choose to get directions to a mapped location, the default start point (the location your directions will originate from) will be your current location (as illustrated in Figure 12-19). You can tap into this field and enter another from location. If you choose to get directions from a mapped location, you'll need to enter a destination (either as a business name or address).

TIP: As with searching for a location, you can use the bookmark button in either search bar to specify start or end locations based on contacts, bookmarks, or recent searches (you might need to clear an existing address or business to see the button). Again, this can be a useful time saver.

With both start and end locations populated, you can click the Route key on the keyboard. Maps will query Google Maps and will then plot your route on the map display, as shown in Figure 12-20. The start location will be indicated by a green map pin and the destination by a red pin. The route itself will be displayed as purple line over the appropriate roads. You will also see that the estimated mileage and time for your trip are indicated.

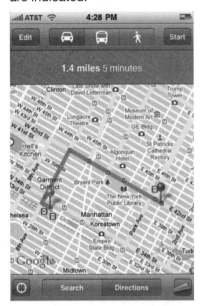

Figure 12-20. *Route plotted in Maps*

If you are using an iPhone 3G and have a GPS signal, the blue dot indicating your position will continuously move to indicate your exact position (the same will occur without GPS, but updates may be less frequent and less accurate).

The Directions Tab

You can also get directions without mapping your destination ahead of time. To do this, tap the Directions tab (as opposed to the default Search tab) in the toolbar at the bottom of the display. You'll notice that this tab looks very similar to the Search tab, except that the search bar now includes both start and end locations, much like the search dialog for a premapped location. In fact, as you can see in Figure 12-21, once you tap one of the fields in the larger search bar, the display will be virtually identical to that shown in Figure 12-19.

Figure 12-21. *Searching from the Directions tab*

Again, you can search using an address, business name, contact, bookmark, or recent search. One difference, however, is that your current location is not automatically assumed as your start point. You can, however, enter that as a start point fairly easily since it is always included as the first item in location bookmarks within Maps. Once you enter a start and end point for a search, clicking the Route button will generate your directions results as I just described.

Getting Reverse Directions

You may have noticed in Figures 12-19 and 12-21 that there is a button with a sort of S-shaped icon to the left of the start and end location fields. This button allows you to quickly swap the content of these fields to get reverse directions (which can be helpful if you need to find your way back from a location, particularly one where there are one-way roads or highway exit ramps that result in return directions being somewhat different).

> **TIP:** This feature can be easily accessed if you use the recent searches feature and simply repeat a directions search and tap the reverse button to swap your locations.

Choosing Driving, Walking, or Mass Transit

One particularly helpful feature about getting directions in Maps is that you can choose your mode of transportation. Although the default results are for driving directions, you can choose to view directions for public transportation or walking using the three icons in the center of the toolbar when directions are displayed. The three options are drive, public transportation (bus, subway, and light rail), and walking (Figures 12-22 and 12-23 shows directions for driving and walking, respectively). The transit times for walking or driving will adjust depending on which option you choose.

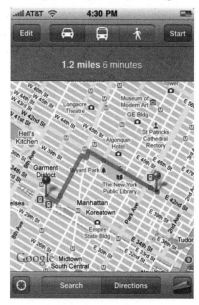

Figure 12-22. *Directions by car*   **Figure 12-23.** *Directions on foot*

Mass Transit Options

When you choose to view directions via mass transit, Google Maps relies on available mass transit routes that are publicly available to compute the quickest way to get from your starting point to your destination. Often this may involve a combination of walking and mass transit (and may even require different modes of mass transit). As you can see in Figure 12-24, icons along your route will indicate where to change methods of transportation.

Figure 12-24. *Mass transit directions*

Also notice that there is a clock icon next to the details about mass transit. This allows you to specify a departure time. By default, Maps will choose the next most available set of transportation options, but you may need to arrive or leave at specific times. If so, you can tap this button and you'll see the dialog shown in Figure 12-25. This dialog allows you to view additional choices based on the schedule of the mass transit options (busses, subway, etc.), and you can select an appropriate time (which may result in different route selections depending on the mass transit system's schedule).

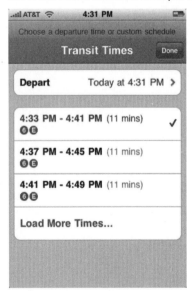

Figure 12-25. *Selecting mass transit times*

NOTE: Mass transit information is available for most major cities and many smaller cities and towns but not all. Google currently supports transit information for over 400 cities across the globe. You can view a complete list of the current cities at `www.google.com/intl/en/landing/transit/text.html`.

TIP: In addition to getting mass transit information from Maps, several city-specific third-party apps can provide detailed information about the mass transit systems in various cities, potentially including some not provided by Google or with additional information and resources. If you will be visiting or living in a city with an extensive transit network, searching for apps specific to that city (such as New York, London, or Paris) in the app store can be a great aid (refer to Chapter 15 for details on the App Store).

Working with Direction Steps and Maps

In addition to simply displaying your route on a map, Maps will include step-by-step directions. This isn't quite the turn-by-turn voice navigation offered by some GPS systems, but it's the next best thing (and for mass transit, it can actually be more helpful). When you click the Start button to the right of the trio of transportation options, Maps will display each step of your trip. Each step is defined by things such as each turn, merge, or exit from a highway, or a change in bus stop or subway station.

NOTE: During the summer of 2009, several companies have developed full turn-by-turn navigation apps for the iPhone (some of which can be used globally and some of which are country/region specific). I'll cover a few the primary choices available in Chapter 16.

When you are viewing direction steps, each one will center in the specific section of map relevant to that step (with that particular portion of the route indicated in dark gray), and will provide written directions as well as estimated mileage at the top of the display (as shown in Figure 12-26). As you complete or wish to view the next step, you can use the arrow keys in the toolbar to step forward and backward through the directions.

Figure 12-26. *Direction steps*

> **TIP:** At any point while following directions, you can use the Edit button to alter your starting point or destination.

Working with Maps Views

Now that you have a good idea about how to find your current location, businesses, and resources, and get directions, it's time to learn about views available other than the basic map view. Although a simple roadmap is very helpful in Maps, there may be times that you'll want to view additional details such as a satellite images, a simple list of directions, or even live traffic updates.

In this last section, I'll focus on how to accomplish these tasks, all of which you can select by tapping the views button—the rightmost button in the toolbar at the bottom of the screen with an icon like a rolled up piece of paper. As you can see in Figure 12-27, when you tap this, the entire map view will roll up (just like the icon) and you can select from the various view options.

Figure 12-27. *Choosing map view options*

There are four primary map views included in Maps, each of which is indicated by the appropriate buttons in Figure 12-27. These include the standard roadmap view (Map; Figure 12-28), a satellite-only view (Satellite; Figure 12-29), a roadmap superimposed over satellite imagery (Hybrid; Figure 12-30), and a list of direction steps (List; Figure 12-31). To select a view, simply tap the appropriate button.

Figure 12-28. *Map view*

Figure 12-29. *Satellite view*

Figure 12-30. *Hybrid view*

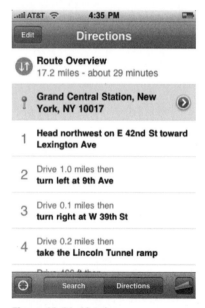

Figure 12-31. *List view*

NOTE: List view encapsulates all the direction steps for a trip in a single view. These are the exact same steps you can see using any of the other views.

Working with Live Traffic View

If you are stuck in heavy traffic conditions (or want to avoid them when driving), the Show Traffic button will quickly become one of your favorite features of Maps. This option will overlay known traffic conditions in real-time over the streets and highways in maps as shown in Figure 12-32. You can disable traffic view by returning to the maps view options and tapping the same button, which will then change to Hide Traffic.

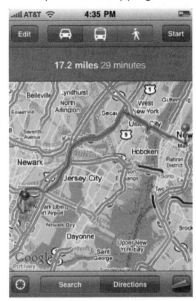

Figure 12-32. *Live traffic conditions*

For streets and highways where such information is available, you will see a green overlay for freely moving conditions, yellow for somewhat congested areas, and red for heavily congested or stopped traffic. This can be particularly helpful in situations where you expect heavy traffic and/or situations where you can see congestion or traffic jams and want to determine the extent of the slowdown.

NOTE: Obviously, traffic view relies on publicly available traffic monitoring tools and may not be available in every location, though it is in many cities in the United States as well as some other countries. Google has consistently expanded this feature since it was introduced as a component of Google Maps in 2007 (when the launch included only about 30 cities in the United States). If traffic data is not available for a given location, you will see that the Show Traffic button changes to say Traffic Unavailable In This Area. If you are traveling to an unknown city or internationally, you may want to try looking up that city/area in Maps before you leave to find out if traffic data is available.

Using Pins to Note Locations

A final capability in Maps is the ability to set a pin. A pin is similar to a bookmark except that it isn't saved permanently. You can drop a pin using the Drop Pin button in the view options dialog. When you drop a pin, a purple map pin is placed in the center of the current map view and it will specify the address of that location, as shown in Figure 12-33.

Figure 12-33. Pin placed at a location

The purpose of a pin is more to serve as a reference point. If you are zooming and scrolling through maps, it can be easy to lose sight of a particular address or even just a particular part of town. By dropping a pin onto the map, you can easily spot a particular location or area without searching for it or making a permanent bookmark. You can also easily move a pin's location by returning to the view options and tapping Replace Pin (shown in Figure 12-34), or simply by dragging it.

Figure 12-34. *Changing a pin's location*

By tapping the pin's arrow icon, you'll see a dialog similar to that for any other business or location that allows you to get directions to/from that point, remove the pin from the map, and perform all the other tasks associated with locations in Maps (including converting the pin into a bookmark).

Google Street View

In recent years, Google has begun to offer Street View—a feature available on the Google Maps web site as well as in Maps on the iPhone—which allows you to view street-level photos of an address. Google has actually done an impressive job in combing the streets of the United States and several other countries block by block to gather the images presented in Street View. If an address is available in Street View (some locations may not yet have been indexed, and some countries have ruled Google's capturing of public images without the consent of people in the area violations of privacy laws), you will see an icon of an orange circle with a white silhouetted head (refer to earlier figures in this chapter). Tapping that icon will display the address in Street View.

As you can see in Figure 12-35, Street View includes a map icon indicating the location and direction that you are facing. You can zoom and pan to get a closer look at an item or turn your view in a complete circle. Arrow icons on the street allow you move to the next block. The toolbar shown when you tap the screen in Street View allows you to return to one of the standard Maps views or to report inappropriate content in a Street View image to Google.

Figure 12-35. *Street View*

WORKING WITH THE COMPASS IN THE IPHONE 3GS

The iPhone 3GS includes a digital compass as part of its hardware, and a compass application (shown in the following image). As you can see, the compass app offers the basic functionality of any physical compass—a nice feature, but not horribly useful for business travelers in and of itself. The real power of the digital compass is illustrated by the ability of the Maps application to not only pinpoint your current location on a map, but to orient the map to point in the same direction you're facing.

Typically, Maps will always orient the map with north facing the top of the screen. However, if you click the locate button to determine your location and then click it a second time, Maps will integrate the compass reading by displaying a blue location dot with an icon that displays a pie-shaped wedge to indicate the direction you are facing on the map, as shown in the following image (the more accurate the compass reading, the narrower the angle of the wedge). For anyone who has trouble reading maps or is disoriented when exiting a subway station, this feature adds a lot of power and ease to the Maps application.

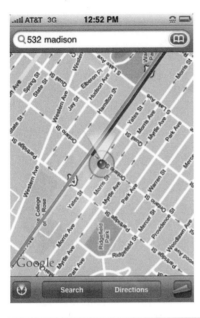

Summary

In this chapter, you learned how to use the iPhone's Maps application and GPS abilities to navigate across town or across the world. It also offered some tips as to how you can use Maps to find businesses, research areas, and communicate your discoveries to colleagues.

In the next chapter, we'll take a look at what may seem like one of the consumer-oriented features on the iPhone: the iPod application. Although this is mainly the center of the iPhone's music and video playback options as a media player, I'll offer some ways in which you can use it for professional purposes as well as for fun and relaxation.

iPod and iTunes

Using the iPod Features of the iPhone As an Aid for Business

For many consumers, the iPhone is, and always has been, a combination of an iPod and a mobile phone. Of the four default apps in the iPhone dock, one is the iPod application. In this chapter, I'll introduce you to the ways that the Apple iTunes and iPod apps can be successfully integrated into business situations. First up is a general reenvisioning of the iPod and iTunes apps and the scope that they offer beyond simply playing back music and video. Then we'll get down in the guts of the iPod app itself and how to work with it as either a personal or professional tool.

Using the iPhone's Media Player Capabilities for Work

The iPhone's ability to work with various kinds of media is one the device's great strengths. The iPod application seems to be most focused on listening to music and watching TV shows and videos from the iTunes Store. However, there are actually a lot of capabilities under the hood that go beyond just listening to your favorite playlists of workout or club music.

Bringing the iPhone's Media Capabilities to the Table

Bringing the audio and visual capabilities of the iPhone to business can range from the basic to the complex. In its simplest form, being able to plug the iPhone into a larger presentation sound system creates an audio solution for scripting and supporting a class or meeting with inspiration. With the right hookups and preselected music (or spoken word recording), an iPhone coupled with a speaker system can set the tone for any class.

Tied into a video production system, the video capabilities can provide an iPhone user the ability to produce a wide range of audiovisual options that include still imagery, audio, and video, all designed to inspire the participants of the meeting or training class.

TIP: As I mentioned in Chapter 10, you can use appropriate cables to connect an iPhone to various outputs typically used for television. However, for broader training and presentation use, you might want to also consider so-called pico-projectors (a new class of small and easy-to-carry multimedia projects), such as the Optoma Pico PK-101 Pocket Projector for iPhone/iPod and the Mili Pro Micro Projector for iPhone, offer the ability to directly connect to the iPhone, turning it into the ultimate in portable presentation option for classes, meetings, or proposals.

Video and Audio for Presentations

Individuals vary in the way that they process and retain information. While some of us learn and retain details simply by reading or hearing, the most effective trainers and presenters know that this approach doesn't work best for everyone. To truly engage an audience (be it one person in a sales pitch, members of a small committee, or a roomful of students that you're training), presenting information in a multimedia manner can help you capture everyone's attention and give them information in a way that each person can digest and take with them.

Traditionally, this approach to training and presentation has involved things like slides, printed charts and handbooks, and PowerPoint-style presentations—all of which require at a fair amount of effort and preparation to produce. The iPhone, with its instant access to audio and visual media, provides you even more opportunities to engage with your audience. If you regularly sync relevant music (or lecture recordings) and video to your iPhone, you can be ready at a moment's notice to enhance any presentation—adding drama and visual interest to help capture people's attention regardless of their learning style.

TIP: There are a few ways to get PowerPoint-style presentation to display on the iPhone. The simplest is to e-mail a PowerPoint file (or if you use Apple's iWork, a Keynote file) to yourself. You can then use the attachment viewing capabilities in Mail to view/show the presentation. PowerPoint (and Keynote) also allow you to export presentations as MOV files, which can be synced to your iPhone though iTunes and viewed using the iPod app. Finally, some office apps and file managers allow you to load and view presentations on the iPhone. Some, such as QuickOffice, even let you edit presentations—check out Chapter 16 for more on office and file manager apps.

Going a step further, the iPhone's ability to access the entire catalog of material available through the iTunes Store allows you to enhance a presentation on the go at any time. If you're on a train and suddenly realize that a particular piece of music or media can enhance your presentation, you can find, purchase, and download it right then and there—though you will want to be aware of presentation rights and copyright laws.

iTunes As a Research Vehicle

While using the iPod capabilities of the iPhone for presentations is impressive, what may be even more valuable to many professionals is the vast catalog of information available to you at any moment. The iPhone gives you the capacity to access the entire iTunes Store from anywhere at any time. While most people associate the iTunes Store with music (and a bit less frequently with movies and TV shows), it has much more potential than the basic consumer focus that most people associate with it.

One great example is the association between the iTunes Store and Audible.com. This allows you to browse a wide range of audiobooks, including many titles geared toward business in general and certain professions in particular. This means that you can easily use your commute or travel times to purchase and listen to any number of books related to your profession.

Another excellent example is iTunes U. Originally conceived as a tool for universities to make lectures available to their students, iTunes U has become a major public educational force that you can tap. This portion of the iTunes Store contains lectures from many noted professors and institutions covering every imaginable academic topic, from historical facts to economic theory to computer science. Whatever your industry, iTunes U can provide a valuable resource for continuing your research and education at any level from anywhere in the world. For anyone in the academic fields or anyone moving into a new field, iTunes U is a massive (and amazingly free) resource that allows you to virtually attend seminars and lectures that might be otherwise inaccessible.

> *We are in a time where we have to embrace lifelong learning. For those of us without the time for traditional classroom settings, ITunes U is a great tool to continue professional development. I can remember the first time I was exposed to this gem. Now, when I forget economic theories I don't have to dust off my old college textbooks to refresh my memory.*
>
> Joanna Palladino, State Government Workforce Development Specialist

Finally, there's the iTunes podcast directory. Like blogs, podcasts may not always be scholarly sources of reference, but they do present professionals with two major advantages. First, whatever your field is, there's likely a few (or possibly a few hundred) podcasters recording information about it. It might be detailed technical information, personal observations, or anything in between, but podcasts do provide a way of learning about topics, demographic groups, and geographical areas. And since you can subscribe to them, you can always have additional information to learn while in the car or on the road.

The second advantage that podcasts—like blogs, YouTube, and other social networking tools—offer is the ability to keep your finger on the pulse of your community. All social networking and related media generally provide up-to-the-minute opinions and information. This can help you stay on top of trends, news, and other information. And again, the ability to subscribe to podcasts ensures that you can always have the latest news from both professionals in your field and your potential customers/clients—all wherever you are.

Finding and Syncing Content with iTunes

As with most other types of information, iTunes is the primary tool for syncing multimedia content between your iPhone or iPod touch and your computer. Using iTunes, you can import audio content from CDs, browse audio and video in the iTunes Store, and subscribe to podcasts. Perhaps most importantly, iTunes gives you the ability to organize all of this content and to choose what content you want to be synced to your iPhone.

Navigating the iTunes Store on Your Computer

The easiest way to add music and video to your iTunes Library is to simply purchase it from the iTunes Store. This easy-to-navigate feature gives you access to the largest online music and media store available—all simply by clicking the iTunes Store icon in the iTunes sidebar.

As you can see in Figure 13-1, the iTunes store is broken down across a broad array of categories and genres. You can browse through the various sections of what's currently popular in the main body of the store's initial display, or you can choose specific portions of the store such as music, movies, TV shows, music videos, audiobooks, podcasts, and iTunes U using the links in the upper left. You can also make a quick search (which includes live search suggestions as you type) using the Search iTunes Store box displayed to the right above the main body of the store to search across all genres and content. Links for working with your iTunes Store account (including initial account setup, redeeming of gift cards and codes, and support) are all included in the Quick Links section to the right of the store.

Figure 13-1. *The iTunes Store*

Quite frankly, the simplest way to discover the iTunes Store is to simply look through it. When you find something of interest, you can read reviews, listen to or watch previews, and see what other people who purchased that same content are also buying. And purchasing a song is as easy as a click of your mouse, as you can see in Figure 13-2.

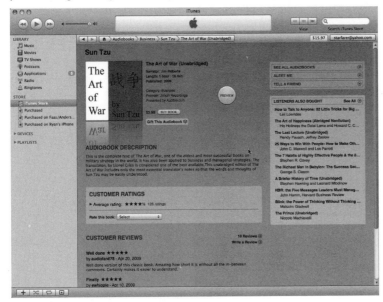

Figure 13-2. *Browsing the iTunes Store*

Podcasts

The iTunes Store contains a very large and very diverse podcast directory, through which you can discover an amazing wealth of original content available for free. If you browse or search through the podcast directory (click the Podcast link shown in Figure 13-1), you'll find that, as shown in Figure 13-3, you have the option to simply listen to/watch a podcast, download individual episodes, and to subscribe to a podcast (after which iTunes will automatically download additional episodes for you). Once you've downloaded podcast episodes and/or subscribed to a podcast, you'll f ind all your podcasts neatly organized by clicking the Podcasts entry in the iTunes sidebar (see Figure 13-4).

Figure 13-3. *Browsing the podcast directory*

Figure 13-4. *Viewing your available podcasts*

You can use the Podcast Settings button to access a dialog (shown in Figure 13-5) that allows you to choose how often iTunes will check for new episodes, whether or not to download them automatically, and how long iTunes should keep podcast files after you've listened to them (either on your computer or your iPhone). You can adjust these as default settings for all podcasts or create custom settings for specific podcasts.

Figure 13-5. *Podcast settings*

TIP: Podcasts are great, but like all media files they can eat up disk space on your computer and storage space on your iPhone, which is why you may want to opt to have iTunes delete them automatically, or choose to periodically delete them yourself by selecting an episode in the list and clicking the Delete key on your keyboard.

Importing Media From Other Sources

You can also import music from CDs into iTunes as well as supported audio and video files purchased or created using applications other than iTunes. To import from a CD, simply insert the CD and click the Import button that appears once iTunes recognizes the CD (by default, iTunes will query Internet-based databases to identify the album, artist, and track names for CDs), as shown in Figure 13-6.

Figure 13-6. *Importing a CD*

For other files, you can typically simply drag the file into the iTunes window while any part of your media library is displayed (note that you cannot drag media files into iTunes while browsing the iTunes Store). You can also use the Add to iTunes command from the File menu.

Depending on your computer's configuration, iTunes may support additional audio and video formats, but your iPhone will only accept those in the following formats: AAC, Protected AAC, MP3, MP3 VBR, Audible (formats 2, 3, and 4), Apple Lossless, AIFF, and WAV. Video formats supported by the iPhone include: M4V, MP4, and MOV (additionally, video must be appropriately sized for display on the screen at 640×480 and encoded using H.264 or MPEG-4 at 30 frames per second). Many video conversion tools can convert video to these formats, and some even provide iPhone/iPod video as a preset option.

Organizing Your Media in iTunes

One of the most powerful aspects of iTunes is the ability to not only store and sync your multimedia files with your iPhone but also organize that media. Whether you look at the iPhone's iPod features as simply entertaining or as a tool for expanding your professional skills or a way to carry training materials with you, keeping that material organized so that you can find what you need at a moment's notice is a key capability.

iTunes provides you with a number of ways to organize your media. On the simplest level, it makes your music browsable by artist, genre, and album with no effort by you at all. It also separates your music from movie or TV show files, podcasts, and audiobooks automatically.

Playlists

And with the ability to create playlists, you can impose whatever form of organization works best for you. In fact, playlists work very well for creating training materials because you can have any audio and video you need not only organized, but in the appropriate order before you show up to a meeting or training.

Playlists are as easy to create as clicking the new playlist button (the + button beneath the iTunes sidebar, as shown in each of the preceding figures in this chapter). After that, simply name the playlist (the default "untitled playlist" name will be automatically selected, so all you need do is type the name and press Enter). To add music or video, simply select the tracks in your library and drag them to the playlist in the sidebar. Then, to arrange items in a playlist, just drag songs, videos, or podcast episodes around in the playlist.

Smart Playlists

While playlists are a natural organizing tool in iTunes, smart playlists are much more powerful. Smart playlists (which can be created using the New Smart Playlist command from the iTunes File menu) don't specify music or videos directly. Instead, you specify criteria—almost like a search. Any items in your library that match those criteria are automatically included in a smart playlist.

As you can see in Figure 13-6, a smart playlist allows you to pick from over 36 different criteria that can be used to identify items in your library. Some, such as artist or album are obvious choices, but others like play count (the number of times you've played a given song or video) or skip count (the number of times you've skipped past something) allow you to create smart playlists that can automatically pull your favorite songs or play just new additions. As you can also see in Figure 13-7, smart playlists allow you to combine multiple criteria—giving you the ability to fine tune what is included in a playlist.

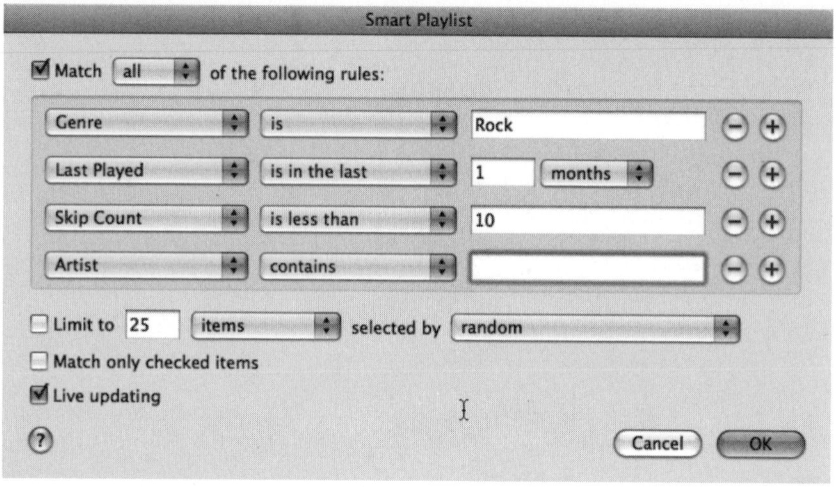

Figure 13-7. *Creating a smart playlist*

Choosing What to Sync

Organizing your media in iTunes is all well and good, but the reason that you want it organized is so that you can control what is synced to your iPhone or iPod touch. You have two basic choices when it comes to syncing either music or video to your iPhone— you can sync everything in your library (or at least everything that will fit on the device) or you can pick and choose. When it comes to picking and choosing, you typically will select specific playlists to sync, which is why using playlists and smart playlists to organize your media is an important step.

Choosing Music and Audio

Figure 13-8 shows the Music tab for an iPhone in iTunes. As you can see, the choices are to sync all songs and playlists or sync specific playlists (which is where having specific predefined choices of music and other audio files such as audiobooks is important). You'll also notice there are options for syncing music videos and voice notes (which I'll cover in the next chapter).

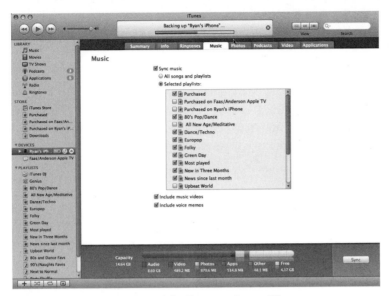

Figure 13-8. *Choosing what music/audio to sync to your iPhone*

Choosing Video

Choosing what video to sync can be a little more granular. You can select to sync movies and TV shows separately. With movies, you can choose all movies or specific movies (note that movies can include things from the iTunes U selection as well as video files you've imported into iTunes). For TV shows, you can choose to sync based on individual shows, whether a show's episodes have been downloaded but not watched, or everything available. Both of these are shown in Figure 13-9.

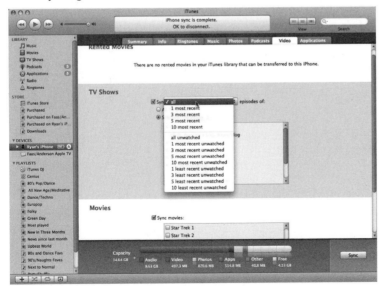

Figure 13-9. *Choosing what video to sync to your iPhone*

Choosing Podcasts

Podcasts, which can be either video or audio in nature and which can be regularly updated, have their own special tab in iTunes for the iPhone and iPod touch. However, as you can see in Figure 13-10, the options are very similar to choosing which TV shows to sync. You can choose to sync all podcasts or just selected podcasts, and you can choose to keep all episodes, unplayed episodes, or only brand-new episodes on your iPhone at any time (as well as how many episodes fall into each of those categories).

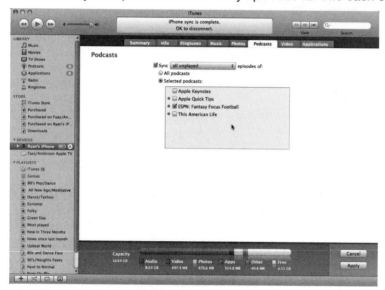

Figure 13-10. *Choosing Podcasts to sync*

Navigating the iPod App

The iPhone iPod app is designed to let you quickly and easily browse and play audio and video content synced to your iPhone as well as purchases made through the iTunes Store app on the iPhone itself (I'll cover purchasing music and video on the iPhone directly later in this chapter). As you can see in Figure 13-11, the iPod app bears some resemblance to the design of the Phone app that you learned about in Chapter 4. Like the Phone app, the iPod app uses a series of tabs at the bottom of the screen to let you access specific portions of the app.

Figure 13-11. *The iPod app showing the default view of tabs*

Browsing Your Music and Media

The iPod app includes five tabs for accessing specific portions of the app. Unlike the Phone app, where each tab provides separate specific feature, the iPod tabs each offer a way to browse your content. As you can see in Figure 13-11, the default view includes tabs for Playlists, Artists, Songs, Videos, and More.

As you might guess, the first three of these allow you to browse through your media by playlists you've created in iTunes, name of the artists that recorded music, or specific track names of songs. When you browse by playlists, songs are listed in the order of the playlist. When you browse by artist or song, they are listed alphabetically and you can use the alphabet along the right side (see Figure 13-12) of the view to jump to specific artist or song names, as well as simply scroll through the list. If you browse by artist, you'll have the option to list all songs by an artist or drill down to a specific album.

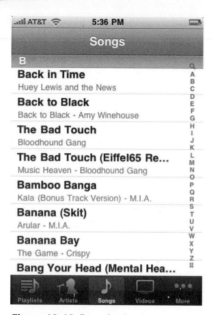

Figure 13-12. *Browsing by song name*

The Videos tab lists all video content available, including TV shows, movies, and video podcasts, as shown in Figure 13-13. Again, you can drill down through TV shows to find specific episodes. As with podcasts, the iPhone will include a blue dot next to items you haven't watched yet on the iPhone, your computer, or any other device synced to iTunes (for items that you've only watched part of, you'll see a half-filled blue dot).

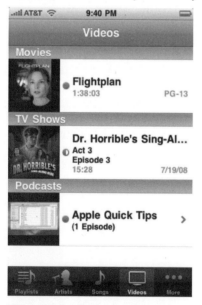

Figure 13-13. *Browsing videos*

The More Tab

The More tab (Figure 13-14) allows you to browse your content in even more ways, such as by genre or album. It also allows you to see audiobook podcasts synced to your iPhone. Each of these tabs allows you to drill down through your content to find specific items. And playing them, as with playing an album or playlist, will play the content in the order it appears on the screen and will only play the content of a selected list (such as all songs in a genre or on a specific album).

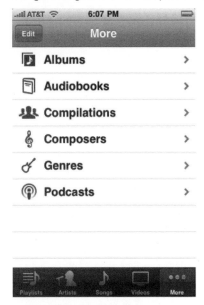

Figure 13-14. *The More tab*

Editing the iPod Tabs

You can change the default tabs in the iPod app. If you find you listen to podcasts a lot but don't watch videos, for example, you can swap out the video tab and replace it with a podcasts tab. To do this, tap the Edit button displayed in the upper left of the More tab (see Figure 13-14). This displays the browser shown in Figure 13-15. To replace the default tabs (or change their order), simply drag tab names from the browser onto the tabs you want to replace. Tap the Done button when you're satisfied to return to the iPod app.

Figure 13-15. *Editing the iPod tabs*

IPHONE VS. IPOD TOUCH

The iPod touch is organized a little differently than the iPhone. While the iPhone has a single iPod app for accessing all of your content, the iPod touch actually breaks the feature out across two apps: Music and Videos. The features and navigation are essentially the same, though the options of tabs at the bottom are slightly different because Music is used only for audio content and Videos for video content (essentially mirroring what you can see in Figure 13-13). Other than that, their functionality is the same as the iPod app on the iPhone.

Playing Music, Video, and Other Content

Playing music or video content on the iPod is pretty simple and straightforward. To start playing any item, simply browse to it and the tap it. As a song is playing, you'll see the album art for it displayed, as well as some controls that overlay the display (as shown in Figure 13-16). Some of these controls are displayed all the time while music is playing while others fade out after a second of not being used.

Figure 13-16. *Playing content using the iPod app*

NOTE: Songs imported from CDs or files may not include album art. If iTunes can identify the album and artist correctly, it will attempt to download the album art. If it can't, you'll see a generic music logo displayed while that song is playing instead.

Pause/Play, Skip, and Volume

Below the album art are the basic playback controls, and they are displayed constantly. These include the pause/play button as well as the skip forward and backward buttons (which also act as fast forward and rewind buttons within a track if you tap and hold your finger on them). There is also a volume slider to give you an onscreen volume control, though you can also adjust the volume using the physical buttons on the side of the iPhone.

Scrubbing, Shuffle, Genius, and Repeat

Another bar of controls appears overlaying the album art (it fades out while content is playing but will reappear if you tap the iPhone's screen). It includes a slider that displays the current position of playback relative to the entire track. The slider can also be used to scrub forward or backward or to jump to a specific portion of the track.

> **TIP:** You can speed up the normal scrubbing speed by sliding your finger down slightly as you scrub with the slider.

Below that are three buttons: the one to left allows you to cycle through the repeat options for the current selection (you can choose no repeat, where this button is white; repeat the entire selection of songs—playlist, album, etc.—where the button will be blue; or repeat only the current track, where the button is blue with a 1 displayed). The center button invokes the iTunes Genius feature (which I'll discuss in a minute). The button on the right is the shuffle button, which will shuffle the songs in the current selection rather than playing them
in sequence. The shuffle button, like the repeat button, turns blue when shuffle is on.

AUDIOBOOK AND PODCAST CONTROLS

If you're playing an audiobook or podcast, you won't see the Genius or shuffle buttons in this bar. Instead, you'll see the buttons displayed in Figure 13-17. The center button acts like an instant replay skips back 30 seconds in playback. This can be helpful if you're listening in a crowded location and miss a word or phrase.

Meanwhile, the button to right allows you to adjust the playback speed. By tapping it repeatedly, you can cycle between normal playback, playback at double speed, and playback at one-and-a-half times normal. This can come in handy if you're listening to a podcast or audiobook and want move through content you've heard before or are simply not interested in listening to—though in both fast speeds, human speech is fairly discernable, meaning

you'll get through content quickly but still be able to tell when you've reached something you're interested in listening to.

Figure 13-17. *Audiobook and playlist controls*

Song Info, Back Button, and Current Album

Above the album art is a bar with three items. To the left is a back button that takes you back to the iPod app to browse for other music or content (though the current selection continues to play until you select something else). In the center information about the track, including the name, artist, and album (for podcasts, the episode name is displayed here, and for audiobooks the current chapter is displayed instead of an album). And to the right is a button that displays the tracks on your iPhone from the current album.

The album browser, shown in Figure 13-18 offers you a couple of features. First, it lets you see all the tracks of an album as well as the duration of each track. More importantly, if you tap a different track in the album, then the iPhone will switch from whatever selection you had been playing to simply playing that album, which can be a lot faster and easier than browsing through the iPod app to locate the album.

Figure 13-18. *Browsing the album of the current song*

The album browser can also be used to rate songs. iTunes allows you to rate music using a system of one to five stars. This allows you to identify your favorite and least favorite music, and it can be used to build smart playlists. To rate or change the rating of a currently playing song, tap the dots above the list of tracks to turn them into the amount of stars that you want to assign as the rating.

Coverflow

If you turn the iPhone sideways while playing music, you'll see the coverflow view (Figure 13-19), this view shows the album art of songs in the current selection. You can flick back and forth though the art and tap the art of a an alternate song to begin playing it.

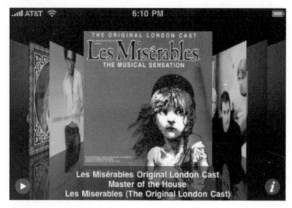

Figure 13-19. *Coverflow*

Video Playback

For video playback, you'll see controllers similar to the ones used when playing video attachments. As you can see in Figure 3-20, these include a bar with volume, pause/play, and skip/rewind buttons (which skip to the next or previous chapter in a video file and also act as fast forward and rewind if you hold them) near the bottom; and a scrubber bar, Done button, and full screen button at the top. Both controllers fade out during playback until you tap the screen.

Figure 3-20. *Video playback and controls*

Genius

Genius is a feature in iTunes that analyzes your music to find songs that fit well together. It does this using a variety of data including beat per minute of songs, genres, your ratings, and the playlists that you've created, and by comparing data about your iTunes library with the data of other iTunes users with similar music tastes (this also allows Genius to suggest music to you from the iTunes Store). iTunes is a free service, and personal information is not stored by Apple. But even without personal details, it does work by sending information about your iTunes library to Apple's server to analyze the results (and update those results every week). Therefore, it is an opt-in service that you can enable from the Store menu in iTunes.

Once you've enabled Genius in iTunes and synced your iPhone, you can create a Genius playlist based on any playing song by tapping the Genius button. The iPhone will then create a playlist based around that song using the Genius information from Apple. The iPod app will display the tracks in a Genius playlist, as shown in Figure 13-21. Using the buttons at the top of the playlist, you can create a new Genius playlist (the iPod app will ask you to choose a different song to base it on), refresh the playlist with different results and ordering, or permanently save the playlist (it will appear in your iTunes library after your next sync). You can select other songs directly from this view or return to the standard view of album art and controls by tapping the Now Playing button.

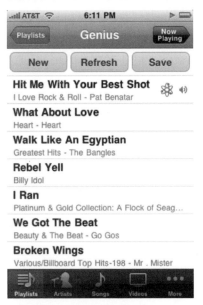

Figure 3-21. *A Genius playlist*

TIP: You can also access Genius from the playlist browse view, which will allow you to select a song that is not already playing to create a Genius playlist.

Browsing the iTunes Store on the iPhone

You don't need to be at your computer to access the iTunes Store. The iTunes app on the iPhone gives you complete access to all facets of the iTunes Store on the go, including music, audiobooks, movies (rent or buy), TV shows, podcasts, and iTunes U. You can also redeem iTunes gift cards directly from the iTunes app. If you make purchases on your iPhone, they are transferred to your iTunes library the next time you sync your iPhone.

As you can see in Figure 3-22, the iTunes app is organized very much like the iPod app. By default, it includes tabs for browsing for music, videos, and podcasts, as well as for searching across the entire contents of the store. Like the iPod app, iTunes includes a More tab that includes options for browsing audiobooks and iTunes U, as well as for viewing downloads in progress after purchase and redeeming gift cards. Also like the iPod app, you can edit which options are included as tabs and which are displayed on the More tab.

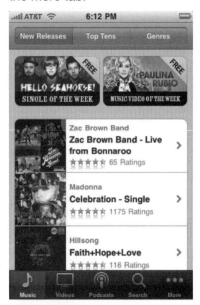

Figure 3-22. *The iTunes app*

Summary

In this chapter, you learned how to use the iPod features of the iPhone for both work and pleasure. You were also introduced to the iTunes Store. In the next chapter, I'll finish off the tour of built-in iPhone apps by looking at the YouTube, Stocks, Weather, Clock, Calculator, Notes, and Voice Recorder applications.

Chapter 14

The Remaining Built-In Apps

Using Other iPhone Tools for Business and Professional Needs

In the preceding chapters, I've focused on explaining the broad capabilities of the staple applications that ship on the iPhone. In this chapter, we'll round out the discussion of built-in apps by taking a look at tools that Apple provides for quickly and easily accomplishing specific tasks. Along the way, you'll see although an app may be simple, it can also be powerful and useful.

The remaining apps fall across a wide range of functions and include YouTube, Stocks, Weather, Clock, Calculator, Notes, and Voice Memos. For some, it's easier to see the business applications of some of these tools than others, but as you'll see, each has something to offer to the professional on the go.

YouTube

Next to the iPod app, YouTube may seem like the most unlikely choice of application for a business device. However, like the iPod features, YouTube can actually be integrated into your professional world in a couple of different ways. Let's take a quick look at how the iPhone's YouTube app functions, and then we'll get into its potential in your business life.

Searching and Browsing

When you first launch YouTube, you'll see a screen similar to that shown in Figure 14-1. As you can see, YouTube relies on a toolbar for browsing content similar to the one used by the iPod app. By default, this toolbar includes Featured (content that is currently featured on YouTube's home page), Most Viewed (which allows you to see the most frequently watched videos of the current day, week, or all time), Search (which allows you to search YouTube), Favorites (which lists videos that you've marked as favorites using your YouTube account), and More (which displays additional browsing options that I'll cover in just a bit). Figures 14-1 shows the YouTube app.

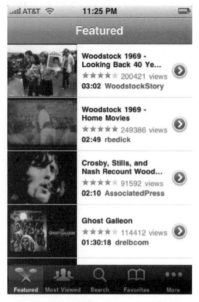

Figure 14-1. Featured YouTube videos (the default view)

NOTE: Although Search in YouTube uses a typical iPhone search dialog, it is not a live updating, nor does it feature auto-complete as do most searches for content on your iPhone, such as Contacts and Mail.

TIP: YouTube favorites are actually server-based (as opposed to being bookmarks sorted on your iPhone). This means that you can mark items as favorites on your iPhone, a computer, or any other device that allows you to log into YouTube—I'll talk more about YouTube accounts later in this section.

More Browsing Options

As with the iPod app, the More view includes additional ways to browse YouTube content. Also as with the iPod app, you can tap the Edit button to rearrange which browsing options are actually included in the toolbar at the bottom of your screen. This lets you customize the YouTube experience to be the most convenient for the features that you use.

The additional browsing options break down into the following: Most Recent (similar to the Featured view, this allows you to browse the most recently uploaded content), Top Rated (which displays the videos that have received the highest overall ratings through YouTube's five-star rating system), History (which acts like Safari's history feature, showing you videos that you have watched on your iPhone), My Videos (which displays videos that you have uploaded using your YouTube account), Subscriptions (which displays any videos to which you have subscribed with your YouTube account), and Playlists (which shows playlists of videos you have created using your YouTube account.

> **TIP:** Although most viewed, recent, and top-rated videos can help you keep a pulse on what's new and popular on YouTube, other browsing methods such as search, history, and options associated with your YouTube account (which I'll cover in more detail shortly) will probably be your better choices for using YouTube professionally on the iPhone.

Playing Videos

Playing a video in YouTube is as simple as tapping it from any of the search or browse views. As you can see in Figure 14-2, while playing, YouTube displays a standard iPhone video controller similar to the one used for video playback in the iPod application. This controller will automatically fade out during playback, but will redisplay if you tap the iPhone's screen.

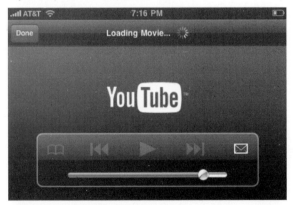

Figure 14-2. *Video playback in YouTube*

The YouTube app has the standard pause/play and skip forward/backward buttons. The forward and backward buttons will skip to the next or previous video or list of search results if you tap them. If you hold either the forward or backward buttons, they will act as fast forward/rewind buttons. The controller also includes a bookmark-style button to add a video as a favorite and a mail button to share a link to the video via an e-mail. There is also a video progress bar/slider along the top of the display, as well as a Done button to stop playback and return to the browse/search features of YouTube without watching an entire video, and a full screen button.

> **NOTE:** If you click a link to a YouTube video in another application, such as in an e-mail or web page, the iPhone will automatically launch YouTube and play the video.

Viewing Video Details

In addition to simple browsing and playback, YouTube on the iPhone supports a range other additional features that are available through the traditional web browser interface of YouTube. These include viewing additional information about a video, viewing related videos, adding the video to a playlist, and rating, commenting on, or flagging a video.

You can view video information in one of two ways. The first is to simply watch a video to its conclusion or tap the Done button during playback. Second, you can click the arrow icon next to each video's thumbnail and description in a browse view or search results. Either option will display the details shown in Figure 14-3.

Figure 14-3. *Video details*

As you can see, video details include a description, current average rating, and related videos suggested by YouTube. There are also buttons to add the video to a playlist associated with your YouTube account, share via e-mail, and mark the video as a favorite (if the video is already listed as a favorite or part of a playlist, you won't see those as options).

Viewing Additional Information (Including Ratings and Comments)

If you tab the arrow icon next to a video's description (at the top of the information display), you'll be able to view even more information, including when the video was uploaded, its category, and any tags listed by the poster for it. You'll also be able to scroll through all the comments that other YouTube users have made about the video.

You can even post your comments, rate the video, or flag it as inappropriate content (which will be followed up by a YouTube staff member) using the button above the comments list. Lastly, from this screen you can view additional videos uploaded by the same user as the one you just watched or browsed using the More Videos tab, and from the list of additional videos, you can subscribe to a user—meaning that you will always be able to easily view their entire stream of videos using the Subscriptions feature.

Using a YouTube Account

As I've mentioned throughout this section, a number of YouTube features (including Favorites, My Videos, Subscriptions, Playlists, and commenting/rating) require a YouTube account. The first time you use one of these features (and periodically thereafter), YouTube will ask you to provide your YouTube account information. You can register for a YouTube account on your computer.

The integration with YouTube accounts is a new feature on iPhone OS 3, and it provides a lot of integration of the YouTube experience between your iPhone and the YouTube web site. It allows you to organize your choices of video very well, it offers the social networking capabilities of YouTube, and it allows you to have easy access to specific videos or content by specific individuals/organizations no matter how you are accessing YouTube. This is particularly handy with three features for professionals on the go (as well as YouTube fans in general): favorites, subscriptions, and playlists.

Favorites

Favorites are essentially bookmarks. By marking a video that you expect to refer to more than once as a favorite, you have immediate access to it on your iPhone, computer, Apple TV or other device. In addition to adding favorites from your iPhone, you can also edit the list as you decide you no longer need to keep track of a specific video. Much like deleting e-mails, you edit the favorites list by tapping the Edit button and then using the red circle with a line icon to display a Delete button in the list. Editing of favorites occurs in real time and will affect what you see in the list on computers and other devices.

Playlists

Favorites are a great help in terms of quickly bookmarking videos, but if you spend a lot of time using YouTube, they can get out of control. That's where playlists come in— playlists allow you to group similar videos together (much like folders for e-mail or Safari bookmarks). You can create as many separate playlists as you like (either using YouTube's web site on your computer or on the iPhone).

To create a new playlist on the iPhone, use the + button above the list of existing playlists. As with Favorites, you can also delete playlists, and you can remove videos from a given playlist. At this time, there is no direct way to move a video from one playlist to another on the iPhone (though this can be done via YouTube's web site).

When you add video to a playlist, you'll be asked to choose which playlist to add it to. Notice that you can choose an existing playlist or create a new playlist on the fly while adding a video.

Subscriptions

Subscriptions are a great feature for YouTube because they allow you to easily locate new and previously posted videos by a particular user. This is a great for professionals, because you can easily follow updates made by a particular company or trade organization (or even a particular colleague) in the same manner that you can subscribe to a podcast. Needless to say, this is great if you rely on YouTube to follow trends or as a way of expanding your skill set.

On the iPhone, you can subscribe to a user from the video details screen. You can then browse your subscriptions. While browsing the videos of a user, you can also unsubscribe from them using the appropriate button.

> **NOTE:** From YouTube on a computer, you may also have the option of subscribing to playlists of a particular user (which can be helpful if they post across a range of topics, only one or two of which may interest you). The iPhone's YouTube app will support these subscriptions, but you cannot create such granular subscriptions on the iPhone, nor can you unsubscribe from them.

YOUTUBE FOR SKILLS AND PROMOTION

Although YouTube is typically seen as an entertainment and hobbyist service, it does have wide potential for professionals. This potential comes in a few different forms: the ability to build your skill set, a method for following trends in an industry, opportunities for networking with other users, and a powerful marketing tool. Of these, the first three can be completely accomplished on the go using the iPhone alone. Even marketing can be accomplished on the iPhone through social networking (though a computer or other facilities are needed to actually produce and upload content).

Many schools and organizations (as well as individuals knowledgeable in a given field) post how-to videos on YouTube. Such content comes in the form of lectures, PowerPoint-style presentations, computer screen captures, and hands-on demonstrations. In many ways, this makes YouTube a broad learning tool that can be used to both build your skill set and demonstrate practical techniques for accomplishing specific (and sometimes very technical) tasks.

If you work in an industry that is at all trend-based, which can include anything from fashion and design (the ultimate trend industries), to technology and medicine, to education, YouTube can help you keep a pulse on what's happening in your field. The rating system and ability to view how popular content is can be a great trend-spotting solution, and can highlight what people are trying that isn't working.

And of course, there is the social networking and therefore marketing aspect of YouTube. This can be an incredibly powerful tool in any industry, whether you're trying to market a product or solution or trying to build a personal network as part of a job search. Although other social networking services (Facebook, Twitter, and LinkedIn all come to mind) tend to be more easily associated with professional networking and marketing, YouTube's ability to be part of the discussion and integrate video and presentation content is very powerful and shouldn't be easily dismissed.

Of course, while networking is easy to do through YouTube on the iPhone, actual content creation is a bit more challenging. Nonetheless, if your company has recently posted content, you can use the iPhone to market that content even if you can't create it.

Another useful marketing and networking capability of YouTube is the ability to build portfolios (either of company products and solutions or of your own work). If you are in a professional situation, such as a conference, or even just meeting someone while waiting for a delayed flight, having immediate and easy access to that portfolio via YouTube (and the My Videos browsing option) can be immensely powerful. The icing on the cake is that you can also immediately e-mail portfolio content directly from the iPhone's YouTube app.

Stocks

The Stocks app, powered by Yahoo Finance, provides a quick and easy tool for monitoring the stock market as a whole or a portfolio of individual companies. As a result, it can be a great tool for anyone in the financial industry or anyone who simply wants to keep tabs on their investments from day to day or moment to moment.

As you can see in Figure 14-4, the overall interface is very basic and divided into three sections: a list of monitored stocks and their recent performance, a detailed display about a selected stock, and a toolbar that includes the Yahoo logo, a dot representing the number of information displays possible for each stock, and an "i" icon that can be used to adjust the app's settings.

Figure 14-4. *The Stocks app*

The top half of the display will always detail the stocks that you are choosing to monitor. It will always display each company's trading code and current value. It will also allow you to cycle through a view of each company's current value, recent growth/loss in the market, and current share price by tapping the values listed in either green or red (as appropriate to the news) in the right-hand column.

Below the list of followed companies is a section that displays details about a selected company. As you can see in Figures 14-5, 14-6, and 14-7, you can choose between views, which include a snapshot of current market data, a graph of recent performance, and recent Reuters news headlines about the company and its industry (which will open in Safari if clicked).

Figure 14-5. *General information about a company*

Figure 14-6. *Recent performance graph*

Figure 14-7. *Recent news*

If you tilt the iPhone into landscape mode, you'll notice that Stocks displays a wide-screen version of the performance graph. As useful as this is, you can also use multitouch gestures to select a range of time periods in the graph, which will display financial details about that particular time frame, as shown in Figure 14-8.

Figure 14-8. *Landscape view of Stocks showing date range detail*

Adding and Removing Stocks

As with other iPhone applications, the "i" icon to the lower right of the screen allows you to adjust the behavior of the Stocks application. You can use this view to add and remove stocks that you want to track, and to change the default view of information displayed about all stocks.

As you can see in Figure 14-9, this view includes %, Price, and Mkt Cap buttons—each of which displays corresponding information about the stocks in the list view. Choosing one of these sets the default view—though you can still tap to view the other details.

Figure 14-9. *Stock options*

Also notice in Figure 14-9 that the list of stocks includes the same red circle icons that you've seen in Mail and Safari Bookmarks—and for the same purpose. Tapping this icon will reveal a delete button that allows you to stop following the stock. You'll also see the three-line icon to the right of each stock that allows you to reorder the stocks you are tracking (just as you can use this icon to reorder favorite contacts or Safari bookmarks).

Also similar to Safari Bookmarks is the triple-line icon to the right edge of any stock you are following. Again, the behavior is the same in that it allows you to tap and drag stocks around to reorder them in the Stocks list. Finally, you can add stocks to the list using the + button in the upper left. You can search for additional stocks across major exchanges the world over by typing either the company name or the stock code used on an exchange into the search field. Once a stock is displayed, complete with code and exchange details in the list, simply tap it to have your iPhone follow it for you. When you're done modifying the selection of stocks that you want your iPhone to follow, simply click the Done button in the upper right to return to the Stocks application.

Weather

The Weather application, as its name implies, provides weather forecasts. As with Stocks, Weather is powered by Yahoo and the Weather Channel. The Weather app provides current conditions and temperatures for cities around the world as a basic five-day forecast, as shown in Figure 14-10. Weather data and forecasts are in real time (provided Internet connectivity is available), but are based on static locations (making Weather one of the few apps to not implement the iPhone's location services).

Figure 14-10. *The Weather app*

You can configure forecasts for multiple cities, and you can flick through them much like you would additional home screens (with each city represented by a dot). As with Stocks, to choose the locations for forecasts, click the "i" icon at the bottom right of the screen.

Editing Weather Settings

As you can see in Figure 14-11, the Weather app includes a list of cities, and buttons for displaying temperatures in either Fahrenheit or Celsius (conditions will be displayed based on your choices regardless of the custom for the location you are viewing).

Figure 14-11. *Editing Weather settings*

Similar to the options for stocks discussed earlier, you can track weather in multiple cities. Cities that you are currently following can be removed and reordered in the same manner (using the red circle icon to display a Delete button to remove cities, and the three-line grip icon to drag and rearrange them). You can also use the + button in the upper left to add a city. When adding a city, you can search/add based on the city name or city and state/province combination, or using a ZIP/postal code). Available cities will be displayed in the list, typically based around the airport conditions nearest to the location that you entered. When finished, again click the Done button.

> **TIP:** Although it seems quite basic, the Weather app can be a very good tool for professionals that travel frequently, work outdoors, or plan events in different locations.

Clock

As I mentioned in Chapter 2, the date and time settings for the iPhone are handled by the Settings app (you can either set them manually or rely on your mobile carrier to provide date and time information). The current time is also always available to an iPhone user from the bar at the top of the display and from the lock screen. So, the Clock app provides time-related functions, even though it's primary purpose isn't displaying the current time. In fact, as you can see in Figure 14-12, the Clock app includes four icons in its toolbar that encompass its functionality: World Clock, Alarm, Stopwatch, and Timer.

Figure 14-12. *The Clock app*

World Clock

As you can see in Figure 14-12, the World Clock feature allows you to easily check the time in different locales around the world. You can add multiple clocks and reorganize them much as you can stocks and weather locations.
To a new clock, tap the + button, type the name (or partial name) of the city or location you want to check the time of, and then select it from the live earch list.

As with similar apps that I've already discussed, you can use the Edit button (upper left) to delete and/or reorder the display of clocks. As with Stocks and Weather, clocks can be deleted using the red circle icon and repositioned using the three-line grip icons.

NOTE: World clocks will display with a black or white face, indicating whether they are reflecting night or day in the selected location.

Alarm

Like most mobile phones, it is possible to use the iPhone as an alarm clock. This can be useful in many travel situations where you may deal with unfamiliar alarm clock models. The Alarm pane, shown in Figure 14-13, can be used to set one or more alarms, each with its own time, repetition, and sound (alarms can use any default or user-installed ringtone). From this pane, you can enable or disable alarms at will.

Figure 14-13. *The Alarm pane*

NOTE: Alarms will remain active as long as an iPhone is powered on, and they will go off, sounding the appropriate ringtone, even if the iPhone is in Airplane or silent mode.

To set an alarm, click the + button and set the Repeat, Sound, and Snooze options. If you enable the Snooze option, a snooze button will display when the alarm sounds, and if clicked will snooze the alarm for nine minutes. You can also add a label or description for the alarm, as shown in Figure 14-14. You can use the clock wheels to choose the time for the alarm, as well as whether it will sound at that time AM or PM.

Figure 14-14. *Setting an alarm*

As with other features discussed in this chapter, you can delete an alarm by clicking the Edit button and using the red circle icons to display a Delete button.

Stopwatch

The Stopwatch is, well, a stopwatch. It supports basic stopwatch timing and lap training. If you use lap training, each successive lap will be listed in the display, as you can see in Figure 14-15. With such a basic interface of start/stop and lap/reset buttons, there's really not much more to say about this feature.

Figure 14-15. *Stopwatch*

Timer

The countdown timer, shown in Figure 14-16, is another basic time tool. Simply enter a length of time using the clock wheels (anything from 1 minute to 23 hours, 59 minutes), choose a sound to be played when the time is up (as with alarms, any ringtones are free game and will play once the time runs out so long as the device is powered on), and tap start. The timer, like any alarm, will continue counting down in the background as you work in other apps, and even if you lock the iPhone. You can also view the current countdown and/or cancel the timer at any point.

Figure 14-16. *Setting a timer*

Calculator

Another one of the more basic but quite useful apps is Calculator. When help in portrait mode, Calculator displays as a basic pocket calculator complete with standard addition, subtraction, multiplication, division, and memory functions, as shown in Figure 14-17. Held in landscape mode, Calculator expands to offer a full-featured scientific calculator with all common advanced and scientific functions, as shown in Figure 14-18.

Figure 14-17. *Calculator with basic functions*

Figure 14-18. *Calculator with full scientific feature set*

Notes

As you might guess from the name, Notes (shown in Figure 4-19) is a basic note-taking application. Although very general in function and interface, the simplicity that Notes offers is that you can use it almost any way you want. You can easily create notes by using the + button in the upper right, view a list of existing notes using the navigation button in the upper left (which reveals a list like the one in Figure 14-20), and navigate through your existing notes using the buttons at the bottom of each note. These include buttons to move to the previous note, convert a note into an e-mail, delete a note, and skip to the next note.

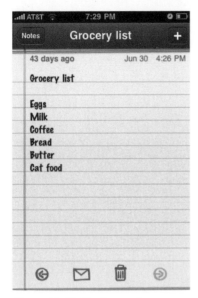

Figure 14-19. *Viewing a note*

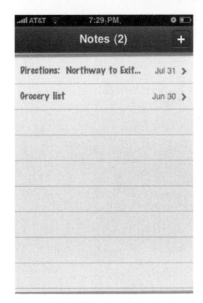

Figure 14-20. *Viewing a list of notes*

Notes can function as a general portable notebook, making the app useful for anything you need to jot down for yourself to remember later, be it a to-do list, a person's name, or even a random quote or reference related to a project that you're working on. On iPhone OS 3, notes can be synced to your computer through iTunes as described in Chapter 1; this can make them particularly helpful since they allow two-way note-taking and reading.

Voice Memos

Much like Notes is a basic tool for jotting down any kind of note to yourself, Voice Memos is a tool for making quick notes to yourself without typing—a great feature if you need to record quick thoughts, take dictation for later transcription, or even record entire lectures or presentations for later processing into podcasts or similar media. In fact, the array of things you can do with recordings made with Voice Memos are somewhat belied by the very basic interface.

As you can see in Figure 14-21, Voice Memos includes the image of a microphone, a sound level gauge, and two buttons—a red one (on the left) to start and pause recording, and one with three black lines (on the right) to view, listen to, and edit existing recordings.

Figure 14-21. *Voice Memos' recording interface*

To a record a memo, simply tap the record button (which will change to a pause button when recording, as shown in Figure 14-22) and start speaking. You can pause at any time. When you're done recording an entire note/event, tap the stop button on the other side of the sound level gauge.

Figure 14-22. *Recording a voice note*

To view your recordings as a list, tap the three-line list button to view the Voice Memos screen (Figure 14-23). You'll notice that the recording list looks very similar to the Phone app's Voicemail screen. To play a recording, tap it and then tap the play icon that appears to the left of it.

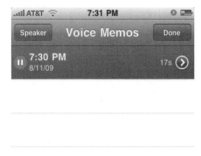

Figure 14-23. *Recordings in Voice Memos*

From this screen, you can also select a voice recording and use the Share button to send it as an MPEG-4 (.m4a) audio file attached to an e-mail or delete it using the Delete button. You can also perform basic editing of the recording and information about it, as described in the following section

Editing a Recording

To edit information about the recording, such as to provide a category or description of it, tap the arrow icon to the right of it in the list. This will show you the time/date of the recording and the length. From this screen, you also have the option to trim the recording (remove any excess sounds or dead air at the beginning or end), as shown in Figure 14-24, and share the recording via e-mail. To enter a description or label, tap the large block that shows when the memo was recorded. You'll then see a list of labels (including Custom, which allows you to create your own labels). Figure 14-25 shows the same memo as Figure 14-24, but with the "Memo" label assigned to it.

Figure 14-24. *Trimming a recording—slide the ends of the yellow rectangle over the blue line representing the recording*

Figure 14-25. *Voice memo with a label applied to it*

Syncing Recordings with iTunes

During a sync with your computer, any recordings that you make with Voice Memos are synced to your iTunes library. They are added as MPEG 4 files. Very little information in included in iTunes about voice recordings, but you can use the Get Info command in iTunes to add information to help identify recordings (see Figure 14-26). You can also export audio or use other audio tools to work with recorded audio further.

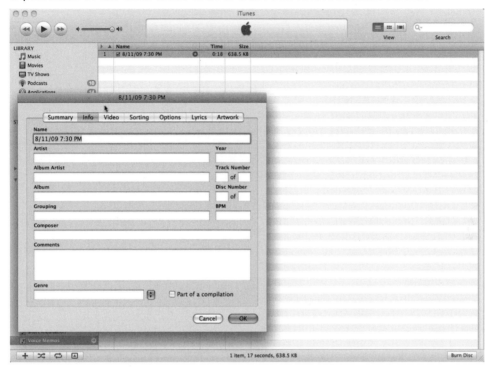

Figure 14-26. *Voice recordings in iTunes*

Summary

In the chapters throughout Part 2 of the book, you've learned about the array of built-in applications and features that Apple ships on the iPhone, and you've learned how to use them to get work done, network, and collaborate no matter where you are. However, some of the real power of the iPhone comes from the tens of thousands of additional applications that you can install on it. In Part 3, I'll introduce you to finding and installing applications, as well as provide you a guide to many of the best third-party business and productivity applications available from Apple's App Store.

PART 3

Getting Even More Done with Additonal Apps

Chapter 15

Understanding iPhone Applications and the App Store

Using Third-Party and Web-Based Apps to Make the iPhone More Than Just a PDA, Media Player, or Phone

As you learned in the first two parts of this book, there's no doubt that the iPhone and iPod touch are amazing devices with a lot of potential straight out of the box. But what makes the iPhone a truly powerful mobile computing platform is that Apple has provided third-party developers with some amazing tools to create their own applications that extend the iPhone in many different directions. In this chapter, you'll learn about the App Store, from which you can purchase and download tens of thousands of iPhone applications, and web-based iPhone applications, which you can access through the Safari web browser on the iPhone.

Web Apps: The First Form of iPhone Applications

When Apple first introduced the iPhone in the summer of 2007, the company didn't provide software developers with the ability to write additional applications that could be installed and run on the iPhone. Instead, the company initially focused developers on creating web-based applications. A web-based application for the iPhone (commonly referred to as a web app) is actually a web site that is specially designed to display content using elements (text, images, forms, and buttons) that resemble the iPhone's interface. Such sites are typically designed to be dynamic and interactive sites that allow you to get something done (such as a viewing and checking off items on a to-do list).

Web apps can accomplish a lot (after all, there are plenty of interactive web sites already out there that allow you to perform a wide range of tasks), but they are somewhat limited because they cannot directly access a number of features on the iPhone. They also require a web server to host the app and any data that you store or want to access using a web app.

Although web apps suffer from these limitations, developers did create a wide range of web apps. Many of those apps tied into other existing web-based services, such as social networking sites, to-do list managers and notes tools, online finance and calculation tools, and project management and CRM services. This actually provides an advantage in some ways because the data is all stored centrally on a server that can be accessed using an iPhone or a computer.

For companies using the iPhone as a mobile platform with custom in-house tools, web apps offer the ability to keep data centrally managed and secure (as opposed to an application that is installed on the iPhone itself), which offers an extra layer of security for sensitive data. Another advantage is that the development process is much faster and easier, particularly for developers not familiar with writing software for the iPhone or Mac OS X. Anyone familiar with dynamic web development can create web apps with a minimal learning curve—making them a viable solution for creating in-house tools for employees with iPhones.

For accessing web apps quickly and easily, Apple added the ability to add web pages to your home screen as icons (as mentioned in Chapter 11). This saves you from having to launch Safari and then navigate through your bookmarks to a web site. It also makes web apps feel much more like extensions of the iPhone rather than separate tools.

> **NOTE:** The phrase "web app" typically refers to a web-based tool with an interface specifically geared to the iPhone. However, the iPhone can readily access most web-based tools regardless of whether they are designed specifically for it, allowing you to easily access virtually any tool that relies on web-based forms. The exceptions are sites that rely on Adobe's Flash technology, which is not available on the iPhone at the time of this writing.

Web Apps vs. Native Apps

Eventually, Apple created a software development kit (SDK) for the iPhone platform and began encouraging developers to create so-called *native apps*. As a tool to make it easy for iPhone owners to find, purchase, download, and install apps, the company also created the App Store as a central marketplace for all native apps. The App store went live in July 2008, and in less than a year offered over 50,000 apps, ranging from free games to high-end CRM tools, and everything in between.

Unlike web apps, native apps are installed directly on the iPhone, and they have the ability to access many of the hardware features of the device, as well as many of the underlying interface elements. They can also be Internet-enabled so that they can directly access and store data on a remote server as well as on the device itself.

> **NOTE:** Apple also provides companies the ability to create their own native apps that will be used only on iPhones used by their employees. This allows companies to develop custom in-house apps and distribute them to employees without using the App Store. Appendix B provides an introduction to this process for companies interested in developing their own native or web apps.

WHY WEB APPS STILL MATTER

In the time since the App Store was introduced, web apps have begun to fade from the thoughts of many iPhone users and developers, as native apps have some distinct advantages. There are, however, still quite a few web apps out there that provide great services (often for free). For businesses looking to develop in-house solutions, web apps can often be developed and deployed faster and more easily than native apps (particularly if the company already has a team of talented web developers, but no one with specific skills for working with Apple's Xcode—the development suite for both Mac OS X and the iPhone).

For apps sold through the App Store, developers must submit their apps for approval by Apple. This ensures the stability and security of the apps sold through the App Store, which is ultimately very good for the iPhone community. However, this also adds some time and a layer of complexity to creating native apps. Also, some apps may not be approved by Apple for one reason or another. Since no approval is needed for web apps, the development cycle can be shortened, and the apps can be produced even if Apple objects to their content.

Finally, it is worth mentioning that through varying software updates to the iPhone, Apple has expanded what developers can do with web apps, and created code that web developers can use that allows web apps to access some built-in iPhone services, such as location services to identify where you are geographically when you access the app. An excellent example of this is Google's Latitude web app for locating friends and coworkers in your immediate vicinity (more information on Latitude is available at www.google.com/latitude).

Finding Web Apps

Unlike native apps, which are all cataloged in the App Store, web apps can be hosted by any web server at any address in the world. However, Apple and others have created web app directories that can help you find and explore useful web apps, including the following (which you can bookmark on your iPhone for easy web app browsing):

- **Apple's Web App Directory:** www.apple.com/webapps
- **AppSafari:** www.appsafari.com
- **Webappuniverse Free iPhone Webapps:** http://iphonewebappdirectory.blogspot.com

The App Store

As I mentioned, the App Store is Apple's solution for making native apps available to iPhone users. When Apple created the App Store, it did so by using the infrastructure of the iTunes Store, which had many helpful and important features like payment processing, user reviews, and download systems already place. As a result, the App Store functions as a part of the larger iTunes Store.

This means that purchases are made using an iTunes Store account and that you can browse, purchase, and download apps through iTunes on your computer. If you purchase apps using iTunes on your computer, they are installed on your iPhone during the next sync operation. You can also use iTunes to specify which downloaded applications you want installed on your iPhone.

You can also browse and make purchases from the App Store directly on your iPhone or iPod touch using the App Store application. When you do so, apps will immediately be downloaded and installed on your iPhone using either Wi-Fi or a 3G/EDGE connection. The files for an application will be transferred to your iTunes library (so that you can install them on other iPhones or iPod touches, and as a backup in you delete an app from your device or need to restore your device).

APP STORE BILLING

One thing that is important to understand about the App Store from a business perspective is how it manages billing through iTunes Store accounts. Although there are a number of great apps designed for business use and productivity, the general approach to purchases follows the more consumer-oriented path of the iTunes Store. Each app that you purchase must be billed to an iTunes Store account. When you purchase an app through either iTunes or the App Store on an iPhone, you will need to enter the password of the iTunes account associated with the iPhone.

For individuals, this doesn't present much of a challenge, as you can just use a single iTunes Store account. For businesses deploying iPhones to multiple employees, however, it does present a challenge, because each company must either allow employees to activate their iPhones using their own iTunes Store accounts (thus allowing them to purchase apps on their own), or use a single company account that can be used to purchase needed apps and install them before giving the iPhones to their users (in which case employees would not be able to make purchases unless provided with the password of that iTunes account).

Neither of these options is a perfect solution. That is why most companies that deliver high-end business tools for the iPhone actually make the applications themselves free and tie the actual use of the applications to a company-wide license for the software. This works well for many network-based applications that employees also access on their computers and/or via the Internet

Exactly what approach your company takes to App Store purchases may vary. If you are a business owner or manager, you may want to take some time to consider which option is the best choice. The biggest question, however, is whether you have a set of apps that you want employees to use. If so, are they paid apps that users would have to buy themselves, or are they free apps that users would not have to pay for if using their own iTunes accounts. Another question is whether you even want to allow users to download apps.

Choosing the Right Apps

Choosing the right apps is key to make the iPhone work as a productive business tool. With such a gigantic catalog to choose from, finding the right app for your needs can be like finding a needle in a haystack. Luckily, Apple divides the App Store into categories, and most (though not all) work-related apps tend to be filed under business or productivity categories, making it a littler easier to browse them. Apple has also added the ability for developers to assign keywords to their apps, making it easier to search for more granular subsections of the broad categories.

The App Store, being part of the iTunes Store, also allows you to search for an app by name. This means that as long as you know what to look for, you can generally find it pretty readily. Many Mac and iPhone news sites regularly promote and review new apps, making them a useful source for finding apps that meet your needs. In the final two chapters of this book, I highlight a number of useful apps for business users and help get you started.

Particularly useful in helping you choose the right app are the user review sections of the App Store and the recommendations by iTunes about what apps other users who purchased a particular app have also purchased. This can help guide you as your browse through and discover what the App Store has to offer.

Browsing the App Store in iTunes

To access the App Store on your computer, launch iTunes and select iTunes Store in the sidebar. Then click the App Store link in the upper-left block of links (refer to Figure 15-1). This will display the App Store section of the iTunes Store, as shown in Figure 15-1.

Figure 15-1. *The App Store in iTunes*

The App Store is laid out much like the rest of the iTunes Store. A column along the left side of the store shows various categories of apps, allowing you to browse for apps in each specific category (see Figure 15-2). On the right side, two sections list the top (most popular) paid and free apps across all categories (similar sections are displayed for top apps within each category as well). In the center of the main display are various featured apps.

Figure 15-2. *The Business category of the App Store (note the top paid and free apps columns and the menu to sort the list of all apps in the category, which are displayed in the middle column)*

TIP: You can also use the iTunes Store search box (located in the upper right of the window) to search for apps by name.

When you click an app's name or icon, you'll see a description of the app with user reviews and screenshots, as well as information about the version and price of the app, as shown in Figure 15-3. To buy an app, click the Buy App button (or Get App in the case of free apps).

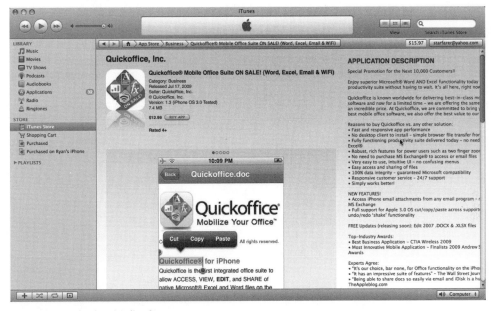

Figure 15-3. *Viewing details of an app*

After you buy an app, iTunes will charge the cost of the app to your iTunes Store account and begin downloading the app. Once the app is downloaded, it can be synced to your iPhone.

NOTE: The iTunes Store allows you to browse and select music and movies using a shopping cart to collect your purchases before actually buying and downloading them. If you've enabled the iTunes Store shopping cart, you'll see a warning when buying apps (or choosing to download free apps) that apps cannot be added to the shopping cart and will be purchased immediately. You can simply click OK in this alert to go ahead and purchase and download the app.

You can view the list of apps for which the install files exist on your computer by clicking Applications on the iTunes sidebar (see Figure 15-4). If you download an app and then later decide that you don't want to keep it, you can delete it from your iTunes library by simply clicking the app in this list and pressing the Delete key on your keyboard.

Figure 15-4. *Apps list in iTunes*

Choosing Which Apps to Sync

You can install as many apps on your iPhone as you have storage space to accommodate. By default, all apps that you download through your computer will be installed your iPhone automatically when you sync it. You can, however, change this behavior so that you can manually choose which apps are synced—something that you might want to do if you sync multiple iPhones or iPod touches to a single computer (you might also choose to manually sync apps if you only periodically need some and don't want to clutter your home screen and fill storage space with certain apps when you don't need them).

> **NOTE:** Remember that although you can install as many apps as you want, if you install more than can fit on the 11 supported home screens (180 in total), you won't see icons for them, and you'll need to use the Spotlight search screen to locate them, as discussed in Chapter 2.

To control syncing of apps manually, connect your iPhone to your computer, select it in the sidebar, and then click the Applications tab (as shown in Figure 15-5). Choose the option to manually sync applications, and then check the boxes for the apps that you want in the list on this tab. During any future sync, no apps will be installed other than those that you select on this tab. If you find that there are apps that you never choose to sync to your iPhone, you may want to consider deleting them altogether, as just described.

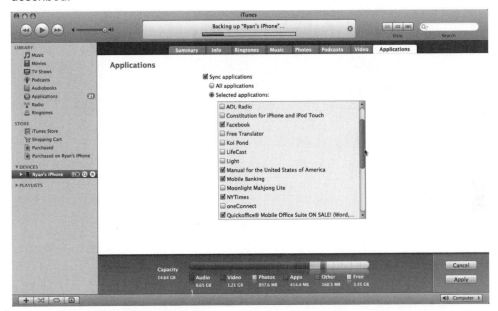

Figure 15-5. *Setting manual app syncing*

WEB-BASED APP STORE DIRECTORIES

As an alternative to browsing the App Store through iTunes or on the iPhone itself, there are a number of useful web-based directories that allow you search and sort through applications. Some offer more detailed reviews of apps while others feature more advanced search capabilities. As great as the App Store is, it can be overwhelming to browse through, and these directories can sometimes make that process easier. Here are my top suggestions for browsing the App Store through the Web:

- **Gizmodo's App Directory:** http://gizmodo.com/tag/app-directory
- **iGoApps:** www.igoapps.com
- **Yappler:** www.yappler.com
- **MacWorld's App Guide:** www.macworld.com/appguide/index.html
- **AppCraver:** www.appcraver.com

TIP Apple allows web sites to link directly to the App Store—the links are designed such that iTunes will open automatically when they are clicked and display the selected app. This makes using web-based App Store directories easy to use, and it also allows app developers, reviewers, and bloggers to link directly to an app. If you want to create an App Store link for your web site or blog, or send the link in an e-mail, right-click (or Ctrl+click if you're using a Mac with a single-button mouse) the app's name or icon in the App Store and select Copy iTunes Store Link from the pop-up menu that appears.

Browsing the App Store on Your iPhone

You can browse and search the App Store just as easily on your iPhone or iPod touch as you can on your computer by launching the App Store application. In fact, the more streamlined interface of the App Store application on the iPhone makes it a little easier to navigate. As you can see in Figure 15-6, browsing the App Store on the iPhone strongly resemble browsing the iTunes Store on the iPhone, as described in Chapter 13.

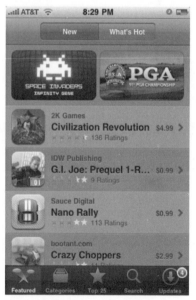

Figure 15-6. *The App Store app*

There are five tabs in the App Store. The Featured tab allows you to view featured apps (those apps that are featured in the center of the main App Store display in iTunes). The Categories tab lets you see the various categories (which you can sort according to top paid or free apps in each category, or by release date). The Top 25 tab allows you to view the top 25 paid and free apps across the entire store. The Search tab lets you search for an app by name, and the Updates tab lets you check for updates.

As with the App Store in iTunes, you can view descriptions, user reviews, and screenshots for each app (see Figure 15-7). To purchase or download an app, tap the price button(or the Free button in the case of a free app) once. The button will turn into a green Buy Now button for paid apps and a green Install button free apps. Tap the green button to purchase or download. You'll see an alert asking you to confirm your purchase/download by verifying your iTunes Store account's password.

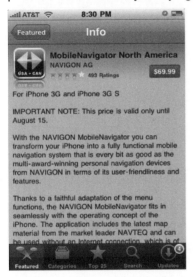

Figure 15-7. *App information in the App Store*

Once you confirm your purchase/download, the iPhone will process the transaction through the App Store and begin downloading and installing the app. Once the download begins, the iPhone will return to the home screen and add and icon for the app (if the current home screen is full, the iPhone will shift to the next available spot). While the app is being downloaded and installed, you'll see a blue progress bar along the bottom of its icon indicating how far along it is in the process. Once the app is installed, the progress bar will vanish and you can start using the app. On your next sync, the app will be copied into your iTunes library.

When I'm out of town on business, apps help me find where I'm going, nearby places to eat, and anything I need to find in towns with which I'm not familiar.

Janet Womachka—Occupational Safety and Health Specialist

> **NOTE:** Downloading most apps is relatively quick, but some apps can be quite large and may take a while to download over slow connections. You can get an idea of how long an app may take by looking at the size of its files, which are included in the description for the app in the App Store. For larger apps, you may find it easier to download through iTunes or over a Wi-Fi connection—in fact, some apps are so large (over 10MB) that they can only be downloaded via Wi-Fi.

Deleting Apps

To delete an app from your iPhone or iPod touch, simply tap and hold one of the icons till they begin to jiggle, indicating you can reposition or delete them (as discussed in Chapter 2). Then click the X icon in the upper-right corner of an app's icon to delete it. When you delete an app, your iPhone will ask if you want to rate it. This rating will be recorded by the iTunes Store and become part of the average user rating that others can use to judge whether or not they want to buy/download the app.

> **TIP:** You can also rate and review apps by clicking the appropriate link on an app's description page in iTunes, though you can only rate and review apps that you have purchased or downloaded.

Application Updates

Like any piece of software, iPhone apps are often updated regularly to add or expand features, fix bugs, or respond to use feedback. Both iTunes and the iPhone will regularly check the App Store for updates to any apps that you have downloaded or purchased (iTunes will do this for any apps, even if they are not currently installed on your iPhone, while the iPhone will only check for updates to installed apps).

When updates are found, iTunes will display the number of app updates next to the Applications entry in the iTunes sidebar. If you click Applications, you'll see a link in the lower-right corner of the window specifying the number of updates (Figure 15-8). Clicking it will display a list of the app updates and provide you the ability to download them either individually or all at once. Once updates are downloaded by iTunes, they are installed on the iPhone during the next sync.

Figure 15-8. *Application updates in iTunes*

When updates are detected by the iPhone, a badge showing the number of updates will appear on the App Store's icon. To view the available updates, launch the App Store and tap the Updates tab. You'll then see a list of updates and have the option to download them all or choose specific apps to update. The update process occurs just like the download and install process on the iPhone. Updates are then copied to iTunes during the next sync.

Summary

In this chapter, you learned about web apps and native apps, and how to browse and purchase apps from the App Store. I strongly encourage you to explore the App Store at this point—one of the best ways of finding apps is to simply explore and learn about the broad range of apps that are out there. It will also help you get comfortable navigating the App Store. In the next two chapters, I'll talk about some of the best apps out there for business in general (Chapter 16) and for specific professions and industries (Chapter 17).

General Business Applications

No Matter What Your Business, Some Apps Apply to Every iPhone Professional

In Part 2 of this book, you learned how to work with the built-in iPhone apps and how to use them for general and specific business functions. In the previous chapter, I introduced the App Store. In this chapter, I'll introduce you to some of the apps that are both well designed and offer valuable business or productivity tools.

Keep in mind that this chapter (as well as the next, in which you'll learn about tools that apply to specific professions or industries) is a starting point for your exploration of the App Store. While I encourage you to check out these apps in particular, you should also feel free to explore the App Store on your own as well as to find out more about and/or purchase the apps listed here.

> **NOTE:** In some sections of this chapter, I'll provide detail descriptions about specific apps, while in others, I'll discuss a general category of tools and provide a simple list of apps. This is because there are categories in which the available apps provide widely different feature sets or user interface, and others in which larges number of apps provide nearly identical capabilities and interfaces. In either case, I encourage you to check out the screenshots, user reviews, and other information available in the App Store for any app in this chapter or the next that might be useful for you.

Office and Document Tools

The iPhone out of the box gives you the ability to view files attached to e-mails in the formats used by the most common office tools (including Microsoft Office and Apple's iWork). However, many professionals on the go don't just want to see files, but also have the ability to create and edit them. The tools listed here provide you the ability to open, edit, and create documents wherever you are. They also provide the ability to store files in a folder-like hierarchy on the iPhone and transfer them to your computer, making your files much easier to manage than as e-mail attachments (in the next section, I'll cover a range of other file management tools as well).

- **QuickOffice:** QuickOffice is available as a suite or a series of individual apps, depending on your needs. As a suite, it offers the ability to create and edit Word and Excel files and a pretty complete set of formatting options. It also offers the ability to transfer files between your computer and iPhone using Wi-Fi (as well as options for organizing files into folders), and the ability to send files to others as e-mail attachments. If you only need to access Word or Excel documents, versions known as Quickword and Quicksheet are available, as is a version solely designed for transferring and organizing files.

- **Documents to Go:** Documents to Go by Dataviz offers similar functionality to QuickOffice, with the ability to edit and format word processing documents (including both Word documents and documents created by Pages, the word processing tool in Apple's iWork suite). Like QuickOffice, it also offers the ability to transfer and manage files. Finally, it offers the ability to view, but not edit, Excel and PowerPoint files (as of this writing, editing of Excel files is a planned feature). Documents to Go is available in two versions: one that is relies on Wi-Fi to transfer files and another that can e-mail files.

- **Documents:** Documents is an app that allows editing of text documents and spreadsheets. The interface in Documents is a little more basic, and as of this writing, features less formatting support than in other apps in this category. But in addition to transferring files using Wi-Fi or e-mail, Documents can sync files with Google Docs (Google's free web-based office suite—http://docs.google.com), and a free ad-supported version called Documents Lite is available.

- **MarinerCalc:** MarinerCalc a spreadsheet app that can create and edit Excel spreadsheets. It includes good formatting options as well as support for over 100 spreadsheet functions.

File Management and Printing Apps

While being able to create and edit documents is a powerful feature, it may not be one that is core to your use of the iPhone (Mail, Notes, and some other apps may provide you all the ability you need to jot down thoughts). But chances are there are still some files from your computer that you may want to carry with you or access on the road from your iPhone (such as PowerPoint presentations, project notes, diagrams, or reference documents). Apps in this category can actually be broken down into three subcategories:

- Apps that transfer and view files
- Apps for printing from the iPhone
- Apps for accessing

These three categories will be described in the following sections.

Apps That Transfer and View Files

The first category of file managers provides essentially that basic ability: transferring files from your computer to your iPhone and vice versa. These apps rely on a Wi-Fi connection to your computer and typically Apple's BonJour networking technology to allow your iPhone and computer to see each other without any extensive configuration. With these apps, you can use your iPhone as a portable wireless hard drive to transfer files between multiple computers, to load files onto it for later viewing, and to organize files in folder-like structures.

While there are quite a number of apps that fit into this category (almost all of which offer the same feature set), here are some of the best that are worth checking out: AirSharing, MobileStudio, FileMagnet, Datacase, Files, and Readdle Docs.

> **TIP:** While these tools for transferring files all offer the same basic functionality, each has a slightly different interface, and they vary in terms of which file types they support viewing. So, you should check the details and screenshots of each option before choosing one.

Printing from the iPhone

The iPhone doesn't offer any built-in printing capabilities, but that hasn't stopped clever app developers from making printing a possibility. By using your computer as a go-between (typically by using an application designed to pair with the app that is installed on your computer), clever app developers have made printing some of the data on your iPhone (photos, notes, contacts, e-mails, web pages, etc.) a reality. You can check out some of the following apps: AirSharing Pro, Print n Share, Print, PrinterShare, ezShare, ACTPrinter, and HP iPrint Photo.

NOTE: When choosing a print app, make sure the app can print the types of items that you need to print (some apps, for example, can print notes, while others can't).

TIP: Some printing apps also offer file manager features, making them a good way to get two important features in a single app.

Accessing Files Remotely

While the file management apps that I mentioned earlier are designed to copy files to your iPhone from your computer, the apps described in this section allow you to access files without copying them to your iPhone, or access files stored on a network or Internet-based server (such as the Apple iDisk service that is included with a MobileMe account).

- **MobileMe iDisk:** This app lets you access files stored on your MobileMe iDisk (as well as public files stored on other people's iDisks). It allows you to view and organize files but not edit them or upload additional files.

- **Box.net:** Box.net is an online storage provider similar to the iDisk. This app allows you to access files stored in that account and upload photos from your iPhone.

- **FTP on the Go:** This app allows you to connect to any FTP site to upload or download files. Once files are transferred, this app functions like a file management app for viewing files.

- **ezShare:** This app allows you to access files stored on your computer, an FTP server, your iDisk, Google Docs, an Amazon S3 account, or a network-attached storage device (such as Apple's Time Capsule). It also functions as a file manager and offers printing capabilities.

- **OneDisk:** This app allows access to your iDisk, Box.net, and other online storage solutions. Unlike Apple's MobileMe iDisk, OneDisk supports uploading files. It also functions as a file manager for downloaded files.

- **Readdle Docs:** In addition to being a file manager, this app provides access to your iDisk, Box.net, and other web-based storage services.

- **Print n Share:** In addition to offering file management and printing capabilities, this app allows you to access your iDisk, Box.net, and other similar web-based storage services.

Better Note Taking

For many people, the ability to edit Word documents on the iPhone isn't a core need, but more note taking power than what's available in the Notes app included with the iPhone is. If you fall into that category, here are a few options that might fill your needs quite well:

- **Evernote:** Evernote is a great tool for not just note taking, but for capturing information and even voice recordings. The app itself is actually the companion to an online service that allows you to record and organize snippets of information. In addition to using the iPhone app, you can create and access notes using a free application for Mac OS X or Windows, or through the service's web site (www.evernote.com).

- **Notebooks:** Notebooks is another great app for recording and organizing notes that you write, as well as images, documents, web sites, to-do lists, and more. The interface is actually designed to mimic a spiral-bound notebook. A free sync tool is available for Mac OS X and Windows via the company's web site (www.alfonsschmid.com/Notebooks).

- **Notebook:** Notebook by Appigo is a very cleanly designed product similar to Notebooks. It offers sync via the Web (www.appigo.com) and integrates with other products the company makes. Notebook also allows you to share your Notebooks with other users.

- **Awesome Note:** Awesome Note is primarily centered around text notes, but has a very nice interface that uses folder metaphors for organizing your notes. It also provides several options for formatting text and the ability to sync to Google Notes (http://notes.google.com).

- **iThoughts:** iThoughts is a mind-mapping tool that allows you to brainstorm, diagram ideas, and develop tasks and goals. This puts it slightly outside the general note-taking category, but also makes it an incredibly useful tool. iThoughts also supports integration with major mind-mapping tools for Mac OS X and Windows and the transfer of files using the free online Box.net service.

To-Do Lists and Task Managers

One of the most common things that we use to help us remember things is the to-do list. There's a whole special set of apps to help you manage tasks better than you can with simple notes. So, here are some apps that will help make sure you don't forget to place a call, check a reservation, or even just pick up the milk on the way home.

- **Things:** This is a simple but very effective to-do list manager that allows you to create individual tasks as well as multitask projects. It offers due date features for easily viewing upcoming tasks.

- **Done:** Simple and with a clean interface, this app allows you to manage individual tasks or lists of tasks. It can also save a snapshot of your current tasks as the wallpaper for your iPhone, giving you an easy way to see what you need to get done.

- **Put Things Off:** This app is built for people who need to manage tasks but don't want to spend too much time organizing them. The interface is built around the concept of quickly viewing tasks and either completing them or putting them off till later.

- **Appigo Todo:** This app offers the ability to build individual tasks into projects or task lists, and allows you to work using either the Getting Things Done methodology (a commonly used system for task and time management and boosting productivity that was developed by productivity consultant David Allen) or your own method of task management. It offers a very customizable interface and integration with Notebook (described previously), as well as the ability to sync data with the Toodledo and Remember the Milk web services (see www.toodledo.com and www.rememberthemilk.com).

Project and Customer Relationship Management Apps

Depending on your job, you may need something more than notes or to-do lists. If you're in charge of keeping projects on schedule or managing your company's customer relationships, you might need something more robust and focused on management and coordination of tasks. Here are some of your best options.

- **Daylite Touch:** Marketcircle's Daylite is a powerful Mac-based productivity manager for businesses. It includes shared scheduling with task, client, and project management tools that enable project managers and team members to effectively communicate and collaborate. Daylite Touch enables iPhone users to access all of these features (see `http://marketcircle.com/daylite/`).

- **Basecamp:** Basecamp is a powerful web-based product that allows you to manage projects and documents. The software offers task management, time tracking, and document sharing features (including document version control to ensure that past and current versions of documents are always available). If your business uses or is considering Basecamp, there are multiple (all good but slightly different) iPhone apps you can use to access Basecamp's feature set, including the following: Encamp, Groundwork, Chieftent, Sherpa, Projects, Mother Camp, Outpost, and Minivan. For more information on Basecamp itself, check out `http://basecamphq.com`.

- **Backpack:** Also by the developers or Basecamp, Backpack is a web-based solution for sharing company documents and resources. The service also allows employees to manage their own schedules and information for sharing and easy access. As with Basecamp, there are a couple of Backpack clients for the iPhone: Satchel and FrontPocket.

- **Omnifocus:** Omnifocus is part of the Omni Group's range of productivity, mind-mapping, and project management tools for Mac OS X. The iPhone version offers powerful task and project management that incorporates contexts for tasks, location services for viewing tasks and contexts near you, and the ability to search and manage tasks. It also offers multiple options for syncing with the desktop version of the product. More details about the Omni Group and its products can be found at `www.omnigroup.com`.

Databases and Other Information Managers

Documents and notes aren't the only way to store information in the business world. Databases give businesses the ability consolidate, organize, and sort of all kinds of records, from simple inventories to customer purchases to HR and customer details. The following apps allow you to create and work with databases on your iPhone.

- **FileMaker to go:** FileMaker produces a line of powerful but easy-to-manage database solutions for individuals and businesses. FileMaker Pro databases are generally easy to create, manage, share, enter data into, and run reports on, but also can scale and offer a fair amount of power, making them ideal for small-to-medium-sized businesses. As a companion to the line of desktop and server solutions for both Mac OS X and Windows, FileMaker to go is a product that pairs with these solutions to allow you to access your databases over a Wi-Fi network or the Internet. FileMaker databases can also be designed for easy viewing and data entry on the iPhone. For more details on FileMaker, visit www.filemaker.com.

- **Bento to go:** Bento is another product produced for FileMaker (only for Mac OS X), but it is aimed at being even easier to use and is designed primarily for the consumer market as a personal database solution. Despite its consumer focus, Bento can serve well as simple way for freelancers and consultants to manage client details, expenses, and product inventory, among other things. Bento to go can serve as a stand-alone customizable database solution or sync with the desktop version of the product. Again, see FileMaker's web site for more details.

- **HanDBase:** DDH's HanDBase is a simple database product that offers many predesigned fields for the iPhone, making it easy and quick to create personal databases or a number of different business solutions (inventory management, time and billing, and field surveys, for example). DDH also produces a range of personal and business solutions for Windows. HanDBase for the iPhone can be integrated with the company's other products to create a desktop and mobile device solution. A free Mac OS X tool is also available for backing up databases on an iPhone (see www.ddhsoftware.com/iPhone).

- **Tap Forms:** Tap Forms is a personal database app for the iPhone (there is no desktop counterpart). Tap Forms is largely aimed at consumer uses (more so than any of the preceding products), but it can still have some business applications for freelancers and consultants, as well as provide a solution for managing personal information.

Secure Information Management

Interestingly, a specific type of database that has become common is a digital wallet of sorts—an information manager where you can store things like passwords, account details, credit card numbers, and other pieces of personal or professional information in a secure form that only you can access. As we go through life and work, we tend to collect more of these types of tidbits of information than most of us can easily remember, and jotting them down on paper and keeping them in your pocket or desk drawer simply isn't safe and secure enough. These specialized tools provide you a secure way to carry that information with you and easily access it whenever you need to. There are a number of apps that provide these features, but as they are largely similar, I encourage you to investigate each of them: Wallet Pro, SplashID, eWallet, mSecure, spbWallet, and Firebox Password Vault.

Apps for Presentations

While you can store and view presentations on your iPhone (either using one of the tools in the preceding sections or by converting the presentation into a video file and syncing it to the iPod app using iTunes, as described in Chapter 13), most presenters work with a computer running a presentation tool like PowerPoint or Apple's Keynote—often being tied to the computer's keyboard to advance slides in the presentation. If you want some more freedom to move around while training or presenting, then you'll want to check out these apps, which turn your iPhone into a remote control for some of the most common presentation tools:

- **Keynote Remote:** Apple's Keynote Remote app is designed to pair with Keynote (the presentation software included with Apple's iWork '09). The app allows you to view slides and presenter notes on you iPhone, as well as preview upcoming slides, in addition to its primary feature of controlling the presentation.

- **mbPointer:** PowerPoint slide show remote control: Similar in concept to Apple's Keynote Remote, this app is designed to control PowerPoint presentations running on Windows or Mac OS X. It features buttons for common uses (first slide, last slide, blank screens) and even offers a pen feature for making annotations, as well as the ability to function as a wireless mouse.

- **iPresenter:** This app is designed specifically for controlling PowerPoint presentations running on Windows. It offers the ability to view slides and preview the next slide.

Billing and Expense Tracking

Keeping track of time and expenses is a daily part of life for freelancers and consultants, as well as for most business travelers. There are plenty of apps for doing that—here are some that let you easily track your time and expenses and even generate reports for invoicing: LiveTimer, Timewerks, Expense, iReciept, TDF Time, Mobile Reciept, Expense Reports, Reciepts, and BizExpense.

Remote Controlling Your Computer

As you've probably realized throughout this book, the iPhone is really a small computer that you can carry with you. But, if you're on the road and you need to remotely access your computer (perhaps to do a task for which there isn't yet an app), these apps will let you remotely connect to and control your computer as though you were sitting right in front of it. There are a number of options for this type of solution, some of which are specific to the platform you're working on and some of which are companions to other services.

For Windows users, Microsoft's Remote Desktop feature is a natural choice because it is part of recent Windows versions. There are a few good options for Remote Desktop clients, including Remote Desktop, iTap, and Jaadu Remote Desktop for Windows.

A commonly used open source tool for controlling remote computers is the VNC protocol, which can be used to control Windows, Mac OS X, and Linux computers. There are a number of VNC clients available for the iPhone, including MochaVNC, Jaadu VNC, iSSH – SSH/VNC Console (iSSH also offers remote command-line access), and RemoteTap.

While both Remote Desktop and VNC are common choices, several companies specialize in providing secure remote control solutions that enable additional features. One such product is Remote Jr. Another is LogMeIn Ignition, which allows you to configure management of multiple computers and specify computer-specific settings, and is a product much more focused on business use than some of the other options in this space.

Web Conferencing

Sometimes you don't need to remotely control a computer, but you need to interact with coworkers, clients, or customers. Web conferencing has changed the way people have meetings with tools that allow you to not just talk on the phone, but also share a joint presentation. Two popular services in this space are Cisco's Webex and Go To Meeting. If you need to access either of these services but aren't near a computer, two iPhone apps are available to you. First is Cisco's own Webex app and second is Callwave's Fuze Meeting, which allows you to connect to either Webex or Go To Meeting calls.

Social Networking

There's no denying that social networking has become a major professional networking tool. LinkedIn may have started as the tool designed specifically for social networking, but Twitter, Facebook, and MySpace are all major ways that you can connect with others in your field, locate jobs, share your knowledge, and keep current on needed skills and trends.

Social networking (for personal or professional uses) has become a major use of the iPhone. In fact, the App Store has an entire category devoted to social networking apps. In some cases, there are obvious choices. Facebook, MySpace, and LinkedIn all produce their own iPhone clients, which are solid and natural choices.

Twitter, on the other hand, has left crafting apps to third-party developers, resulting in a number of different Twitter apps that offer different interfaces and capabilities. If you're looking for a Twitter client, some of the top choices for the iPhone include Twitterific, Tweetie, SimplyTweet, TweetDeck, and TwitterFon.

Then there are applications that allow you to post to and see updates from multiple social networking tools at one time. This approach can be good if you routinely use multiple services, but post the same information to each one. Some good apps to check out in this arena include TweetMyFace and Twitbook, which allow you to manage Facebook, Twitter, and MySpace accounts.

Job Searching Apps

Sometimes using your iPhone for work is about finding work, and there are some helpful apps for that as well. CareerBuilder offers a free iPhone app to help manage your job search on the go, and JobCompass is a paid app that allows you to search for jobs from multiple services like CareerBuilder, Monster, and HotJobs. If you're a freelancer, iFreelancer helps connect you with jobs in your field and region.

Once you've found the perfect job and need to focus on getting it, there are a couple of helpful apps. Interview Questions helps prepare candidates for interviews and Resume Pro is a rather impressive tool for crafting or updating a resume and e-mailing it directly from your iPhone as a PDF.

Summary

In this chapter, you learned about some of the many applications that are out there for professional iPhone users, ranging from tools to help you get things done to tools that expand the iPhone's general capabilities. In the final chapter, I'll discuss some even more specialized tools that apply to specific professions and industries.

But remember that this discussion is just the beginning, and the App Store is an ever-expanding box of tools. So keep exploring it on your own and don't limit yourself to just the business and productivity sections. Useful business apps can be found scattered across almost every category.

Chapter 17

Apps for Specific Professions

Find Out About the Apps That Can Make Your Job Easier

In the last chapter, you read about a number of apps that can make the iPhone easier and more effective as a business tool for any professional. In this final chapter, I'll take a look at ten different areas of the professional spectrum, highlighting individual apps that can enhance your work experience and abilities, and discussing some broader thoughts on how the iPhone can relate to each industry.

Even if you don't work in some (or any) of these fields, I encourage you to read through the entire chapter. Some tips may still apply to how you use the iPhone. Even if nothing specifically applies to your job, this chapter as a whole provides you with a broad overview of the types of work that can be done with the iPhone, including some of the unique solutions app developers have created for professionals.

Medicine

Health care is one of the industries where technology is becoming more integrated as part of the daily workflow than ever before. Hospitals and doctor's offices continue to move steadily toward the goal of electronic medical records, integrated patient care across multiple offices, and making medical imaging and lab results more accessible than ever before. The iPhone stands to offer health care workers and students an unprecedented platform for easily tracking patients, viewing lab results, and recording notes and instructions; it can also serve as a portable reference guide to diagnoses and drugs.

NOTE Several additional medical apps have been announced that take advantage of the iPhone for medical monitoring equipment and allow physicians to remotely monitor patient vital signs and conditions. As of this writing, these applications are still pending FDA approval.

- **Epocrates:** Epocrates is a medical reference suite that comes in free and subscription versions. The free version includes a complete drug reference with medical news updates, The paid subscription versions also include disease treatment guides, monographs, images, and tests. Visit www.epocrates.com/platforms/iphone to view the varying services and rates.

- **Skyscape's Medical Resources:** Skyscape is a suite of medical reference tools including a medication guide, evidence-based clinical information in outline form, a medical calculator, and a medical news service that provides information from more than 50 medical publishers.

NOTE: Skyscape also produces several targeted medical guides for the iPhone, including several Netter's Anatomy guides; clinical nursing and diagnostic guides; and guides to cancer treatment, anesthesia, and emergency diagnosis and treatment; among many others.

- **Taber's Medical Dictionary:** This is a free electronic version of Taber's Medical Dictionary (which is also included in some other products).

- **Netter's Guides:** These are electronic versions of the Netter's Anatomy Guides.

- **ReachMD CME:** This is an iPhone app for accessing the ReachMD online service for continuing medical education (CME).

- **MacPractice:** This is the iPhone version of the popular Mac-based MacPractice suite that can be used for complete practice management for doctors, dentists, and eye doctors.

- **Merge Mobile:** This app is designed to allow users to retrieve and review medical images (such as CT scans, MRIs, and X-rays) and perform standard radiologic manipulations on them.

- **Nursing Central:** This is a suite of reference guides for nurses that includes comprehensive guides to drugs, lab tests, diseases, and Medline journals.

TIP: There are several ICD-9 medical coding guides available for the iPhone, many of which offer excellent search and browse features. You can find them by doing a web search on "ICD-9."

TIP: There are several good medical calculators available for the iPhone, including MedCalc, DoctorCalc, and Mediquations.

Law

Much of the work of lawyers, paralegals, and others in the field of law requires reference tools and the ability to draft and file written documents. The iPhone can serve as a powerful tool for general communication, making notes, checking electronic versions of law books, and keeping track of court dates, among other things. Given the amount of sheer typing up of legal documents, it is hard to imagine the iPhone replacing a computer completely in any law office, but that doesn't mean that there aren't some very helpful apps specific to the legal field.

- **Black's Law Dictionary:** This is a copy of the complete eighth edition of Black's Law Dictionary, available in electronic form complete with browse and search features for the iPhone.

- **Court Days:** This app allows you to quickly and easily calculate the date that a response to legal action is due, using either straight calendar days or days when court is in session in various US jurisdictions (which can vary depending on the observance of holidays).

- **Law Pod:** Law Pod produces a series of electronic reference guides, including Federal Rules of Civil Procedure, Federal Rules of Criminal Procedure, Federal Rules of Appellate Procedure, Federal Rules of Bankruptcy, Federal Rules of Evidence, and the US Constitution.

- **Cliff Maier's legal reference apps:** Cliff Maier is a lawyer and iPhone developer who has created electronic versions of many legal references covering sections of federal law, as well as many references for laws in different states. You can view a complete list at his web site—www.waffleturtle.com.

- **myMCLE:** From the same producers of Court Days, this is s series of apps for keeping track of state-mandated continuing legal education credits. Apps are currently available for a handful of states, which you can find at www.lawonmyphone.com.

> **TIP:** iPhone J.D. is a great blog and resource site full of tips and general information for lawyers using the iPhone professionally. Check it out at www.iphonejd.com.

Real Estate

When it comes to fields where the iPhone is a natural match, real estate is probably one of the most obvious fits. Real estate agents are always on the go locating and showing properties to clients. The iPhone offers the ability to connect with clients, research and review listings, calculate mortgage payments, and research neighborhood amenities and home values. Here are some of the best tools to accomplish all those feats quickly and easily:

- **Real Estate Search apps:** Several apps are available to perform mobile real estate listing searches that incorporate the iPhone's location service to help you locate listings either in a given area or nearby. These apps include Puluwai, Trulia, Homes.com, and Apartments.com. Each of these apps can be used to search real estate listings using Internet databases (in the case of Homes.com and Apartments.com, the only databases searched are the ones that can be viewed at the web sites of the same-named apps).

- **Mortgage calculators:** Being able to help clients estimate the mortgage payments for a property is a no-brainer for real estate professionals. Mortgage Calculator and Mortgage Calculator Pro are a couple of apps that let you do that on site quickly and easily.

- **RulerPhone:** This app is a must for real estate professionals (or anyone in a related field). It allows you to calibrate the iPhone camera by photographing an object of a known size and then get relatively accurate measurements of a room or object by simply snapping a picture.

- **iLiving:** This is a unique tool that allows you to photograph a room with the iPhone and then position virtual furniture within it. It can be a great way to help clients visualize a space with different furnishings or picture their furniture in it.

- **Neighborhood Information Tools:** Many tools are available for the iPhone that allow you to locate points of interest (shops, restaurants, schools, parks, etc.) near a given address or your current location. These can help you research neighborhoods for clients or even provide clients on the spot with details about a neighborhood that they may be unfamiliar with. Some of the best apps for this include Nearby, Around Me, Yelp, and Where To.

Sales and Marketing

Like real estate agents, sales and marketing professionals are often on the go and regularly meeting with various teams within their organization, as well as with clients and potential clients. The iPhone has a lot of potential for them, as well as for assuring fast communications and responses, keeping contact and product information ready, providing a research vehicle for future accounts, and quickly delivering proposals, quotes, and even invoices.

- **Surveyor:** Surveyor is a combination iPhone app and online service that allows you to use the iPhone for survey creation and data collection, useful in market or sales research. The service offers a variety of options and quick and easy mobile data collection. More service details are available at `http://touchmetric.com/en`.

- **Stay in Touch:** This is a simple tool for ensuring that you stay in touch with clients or customers regularly. This app lets you select contacts and set a specified or random period of time after which it will remind you to touch base with those individuals.

- **Bump:** Bump is a simple tool for exchanging contact information with other iPhone users. Although you can do this in the Contacts app (as I mentioned in Chapter 8), Bump makes the process faster and easier by simply bumping two iPhones gently together.

- **Sales and Commissions:** This is a simple and easy-to-use tool for tracking sales and associated commissions. You can use this to track your own sales or the sales of others (such as employees).

- **Daylite Touch:** I mentioned Daylite in the last chapter as an excellent CRM and project management tool. Its overall nature and focus on team-based customer relations capabilities make it an excellent tool for sales and marketing professionals.

- **SalesForce Mobile:** If your company uses Salesforce.com as a CRM tool for sales, marketing, or customer relations, this app provides you access to your Salesforce.com account and information.

- **Analytics Pro:** This is a tool for accessing Google Analytics, an enterprise-grade solution for analyzing data about your web site and customers that access it.

- **Oracle Mobile Sales Assistant and Mobile Sales Forecast:** These are two components of Oracle's suite of iPhone applications for businesses. They implement various components of the company's business intelligence, management, sales, and CRM services. These two are, respectively, tools for accessing CRM and sales forecast data.

- **Omniture SiteCatalyst:** This app is the companion to Omniture's SiteCatalyst service, which helps marketing professionals with information regarding online marketing campaigns (including web, mobile browsing, and social networking initiatives).

Retail and POS

If you own a retail business or need to be able to offer electronic payment of invoices to customers (which can help speed the payment process of traditionally mailed invoices), then POS (point-of-service) tools that allow you accept payment by credit/debit cards may be a need for you. Here are three iPhone POS solutions to consider: Process Away, Ring It Up POS (available in both free and paid versions depending on your needs), and iPOS.

> **NOTE:** While these apps allow you to accept payment via your iPhone, you will need an appropriate merchant account with a credit card processing company to process payments (check with the details about each app to determine which companies are available for use with each app).

Finance

Financial services run the gamut of job roles from accounting services to retirement planning and investing. The tools in this section cover a broad swath, from helping analyze accounts and managing a small business's financial needs to researching investment options.

- **Biz Analyst+:** This is a general-purpose business analysis app that includes a very wide range of common business, financial, and statistical math functions and worksheets for many common financial and business tasks.

- **Loan-U-Later:** This is a general-purpose loan and investment calculator.

- **Currency:** This is a currency conversion app that includes over 90 currencies used in more than 100 countries.

- **Dictionary of Accounting Terms:** This is a general-purpose dictionary of accounting terms in electronic format. It is useful for those new to working in the financial services industry or who are working in unfamiliar segments of it.

- **QuickBooks Data on the Go:** For individuals and small businesses that rely on QuickBooks for accounting needs, this app provides mobile access to QuickBooks data.

- **FastFigures:** This is a professional financial calculator that includes multiple built-in templates for quick and easy operation.

- **Dow Jones Sales Triggers:** This is a tool for monitoring events that could trigger sales of stocks, such as management entering/leaving publically traded companies, mergers and acquisitions, and new investments.

- **Bloomberg Mobile:** This investment tracking tool provides greater depth of information, monitoring, and analysis than the iPhone's built-in Stocks tool.

Human Resources

At the end of the last chapter, I talked briefly about some of the tools out there for job seekers. Now I'll discuss the flip side of that coin. Human resources is often charged with hiring new candidates for positions throughout an organization and then helping employees understand such things as payroll and benefits. Here are a few apps that can help with those specific job functions:

- **Interview Assistant Lite and Interview Assistant Pro:** These two apps (one for small business and one for larger firms) assist in developing interview questions. The app is designed to help you develop questions and frame them such that they do not violate privacy or discrimination laws. It also offers some advice on making decisions.

- **Recruiter:** This is a candidate and client database tool for recruiters and HR professionals. It allows you to store candidate information and notes, track changes, and highlight candidates that are nearing completion of current projects.

- **Per Diem FY09:** This is a tool that you can use or provide to employees to determine the standard per diem rate allowances set by the US government.

Management

Some of the most effective tools for managers are general productivity and communications tools. In fact, some of the most effective tools are ones that I cover in the last chapter, such as project and task management tools. Depending on the specific department or business that you manage, some other tools throughout this chapter may also be helpful to you. However, there are also some very powerful business intelligence and CRM solutions for the iPhone that you should be aware are out there (some of which I mentioned in the last chapter and in the "Sales and Marketing" section earlier in this chapter). Typically, these pair with existing tools and services that you may be using or want to consider investing in.

- **Oracle Business Indicators, Oracle Business Approvals, and Oracle Enterprise Asset Management:** In addition to Oracle Mobile Sales Assistant and Mobile Sales Forecast (which I discussed earlier in this chapter), these make up the complete set of Oracle apps available on the iPhone. These pair with a range of other Oracle products, and used all together or individually can provide you an immense resource for business intelligence, asset management, sales figures, and managing business approval processes. (Oracle actually has several different versions of business approvals, each geared to specific types of management.) For more on the range of mobile and desktop/server-based solutions from Oracle, visit www.oracle.com.

- **SalesForce Mobile, Analytics Pro, and Omniture SiteCatalyst:** All of there were discussed in the "Sales and Marketing" section earlier, and each of them also has potential for managers to keep abreast of the initiatives within their organizations.

- **Daylite Touch, Basecamp, Backpack, and Omnifocus:** Each of these was profiled in detail in the last chapter. Again, these are all excellent tools to consider using within your organization both for your employees' abilities to collaborate and for your ability to stay aware of projects and strategies being implemented.

- **Active Strategy Mobile:** Active Strategy offers a series of enterprise-level software solutions and management consultation services to develop, track, and implement strategic plans. The company's iPhone application pairs with its software to help your measure effectiveness both across business units and individuals. Visit Active Strategy's web site for more information, at www.activestrategy.com.

Education and Training

For educators, the field of iPhone apps is truly so broad that virtually any reference application or educational game has the potential to be used in the classroom. Likewise, any presentation tools mentioned in the last chapter or presentation techniques mentioned in earlier chapters of this book are tools that directly empower teachers and trainers alike in the classroom. They enable you to engage students in an interactive mechanism. Social networking tools also make a nice fit in the classroom and enable you to connect and bring learning beyond the classroom.

Rather than trying to provide a guide to all the reference tools on each possible school subject (which would be quite a vast undertaking), I'll stick to a few core reference- and education-related tools, and advise that you search the categories of the App Store that apply to the subjects that you teach to find exactly what you need.

- **FlashMyBrain and StudyCards:** These are both tools for generating iPhone-based flash cards. Additionally, both tools offer online repositories of flash cards that other users have created.

- **iHistory:** This is a good general-purpose tool for learning about history.

- **Google Earth:** This provides the power to investigate any part of the planet and discover information across many areas: geographic, cultural, political, historical, and linguistic, among others.

- **TED:** This is a collection of resources and recordings from the TED (Technology, Entertainment, Design) conferences.

- **Wikipanion:** This is an app for accessing, searching, browsing, and bookmarking Wikipedia.

- **Attendance:** This is an easy-to-use graphical attendance sheet application.

- **iGrade:** This is a complete student information and grading system. It provides a range of customizable grading options and statistical monitoring tools.

- **GradePad:** This is a general assessment tool that can apply to teachers, trainers, coaches, or anyone else that needs to evaluate and maintain assessment records.

- **GradeAider:** This is a simple but effective tool for grading papers. Simply enter the number of questions and the number of right or wrong answers.

- **Educate:** This is an app for developing lesson plans and schedules (useful for teachers and trainers alike).

- **Teacher's Pick:** This is a tool that generates random lists of students in your class so that you can ensure that each student is asked to answer questions in an even manner.

- **GPA+:** This is a tool for calculating student GPA.

Information Technology

For Information Technology (IT), the iPhone can be just as much of a task manager and general productivity tool as it can for any other profession. However, the fact that the iPhone is essentially an ultraportable computer and network device means that it can be used directly as a tool for verifying the status of networks, servers, and individual computers, and troubleshooting and configuring them. For IT staff that need to travel or keep systems running day and night, the iPhone can be a convenient way to constantly provide monitoring and support without your having to be on site or carry a laptop around all the time.

One the most commonly used type of apps for IT professionals are tools that allow remote control and management of computers or servers. These can include command-line access via SSH (such as iSSH – SSH/VNC Console, TouchTerm Pro

SSH, and pTerm) or screen control solutions that function securely to control one or more platforms (such as LogMeIn Ignition, Remote Desktop, iTap, Win Admin, Jaadu, and MochaVNC). For Mac OS X Server administrators, an iPhone app called Server Admin Remote provides an iPhone-formatted interface to Apple's Server Admin tool. If you use these tools, however, be sure that they provide adequate security or that you use them through a VPN tunnel.

The second most common set of tools are those that can be used monitor the performance of network devices and servers. There are a range of tools that do this simply by sending a ping request to a single or specified set of IP addresses (the effect of which is functional, albeit typically further troubleshooting will likely require more advanced tools). Some of these solutions worth considering are What's Going Down, Server Status, and Server Stat+.

A few tools provide more detailed network and Internet utility features. These include the following:

- **WiFiFoFum:** This is a Wi-Fi signal detector that provides information about available Wi-Fi networks and can help you find low-signal spots and incidents of radio interference with your Wi-Fi network, helping you improve or trace problems.

- **Lookup:** This is a standard DNS lookup tool.

- **Snap:** This is a simple tool for scanning for machines connected to a Wi-Fi network. It can also use portscan to provide additional information about what services they may be offering (and what they might vulnerable to).

- **iStat:** This is a tool that allows you to display hardware status about both your iPhone and remote Macs and Mac servers on your network.

- **Prowl:** This is a Growl client for the iPhone. Growl is a package that can be installed on Mac OS X and Mac OS X Server, and allows applications and utilities that are Growl-aware to display notifications about current activity or application events. Prowl supports push notification, meaning that your iPhone will update with Growl events even if Prowl isn't running—making this an excellent tool for monitoring remote Macs and servers. For more information on Growl, check out http://growl.info.

- **iNetUtil:** This tool is designed as a web monitoring tool, but it offers a lot of general network tools, and includes the ability to view information about remote IP addresses (including server software versions) and perform DNS lookups.

- **Network Utility Pro:** This app offers a handful of helpful network tools that make it well worth keeping as part of your mobile toolkit: ping, TCP/IP port scanning, GeoIP lookup (with geotargeting via Google Maps), and DNS lookup, as well as general information about the machine at a given IP address.

Summary

In this final chapter, you learned about a number of diverse applications and how they can be applied to specific industries and professions. You also got a glimpse of the iPhone's potential for use in the business world. You also saw the level of granularity that iPhone developers are bringing to the iPhone and how the iPhone is turning from being just a general tool for business into a device that can be very specific to your business.

My hope is that throughout this book, you've learned how to use the iPhone both in general and in a business setting, as well as how to expand upon the basics and make the iPhone your own professional solution—one that is customized to you and your needs through the built-in tools, the ability to connect to the Internet, the capabilities for collaboration, and the ability to find and choose apps that empower you personally as well as professionally.

Resources for iPhone Management in Business and Enterprise Environments

Information for IT Professionals That Activate, Deploy, Manage, and Support the iPhone

One of the challenges for businesses looking to provide iPhones to their employees is deciding how to deploy and manage them. For small companies, this may not pose a significant challenge (particularly if only a handful of users will be receiving iPhones. Larger companies, for whom a rollout could include dozens or even hundreds of iPhones, however, will need to develop policies and processes for configuring and deploying them, as well as ongoing management and user support. The following resources can help you understand the tools and techniques that can be implemented to ensure a smooth and secure iPhone experience for both the IT team and the users who will be receiving iPhones.

- **Apple's iPhone Enterprise Deployment Guide:** This guide provides a solid reference to how to configure iPhones in large business environments, including how to provision the iPhone with digital certificates, preconfigure settings, and set access restrictions (see http://manuals.info.apple.com/en_US/Enterprise_Deployment_Guide.pdf).

- **iPhone Configuration Utility:** This is the tool that administrators use for provisioning, creation, and distribution of iPhone configuration profiles. It is available for Mac OS X (http://support.apple.com/downloads/iPhone_Configuration_Utility_2_0_for_Mac_OS_X) and Windows (http://support.apple.com/downloads/iPhone_Configuration_Utility_2_0_for_Windows).

- **Apple's iPhone in the Enterprise support site and knowledgebase:** This is Apple's repository of support documentation for deploying the iPhone in a business (www.apple.com/support/iphone/enterprise).

- **Apple's iPhone in Business site:** This site describes the various ways Apple recommends to integrate the iPhone into a business environment and workflow (www.apple.com/iphone/business).

- **Seven Ways to Push Mail to the iPhone - Without Exchange:** This is a guide to mail and collaboration systems other than Exchange that can be can be used with the iPhone to deliver push notifications of e-mails, new calendar items, and updates to contacts (http://ryanfaas.com/index.php/2008/11/21/seven-ways-to-push-mail-to-the-iphone-without-exchange).

- **Planning for and Supporting the iPhone in Business Environments:** This provides general information on how to support the iPhone in a business environment (http://ryanfaas.com/index.php/2008/07/31/planning-for-and-supporting-the-iphone-in-business-environments).

- **How to Configure and Support the iPhone 3G for Business, Part 2:** Integrating with Exchange: This guide provides details for Exchange administrators on ensuring that their environments are properly configured to support the iPhone, as well as some common problems faced when integrating the iPhone into an existing Exchange environment (http://ryanfaas.com/index.php/2008/09/17/how-to-configure-and-deploy-the-iphone-3g-for-business-part-2-integrating-with-exchange).

Resources for Developing In-House iPhone Applications

Information for Businesses Looking to Develop Their Own Internal iPhone Applications

While there are many useful business and productivity tools for the iPhone available in the App Store, there may be situations where available apps don't quite meet the needs of a company (most typically because the iPhone needs to interact with existing network applications such as custom databases). In such circumstances, the best option may be for a company to develop one or more custom apps in-house. These could be either web apps or native apps. The following resources and related books can help developers working for such companies to learn how to develop such in-house applications.

Online Resources

- **The iPhone Dev Center:** This is Apple's central hub of information and resources for iPhone developers, including guides, articles, video content, and sample code (`https://developer.apple.com/iphone`).

- **Apple's Web App Development Guidelines:** These are Apple's interface and coding guidelines for creating web apps for iPhone users (`http://developer.apple.com/webapps/designingcontent.php`).

■ Saf**ari Dev Center (includes resources for developing web apps):** This is Apple's site for developing web applications and web sites that make use of specific technologies available in Safari (both on the desktop and on the iPhone) (`http://developer.apple.com/safari`).

■ **Apple's iPhone Developer Program:** This provides information about and the ability to join Apple's iPhone Developer Program (membership of which is required to be able to load applications onto an iPhone for testing or submit them to the App Store. (Note that if you are building in-house applications, you will need to join the enterprise version of the program for $299 per year, not the $99 program aimed at developers who will be distributing apps via the App Store) (`https://developer.apple.com/iphone/program`)

■ **iPhone Development Central:** This is a great all around resource site for iPhone developers that includes helpful information as well as blogs and forums (`www.iphonedevcentral.org`).

■ **iPhone Development Blog:** This is the blog of Jeff LaMarche, an iPhone developer and author of multiple iPhone development books by Apress (`http://iphonedevelopment.blogspot.com`).

■ **iPhone Development Bits Blog:** This is an iPhone development blog that has a number of good tips for new and experienced iPhone developers (`http://iphonedevelopmentbits.com`).

Related Books by Apress

■ *Beginning iPhone 3 Development: Exploring the iPhone SDK*, by Dave Mark and Jeff LaMarche (Apress, 2009)

■ *iPhone User Interface Design Projects*, by Dave Mark (Apress, 2009)

■ *More iPhone 3 Development: Tackling iPhone SDK 3*, by Dave Mark (Apress, 2009)

■ *Practical iPhone Web Applications*, by Jack Herrington (Apress, 2009)

Index

Symbols & Numerics

A

G

H

I

W

X

You Need the Companion eBook

Your purchase of this book entitles you to buy the companion PDF-version eBook for only $10. Take the weightless companion with you anywhere.

We believe this Apress title will prove so indispensable that you'll want to carry it with you everywhere, which is why we are offering the companion eBook (in PDF format) for $10 to customers who purchase this book now. Convenient and fully searchable, the PDF version of any content-rich, page-heavy Apress book makes a valuable addition to your programming library. You can easily find and copy code—or perform examples by quickly toggling between instructions and the application. Even simultaneously tackling a donut, diet soda, and complex code becomes simplified with hands-free eBooks!

Once you purchase your book, getting the $10 companion eBook is simple:

❶ Visit **www.apress.com/promo/tendollars/**.

❷ Complete a basic registration form to receive a randomly generated question about this title.

❸ Answer the question correctly in 60 seconds, and you will receive a promotional code to redeem for the $10.00 eBook.

Apress®
THE EXPERT'S VOICE™

233 Spring Street, New York, NY 10013

All Apress eBooks subject to copyright protection. No part may be reproduced or transmitted in any form or by any means, electronic or mechanical, including photocopying, recording, or by any information storage or retrieval system, without the prior written permission of the copyright owner and the publisher. The purchaser may print the work in full or in part for their own noncommercial use. The purchaser may place the eBook title on any of their personal computers for their own personal reading and reference.

Offer valid through 4/10.